In Place/Out of Place

Geography, Ideology, and Transgression

Tim Cresswell

University of Minnesota Press
Minneapolis
London

Published by the University of Minnesota Press
111 Third Avenue South, Suite 290, Minneapolis, MN 55401-2520
Printed in the United States of America on acid-free paper

Library of Congress Cataloging-in-Publication Data

Cresswell, Tim.
    In place/out of place : geography, ideology, and transgression /
  Tim Cresswell.
       p.   cm.
    Includes index.
    ISBN 0-8166-2388-0
    ISBN 0-8166-2389-9 (pbk.)
    1. Geography—Philosophy.   I. Title.
  G70.C74   1996
  910—dc20   95-25660

Contents

Acknowledgments   vii

Part 1. The Terrain of Discussion: Definitions, Concepts, and Arguments   1

1. Introduction   3

2. Geography, Ideology, and Transgression:
   A Relational Ontology   11

Part 2. Heretical Geographies   29

3. Heretical Geography 1: The Crucial "Where" of Graffiti   31

4. Heretical Geography 2: The Sacred and the Profane—
   Stonehenge and the Hippy Convoy   62

5. Heretical Geography 3: Putting Women in Their Place—
   Greenham Common   97

Part 3. Conclusions   147

6. Place and Ideological Strategies   149

7. Place, Transgression, and the Practice of Resistance   163

Notes   177

Index   197

Acknowledgments

This book was researched and written between 1988 and 1994. The University of Wisconsin provided a Research Scholarship for Travel Abroad. Most of the archival research took place in the Wisconsin State Historical Society Library (chapter 3) and the Bodleian Library in Oxford (chapters 4 and 5). I was also allowed to make use of the archives of the Campaign for Nuclear Disarmament in London (for chapter 5). The use of these resources was invaluable. The following people have provided encouragement and criticism along the way: Yi-Fu Tuan, Robert Sack, Joel Rogers, John Paul Jones III, David Delaney, Peter Jackson, Carol Jennings, Donna Baron, Steven Silvern, Drew Ross, Denis Cosgrove, and Mary Braun — thanks to all of them. Finally, many thanks to all at the University of Minnesota Press who made this a smooth and painless process, particularly Lisa Freeman, Janaki Bakhle, and copy editor Anne Running.

Part 1

The Terrain of Discussion:
Definitions, Concepts, and Arguments

Chapter 1

Introduction

In the case of ideologies of what is good and right it may be space rather than time that is crucial. Something may be good and just everywhere, somewhere, here or elsewhere.
— *Goren Therborn, 1980*[1]

There are many instances in our everyday existence when we use the word *place*. On some occasions we use it to refer to a building or a location — a rendezvous or site of significance. On other occasions the word *place* turns up in common phrases such as "a place for everything and everything in its place" or "know your place" or "she was put in her place." In these expressions the word *place* clearly refers to something more than a spatial referent. Implied in these terms is a sense of the proper. Something or someone *belongs* in one place and not in another. What one's place is, is clearly related to one's relation to others. In a business it is not the secretary's place to sit at the boss's desk, or the janitor's place to look through the secretary's desk. There is nothing logical about such observations; neither are they necessarily rules or laws. Rather they are *expectations* about behavior that relate a position in a social structure to actions in space. In this sense "place" combines the spatial with the social — it is "social space."[2] Insofar as these expectations serve the interests of those at the top of social hierarchies, they can be described as ideological.[3] The example of the business can be extended to society as a whole. Just as the business has a social hierarchy, society has levels of power and influence related to class, gender, race, sexuality, age, and a host of other variables. Similarly, the building in which the business is located has spatial divisions, and the world outside is divided up into segments — houses, streets, public places, libraries, shops, and so on. Just as in the business, there are expectations about behavior in these places that are related to positions in the social structure. Many of these expectations are written into law. Most, however, remain unstated and taken for granted.

In this book I examine the basis for expressions such as "everything in its place." I argue that expectations about behavior in place are important components in the construction, maintenance, and evolution of ideological values. In order to illustrate this argument I examine reactions to three events that upset expectations about place and behavior. First, however, it is helpful to provide some brief illustrations for the more theoretical sections of the book.

"True" Stories

In the early 1980s thousands of homeless people appeared on the streets of New York City—in parks like Tompkin's Square, on the sidewalks of Fifth Avenue, and on the floor of Grand Central Station. The majority of these people were trying to survive, to eat and sleep and find shelter—the basic conditions of survival. In general they were not organized into a movement of resistance. The act of sleeping on the floor of a railroad station or defecating on the sidewalk outside million-dollar apartments was not, I would surmise, an act of intentional resistance. Most of the homeless people would not think twice about swapping places with those inside the apartments. Homelessness is not, in general, a political movement; it is reasonable to assume that most of the actions of homeless people are simply strategies of survival.

The mayor of New York at the time, Ed Koch, was upset by homelessness—it did not fit into his image of a wealthy and improving metropolis. He was particularly disturbed by the sight of homeless people in the fine, grand railroad station where people left and entered the city. His reaction was to introduce an "anti-loitering" law under which police would have powers to remove the homeless from public spaces. The State Supreme Court of New York overturned the law.

Mayor Koch's reaction to this was to appeal to "common sense" in a speech to the American Institute of Architects discussing the subject of "art in architecture." In the answer to a question at the end of the speech Koch reminded the architects of the presence of homeless people in Grand Central Station:

> These homeless people, you can tell who they are. They're sitting on the floor, occasionally defecating, urinating, talking to themselves ... We thought it would be reasonable for the authorities to say, "you can't stay here unless you're here for transportation." Reasonable, rational people would come to that conclusion, right? Not the Court of Appeals.[4]

Rosalyn Deutsche suggests that having been denied *repressive* powers, Koch resorts to *ideological* ones by declaring that reasonable people would know that a railroad station is for traveling and not for urinating. This is stated as though it were transparent, obvious—what all people think—a truism that benefits all people. I can certainly imagine readers nodding their heads in agreement. Of course train stations are meant for travel!

There are, however, a great number of other behaviors "appropriate" for Grand Central Station. People use it as a meeting place and as a place to eat. Architecture students may walk around it simply to admire its cathedral-like construction and decoration. Artists might even erect an easel in the station and paint the rush-hour crowds against the majestic background of the station. Husbands buy their wives flowers there. None of these activities count as travel. They are all, however, "acceptable." In making his ideological case, Koch resorts to defining the "proper" use of a place. In doing so he exploits the "naturalness" of the social geographical environment.

By concentrating on the apparent discrepancy between the behavior of homeless people and the demands of a place like Grand Central Station, Koch takes the station out of a context—the context of New York in the 1980s. Homelessness is treated as an instance of people out of place, dislocated from the urban politics and economics of New York. At the same time as urban "development" creates more and more homeless people, Koch denies the homeless any right to the public spaces of the city. By divorcing the homeless issue from a wider context and referring instead to a single place, he removes the issue from the realm of the social and the political and simply asserts the out-of-place nature of the homeless.[5] Indeed nothing could seem more natural. It is this naturalness of the environment that makes it so useful in defining what is and what is not "the right thing to do." Here geography and ideology intersect.

On 20 December 1986, early in the morning, a car driven by three black men stalled on a major road in Queens, New York. Not knowing how to remedy the situation, the three men walked into the nearby Howard Beach neighborhood and ordered a pizza. Within a few hours the three men had been chased three miles. One was killed by a car as he tried to cross a highway to escape the eight white attackers. Another became blind in one eye from the continuous beating he received during the three-mile chase. Even before the three men were confronted by the eight white men, an anonymous caller had informed the police of the presence of troublemakers. The police had arrived at the pizzeria and found no signs of trouble—just three black men having a pizza.

During the investigation that followed, surprisingly little attention was paid to the motivations behind the brutality that had been inflicted on the three men. The most persistent line of questioning was, "Why were the three black men in Howard Beach if they weren't causing trouble?" The attention was on the place of the assault rather than the assaulters. Patricia Williams remarks that this emphasis was the result of a constant stream of statements from defense lawyers and Howard Beach residents that indicated that the mere presence of the three men in that particular place was good enough reason to drive them out.[6] A *New York Times* article reported the following:

> The [defense] lawyers questioned why the victims walked all the way to the pizza parlor if, as they said, their mission was to summon help for their car, which broke down three miles away.... At the arraignment, the lawyers said the victims passed two all-night gas stations and several other pizza shops before they reached the one they entered.[7]

The story goes on to report how many working telephones there were between the car and the pizza joint. Williams wonders why this is of any relevance to the issue of the brutal assault. The fact was that no trouble had been caused. Neither was there any reason for the white people to believe that the black people were going to cause trouble. The clear suggestion was that the black men were out of place—that they did not belong—that the laws of place itself were being violated. The "trouble" caused by the three men was purely a transgression of expectations—expectations concerning where black people do and do not belong.

Two cases of brutal rape that received considerable media attention in recent years are worth comparing. One is the case of a woman gang-raped in a Massachusetts barroom on a pool table.[8] The other is the rape of a white woman jogger by a group of black boys in Central Park. The woman raped in the barroom was a white working-class woman. The rapists were also white and working-class. In the Central Park case the woman was white and affluent while the attackers were black and poor. Both cases involved incredible violence. In the barroom case the media story gradually centered on a fascination with the location of the event. The question (sometimes explicit, often implicit) was, "What was a single woman doing in a barroom?"—the implication being that she must have been looking for sexual favors, that she got what she was looking for. In the Central Park jogger case the media reports used the place of the event in a different way. The public nature of Central Park was emphasized. The rape was more horrific because it occurred in Central Park—it could have happened to anyone. The barroom case clearly reflects the Howard Beach case, as attention gradually turned to the site of the event and the supposed implications of particular types of persons (black man, single woman) being in places they do not belong. No one suggested that the Central Park jogger was out of place. All attention was on the brutality of the (poor and black) attackers.

A man walks into a restaurant in Argentina and declares in a loud voice, "I'm hungry and would like a meal without wine or dessert." The waiter finds him a table and brings him a beefsteak and potatoes. The man eats them and expresses his satisfaction. The waiter brings him a check and the man produces an identity card and shows it to the other diners before signing his name on the bill. He then recites a recently passed Argentinian law that states: "No Argentine shall go hungry. An Argentine is entitled to a meal, so long as it does not include liquor or dessert." "But who pays?" the waiter protests. The man shrugs his shoulders and confesses his ignorance in this matter. After some argument the manager threatens to call the police and another diner gets up, says he is a lawyer and wishes to defend the man. By this point the other diners in the restaurant are arguing about the fairness of the law. Eventually a third man offers to pay the bill and the dispute is settled.[9]

This event seemed like a strange episode in an otherwise normal meal to the diners and staff of the restaurant. In fact they were witnessing "invisible theater." The three men were all actors involved in propaganda theater under the tutelage of Augusto Boal—the Brazilian creator of the "theater of the oppressed." The diners did not know that they were an audience, as the actors never revealed themselves as such. By conducting theater in this way they turn the audience into "Spect-actors." The creation of the scene led to the involvement of the restaurant-goers in a way that standard theater—in its proper place and time—cannot. The theater was "invisible" because the normal context of theater was not present. In addition there was no clear distinction between actors and audience so the spect-actors could not distance themselves from the proceedings. The actions of the man who refused to pay were actions "out of place" in that they constituted behavior that deviates from the established norms of restaurant ritual. Theaters and restaurants are specialized places that demand appropriate behavior. By behaving out of place the actor drew attention to the function of the restaurant and to the legitimacy of a law. By jarring the diners out of their everyday expectations the actor forced them to confront a political issue that would otherwise have been far from their minds.

The apparently commonsensical notion of "out-of-place" plays a clear role in the interpretations of particular events. In many instances these interpretations have intensely political implications. Mayor Koch and the defense lawyers in the Howard Beach case manipulate the properties of place to make ideological and political arguments. They use the taken-for-granted aspects of place to turn attention away from a social problem (homelessness, racism) and reframe a question in terms of the quality of a particular place. Never mind the growing problem of homelessness in New York, people shouldn't sleep in stations. Never mind the racism of a group of white men whose actions resulted in the death of a black man—why was the man in Howard Beach? The same switch from wide social issues to questions about place occurs in the barroom rape case.

But the effect of place is not simply a geographical matter. It always intersects with sociocultural expectations. This is evidenced by the Central Park case. Here the place of the attack serves to underline the horror of the attack. During the same day on which the white woman was attacked in Central Park a black woman was raped in her own home and eventually thrown off a high roof and killed. The attacker was also black. The event was almost unreported. The victim was not white or wealthy and the attack occurred in her own private place.

In this book I use three in-depth stories to illustrate the relationships between place and sociocultural power. I have chosen to look at events that transgress the expectations of place. In each illustration we will see this general situation repeated. A particular set of places and spaces exists, an event occurs that is judged by some "authority" to be bad, and that authority connects a particular place with a particular meaning to strengthen an ideological position. These events are referred to here as *transgression*. The first illustration is the example of reactions to graffiti in New York City during the 1970s; the second is the outcry surrounding the attempt of a convoy of travelers and young people to hold a free music festival at Stonehenge during the summer solstice every year throughout the 1980s; the third is the case of the establishment's condemnation of the Greenham Common Women's Peace Camp through the early 1980s.

Central Themes

There are two connected central themes that run throughout this book. The first is the way in which space and place are used to structure a normative landscape—the way in which ideas about what is right, just, and appropriate are transmitted through space and place. Something may be appropriate here but not there. The effect of spatial structures on what is deemed appropriate is dealt with in some depth by Pierre Bourdieu in his study of the Kabyle.[10] He shows how certain orderings of space provide a structure for experience and help to tell us who we are in society. He writes, "The spatial structures structure not only the group's representation of the world but the group itself, which orders itself in accordance with this representation." He goes on to suggest that it is through "the dialectical relationship between the body and a structured organization of space and time that common practices and representations are determined."[11]

Spatial structures structure representations of the world as they are held in a taken-for-granted way. But value and meaning are not inherent in any space or place—indeed they must be created, reproduced, and defended from heresy. It is exactly this process that I illustrate. In the first half of the conclusion I return to this theme and suggest that the fundamental human experience of the world *as* the world—a set of places—gives geography a fundamental role in ascribing particular sets of values to particular actions. The geographical setting of actions plays a central role in defining our judgment of whether actions are good or bad.

The second theme is that of transgression. Just as it is the case that space and place are used to structure a normative world, they are also used (intentionally or otherwise) to question that normative world. There has been a great deal of discussion about marginality, resistance, and the construction of difference recently. Here I wish to delineate the construction of otherness through a spatially sensitive analysis of transgression. Transgression, I shall argue, serves to foreground the mapping of ideology onto space and place, and thus the margins can tell us something about "normality." I am also interested in thinking through the implications of transgression as a form of politics.

In each of the illustrations that form the body of the book the twin themes of normative geographies and transgression interplay to raise questions about each other. To summarize, there are two processes at work: the discursive attempt to create and maintain normative geographies (where everything is in place) through and by the media and, second, the effect of place on the interpreted meanings of transgressive actions. The media reaction to a perceived transgression (such as homeless people in Grand Central Station), then, is affecting place through its discourse at the same time as this discourse is affected by the already existing meanings of place (the idea that Grand Central Station is not for sleeping in).

A Method

How, then, can we interpret the connection between commonsense assumptions about place and normative judgments of behavior? We can hypothesize the existence of a set of commonsense assumptions about appropriate behavior that is heavily determined by the qualities of particular places serving as experiential contexts for behavior. We also know that there is not, in everyday life, a direct correlation between place and appropriate behavior. That is to say we cannot take a place such as a corner on Main Street and list all the activities that would be appropriate there. In fact our consciousness of place all but disappears when it appears to be working well. My approach is to examine situations where things appear to be wrong, those times when we become aware of our immediate environment—when the heating fails or the lights go out. We rarely sit and think of a working electric light. The light's failure to work when we are reading a book, however, leads to an instant and heightened awareness of the particular place we are in.

One way to illustrate the relation between place and behavior is to look at those behaviors that are judged as inappropriate in a particular location—literally as actions out of place. It is when such actions occur, I argue, that the everyday, commonsense relationships between place and behavior become obvious and underlined. The labeling of actions as inappropriate in the context of a particular place serves as evidence for the always already existing normative geography. In other words, transgressive acts prompt reactions that reveal that which was previously considered natural and commonsense. The moment of transgression marks the shift from the unspoken unquestioned power of place over taken-for-granted behavior to an official orthodoxy concerning what is proper as opposed to what is not proper—that which is in place to that which is out of place.

Clearly different groups of people have different ideas about what is and is not appropriate, and these different ideas get translated into different normative geographies. The stories I presented earlier illustrate this point well. It is when different spatial ideologies come into conflict that they are taken out of the role of "common sense" and are stated as "the right way"—the "orthodoxy." It is at this point, when different cultural values clash, that normative geographies are defined by those with the power to do so. This process of reaction and definition in the media and elsewhere constitutes a rich source of evidence for the normally unstated relations between place and ideology.

Chapter 2

Geography, Ideology, and Transgression: A Relational Ontology

Geography

Geography has traditionally been ignored in critical theory. Class, gender, and race are often treated as if they happened on the head of a pin.[1] There is no intention here to supersede or somehow replace discussion of social processes. Rather I hope to add to these important discussions in a critical way. A discussion of the role of the geographic environment—the power of place—in cultural and social processes can provide another layer in the understanding and demystifying of the forces that effect and manipulate our everyday behavior. It should be read in addition to, rather than instead of, wider discussions of the interaction between social groups. It will become evident in later discussions of an array of geographical conflicts that the structure of the environment has something to say about issues of class, gender, ethnicity, age, and sexuality—each of which has its own distinct and peculiar "heretical geographies."

That said, I do not wish to suggest that we simply "add geography and stir"; rather I insist that the social and the spatial are so thoroughly imbued with each other's presence that their analytical separation quickly becomes a misleading exercise. Indeed, a sustained investigation of the "out of place" metaphor points to the fact that social power and social resistance are always already spatial. When an expression such as "out of place" is used it is impossible to clearly demarcate whether social or geographical place is denoted—place always means both.

A recent direction of theoretical human geography has been toward an analysis of the spatiality of social life. Neil Smith's "uneven development," Edward Soja's "socio-spatial dialectic," Robert Sack's theory of "territoriality," and David Harvey's "time-space compression" are all examples of this.[2] Such work is, in part, a response to geography's traditional contentment to study the regional distribution of "things." Regional geography (the characteristic "paradigm" of the first half of the century) found its calling in the mapping of populations, resources, climates, soils, languages, religions, and a host of other variables. Introductory human geography is still taught this way in the colleges of the United States. The object of the study is the region and everything that makes it unique. This type of geography was and is descriptive in nature.

In this form of geography the object of geographical study exists *as a result* of processes (migrations, "culture," urbanization, and so on). It is the product of wider forces that arrives fully formed at the end of an intellectual conveyor belt. Recent theoretical geography has attempted to put the object of geographical analysis somewhere *on* the conveyor belt — helping in the production process. The new object of geography, then, is in some sense explanatory. Thus territoriality is an intrinsic part of the organization of power and the control of resources and people. Uneven development helps explain the frustrating problem of the continuation and expansion of capitalism, and the time-space compression goes some way to explaining the cultural form called "postmodernism."

The direction of recent critical geography, then, has been away from seeing its object as the *description of regions* and toward the *analysis of the role of geographic forces in the explanation of other things*. This is not to fetishize the role of space and place, nor to claim that geographical explanation can explain everything. Geographers (including myself) simply want to insist on the geographical component in the social and cultural and, in doing so, make up for a void in previous social and cultural theory. Keeping this in mind, we can avoid geographical reductionism.

The explanatory enterprises of Harvey, Soja, Sack, and others are linked by their exploration of the society-and-space dialectic. They wish to show that space is not simply formed and molded but plays an active role in the formation of society. Society produces space and space reproduces society. The end point, as I mentioned above, is to undermine altogether this binary form of the society-space relationship.

A similar project has been at the heart of the so-called new cultural geography.[3] This project, inspired by the coming together of humanist and Marxist agendas, has raised questions concerning the role of geography in the creation, maintenance, and transformation of meaning.

The chief inspirations behind the new cultural geography are the various and contested forms of "cultural studies."[4] Interdisciplinary approaches to the study of culture have focused on examining culture as an actively contested political arena. This contrasts with both the traditional conservative view of culture (as "the best that has been thought and said") and with the Marxist view of culture (as a decorative "superstructure" to an economic base).[5] The approaches of cultural studies seek to explain how myths and beliefs are created and sustained through culture, both elite and popular. In addition, the multiple resistances of subordinate cultures are brought to the foreground. The importance of cultural studies for geography is that it changes the way we look at geographical phenomena such as place and landscape. If place and landscape are seen in the context of a broad and unitary culture they appear as static and already formed material reflections of a superorganic culture.[6] Places are seen as rooted and intransient. The new cultural geography critiques this view and emphasizes in its place the active constitution of places through cultural struggle.

Peter Jackson's book *Maps of Meaning* provides an overview of possible and actual contributions of a geography informed and inspired by critical cultural studies. On the whole, however, radical cultural geography has remained, in its early stages, suggestive rather than concrete.[7] This project, then, is an example of radical cultural geography that begins to explain how and why place is a powerful force in the ongoing hegemonic and counterhegemonic struggles.

The central geographical concept here is that of "place." In geography the concept of place has been rejuvenated by the humanistic and radical reactions to spatial analysis,[8] which concentrated on the abstract rather than experiential properties of space and location.

Humanistic geography's most important reminder has been that we do not live in an abstract framework of geometric spatial relationships; we live in a world of meaning. We exist in and are surrounded by places—centers of meaning. Places are neither totally material nor completely mental; they are combinations of the material and mental and cannot be reduced to either. A church, for instance, is a place. It is neither just a particular material artifact, nor just a set of religious ideas; it is always both. Places are duplicitous in that they cannot be reduced to the concrete or the "merely ideological"; rather they display an uneasy and fluid tension between them.

Because places are meaningful and because we always exist and act in places, we are constantly engaged in acts of interpretation. This has led some to talk of places and the landscape as a text.[9] Like a book, the landscape is created by authors, and the end product attempts to create certain meanings. But also, like a book, the people who "read" the landscape and its places can never be forced to read it in only one way. The text is subject to multiple readings despite the fact that some readings are encouraged more than others. We can thus talk of a hierarchy of readings, with favored, normal, accepted readings and discouraged, heretical, abnormal readings—dominant readings and subordinate readings. This leads us to the concept of ideology.

Ideology and Doxa

In many ways my use of ideology follows that of Goren Therborn. He argues that the operation of ideology in human life "basically involves the constitution and patterning of how human beings live their lives as conscious, reflecting initiators of acts in a structured meaningful world."[10] Ideologies work at three levels in Therborn's analysis. They define (1) what exists and what does not exist; (2) what is good, just, and appropriate and what is not; and (3) what is possible and impossible. These three "modes of interpellation" form three lines of defense for any given order. For instance, it is an ideological position that racism does not exist in the university system of the United States. If this does not convince people, then the second "mode of interpellation" can be called upon. We admit that racism exists but claim that it is just, for some reason. Third, we may have to admit that racism exists and that it is bad and unjust. In this case we may resort to the next line of defense and say that although it is deplorable that racism exists, there is nothing we can do to change it. In order to change something we must first recognize its existence; second, recognize that it is "bad"; and finally conclude that there is some hope of effecting change. As you can see, these three elements form part of an interrelated argument that covers for itself should one element fail.

It is my claim here that place plays a role in the constitution of ideology at all three levels. In general, though, I shall concentrate on the role of place in the second mode of interpellation—the definition of what is good, just, appropriate, and so on. Ideological judgments of actions vary according to geographical context. As Therborn argues, judgments of what is good as opposed to what is bad vary according to the place of a particular act.

Ideology, though, should not be thought of as another way of saying "cultural values" or "belief systems." The analytic power of the concept comes from the way it connects ideas of what exists, what is good, and what is possible to various forms of power relations. Ideology, as J. B. Thompson suggests, is "meaning in the service of power."[11]

Before going on to examine more closely the relation between place and ideology, it will be helpful to make two more remarks concerning the nature of ideology. First, ideology is not purely a class phenomenon. There are many other basic forms of human subjectivity related to a whole range of power relations. Throughout this book I consider the multitude of ideologies and their interrelationships. Each case study illuminates and is based on different ideological structures—the chapter on graffiti includes ideologies of race, the chapter on Greenham Common is based on ideologies of sexuality and gender, and the chapter on Stonehenge involves ideologies of nationalism, religion, and age. Even within the case studies there is more than one ideology at play. Place can play a role in the maintenance of all ideologies and the power relations they support.

When I use terms such as *dominant* and *dominated* I do not intend to suggest that there are two mutually exclusive groups of people in the world who fall into one or the other of these categories. I do mean to suggest, however, that in given contexts we can make judgments concerning who has power over whom. Take the first of my illustrations as an example—graffiti in New York City. The main actors in the story are graffiti artists (usually poor, often black or Hispanic, mostly male), city government (mostly male, wealthy, and white), and the art world (male and female, mostly white, wealthy). It seems quite reasonable to suggest that the graffiti artists are less powerful than the city government and the art world. Within the art world there are probably different groups, such as traditionalists and the avant-garde. Traditionalists tend to define what counts as art and are more often white and middle or upper class than the avant-garde upstarts. Nevertheless the avant-garde upstarts who bring graffiti into the gallery have more power than the graffiti artists. Graffiti artists in turn are mostly male and often refuse to include women in their groups. The graffiti artists are thus subordinate in relation to the art world but dominant in relation to women in their own community. The story could become more and more complicated. The point is that domination needs to be conceived of in relation to the story that is being told.

Second, it is important to note (as Therborn does) that many ideologies define a position within a wider structure. A positional ideology "subjects one to, and qualifies one for, a particular position in the world of which one is a member."[12] This can be contrasted with an "inclusive" ideology, which defines an individual as a member of a world. Nationalism is an inclusive ideology, as it defines an individual as a member of a nation. An important point about positional ideologies is that they have a "dual character" in that by becoming aware of one's position one becomes aware of others in different positions. Positional ideologies have "alter-ideologies." Sexism, for instance, has an "ego-ideology" of maleness and an "alter-ideology" of femaleness. Even the inclusive ideology of nationalism has an "alter-ideology" in the definition of "aliens." This, of course, is easily translated into geography, as we shall see. One's awareness of being "in place" is structured within an awareness of being "out of place." Place is one of the easiest ways of being "included" and recognizing "other" positions. The very concept of "position" has a geographical basis. When Therborn uses the term *positional* he is using a geographical metaphor that is comprehensible to anyone because of the basic awareness of being in space.[13] Alter-ideology then, relates to the ideological dimension of the way in which one relates to the "Other."

The argument here is that spatial structures and the system of places provide historically contingent but durable "schemes of perception" that have an ideological dimension. In particular, the place of an act is an active participant in our understanding of what is good, just, and appropriate. How does this work? To understand this we have to understand the importance of "practice."[14]

Ideological beliefs are important because they affect what people do. Ideologies are not simply sets of ideas. They are ideas that influence and guide actions. These actions are referred to as "practice." The geographical environment forces people to relate beliefs to actions. People read places by acting in them. Our actions in place are evidence of our preferred reading. Just as a book comes to have meaning through our reading it, so a place comes to have meaning through our actions in it — by "practice" — and through our reactions to this practice. When we are silent in the library or kneeling in the church we are "reading" the place. This practice is, in turn, informed by the always already existing meanings of the place. Kneeling in church is an interpretation of what the church means; it also reinforces the meaning of the church. Place is produced by practice that adheres to (ideological) beliefs about what is the appropriate thing to do. But place reproduces the beliefs that produce it in a way that makes them appear natural, self-evident, and commonsense. We are silent in a library because we believe that it is appropriate to be silent in libraries, and by being silent in libraries we contribute to the continuation of silence. Thus places are active forces in the reproduction of norms — in the definition of appropriate practice. Place constitutes our beliefs about what is appropriate as much as it is constituted by them.[15]

Dick Hebdige, in his study of subcultures, discusses the "everyday" nature of ideology. He chooses to illustrate this with a discussion of a university. He describes how the faculty of arts is divided from the faculty of science by having them in separate buildings and how the hierarchical division of the teacher and the taught is reflected in the layout of the lecture theaters, with the seats directed to emphasize and naturalize the authority of the distinguished professor. The spatial construction of the university thus sets limits on what is possible and what is impossible in an educational setting. More critical lecturers are often the first to suggest the rearrangement of a seminar room into a more equalizing pattern such as a circle. Decisions made in the very spatial planning of our educational places set limits on what is taught and how it is taught:

Here the buildings literally *reproduce* in concrete terms prevailing (ideological) notions about what education *is* and it is through this process that the educational structure, which can, of course, be altered, is placed beyond question and appears to us as "given" (i.e. as immutable). In this case, the frames of our thinking have been translated into actual bricks and mortar.[16]

A place such as a university, then, does not "reflect" ideology; it is not just an "expression" of values. It is better to think of place as something produced by and producing ideology. Places are not *only* simple reflections of ideology—they are a lot more. There is no intention here to imply that social actors are completely "fooled" by their misrecognition of places as natural. Places do not have intrinsic meanings and essences, they simply have meanings that are more conventional and "appropriate." As I have argued here, the meanings of place are created through practice.

Practice is simultaneously a form of consumption (insofar as the actor acts according to assumed norms, he or she "buys" them) and a form of production (as the actor, by acting in accordance with assumed norms, contributes further to the continuation of accepted, "commonsense" place meanings). By acting in space in a particular way the actor is inserted into a particular relation with ideology. Importantly, the actor has the ability to recognize a particular spatial "text" and react to it in a way that is antagonistic to a particular ideology.

Meaning is invoked in space through the practice of people who act according to their interpretations of space, which, in turn, gives their actions meaning. This is a fluid process that changes over time. Any given set of interpretations of space can be and have been overthrown historically.

The question remains as to how ideology works. One largely discredited model of explanation is the simplest and most convenient one. This model is the one that says that there are a small group of powerful people in society who impose ideology from above on the masses below. They create stories that, when believed, prevent the masses from realizing their position as exploited individuals. This model posits a very smart group of conspirators planning things and a large group of blind and foolish followers who are easily persuaded. This can be called the "dominant ideology thesis." Subsequent theories have given more respect to the savoir-faire of the exploited and have assigned considerably less power to small elites. Sophisticated theories of ideology allow for the possibility of the exploited and the subordinate to actively resist their exploiters, for the possibility that the exploited are fully aware of the injustices that beset them but choose to "play the game" anyway, and even for the possibility that the powerful themselves believe their own stories—that they are not deliberately making them up. In short, theories of ideology have become far more subtle. In general this subtlety involves a recognition that our consciousness is a fragmented and contradictory cocktail of values learned from "above" and strategies learned from everyday experience, which both "rewards" good and appropriate behavior and makes life miserable for those who transgress. An increasing amount of attention has been directed toward the "commonsense" and "everyday" nature of ideology.

Sophisticated theories of ideology insist that everyday common sense is an essential part of history and power. A group cannot become dominant and rule effectively without claiming common sense as their own. This was the major insight of Antonio Gramsci in his *Prison Notebooks,* and it has been developed most famously by Raymond Williams.[17] Gramsci's concept of hegemony insists that people are not simply imposed upon by dominant groups but are convinced that the ideas of dominant groups will also benefit subordinate groups. Domination thus occurs through common sense. The concept of cultural hegemony places a significant burden on the concept of culture, as power is seen to occur in the realm of meaning rather than in the formal political arena. Thus hegemony has played a central role in the new field of cultural studies. This is reflected in the work of Pierre Bourdieu:[18]

> The cognitive structures which social agents implement in their practical
> knowledge of the social world are internalized, "embodied" social
> structures. The practical knowledge of the social world that is
> presupposed by "reasonable" behavior within it implements
> classificatory schemes..., historical schemes of perception and
> appreciation which are the product of the objective division into classes
> (age groups, genders, social classes) and which function below the level
> of consciousness and discourse. Being the product of the incorporation
> of the fundamental structures of society, these principles of division are
> common to all the agents of the society and make possible the
> production of a common, meaningful world, a common-sense world.[19]

Throughout his work Bourdieu has attempted to theorize the importance of common sense as a mechanism of domination. He describes common sense as a *sense of limits* or as *doxa.* The core of his argument is that agents have permanent *dispositions* embedded in their very bodies. A disposition is a preferred and unselfconscious mode of acting reflected in a multitude of actions from bodily posture to modes of speech. These dispositions reveal a connection between a person's "objective" position (for example, as a worker, a female, or an old person) and their subjective beliefs.

It is the relationship between objective positions and subjective beliefs that is the key to the notion of a sense of limits:

> Every established order tends to produce ... the naturalization of its own arbitrariness. Of all the mechanisms tending to produce this effect, the most important and the best concealed is undoubtedly the dialectic of the objective chances and the agents' aspirations out of which arises the *sense of limits,* commonly called the *sense of reality.*[20]

Bourdieu is arguing that an established order, if it is successful, must make its world seem to be the natural world—the commonsense world. People must aspire to that which they are meant to aspire to. If the objective position of a person (as a worker, woman, and so on) corresponds to his or her "mental" position ("taken-for-granted" beliefs about the world), the result is "ineradicable adherence to the established order." This is because the social world appears as a natural world. By acting in accordance with these commonsense beliefs about the naturalness of the social world, the objective conditions are reproduced.

The importance of the commonsense "sense of limits" (or sense of one's place) is that it is the most effective way to reproduce the (contingent) conditions that produced it. The "quasi-perfect" fit of objective order and subjective beliefs makes the social world appear self-evident— "a sense of one's place ... leads one to exclude oneself from the goods, persons, places and so forth from which one is excluded."[21] Dominated subjects come to have beliefs about their being in the world by applying categorizations and schemes of perception that are produced by the dominant, and thus they refuse what they are refused—they define themselves according to established definitions. When this fit (between objective position and subjective beliefs) is close to perfect, Bourdieu refers to people's experience as *doxa.*

Doxa is opposed to orthodoxy, which, unlike doxa, implies some awareness of alternative experiences. While doxic experience is the only experience (as it is unquestioned and taken for granted), orthodox experience is merely the "right" experience as opposed to the wrong experience. Doxa is the most effective way to maintain the established order:

> When, owing to the quasi-perfect fit between the objective structures and the internalized structures which results from the logic of simple reproduction, the established cosmological and political order is perceived not as arbitrary, i.e. as one possible order among others, but as a self-evident and natural order which goes without saying and therefore goes unquestioned, the agent's aspirations have the same limits as the objective conditions of which they are a part.[22]

With the doxic mode of experience there is no conflict, as individuals aspire to that which fits with what their objective position allows—the woman aspires to be a mother, the worker aspires to be good at his or her job, the schoolchild aspires to be like his or her parents. Agents recognize the "legitimacy" of the social order because they "misrecognize" the contingent nature of that order. In effect they are not aware of the question of legitimacy in the first place. People are only aware of the question of legitimacy when an alternative is presented to them and social groups compete over claims to legitimacy.

If a person's subjective beliefs do not correspond to his or her objective position, he or she may start to question the legitimacy of the objective limits. For example, a worker may come to realize that she could be the manager and do the job more effectively. At this point doxa evaporates and there is a mismatch between the objective structure and the subjective beliefs.

A prime subject of social struggle, then, is the claim to legitimacy from opposing forms of commonsense classification. The dominating groups have an interest in defending the taken-for-grantedness of things—the prevailing doxa—while the dominated groups seek to push back the boundaries of what is taken as natural. If the natural is shown to be arbitrary, then the ruling groups can replace it with its imperfect substitute—orthodoxy. The constitution of common sense is a major stake in all kinds of struggle.

By revealing what was formally hidden (the contingent nature of social distinctions), a dominated subject causes "the establishment" to clarify the formally commonsense categories; they are forced to produce official categories with official boundaries:

> Only in and through the struggle do the internalized limits become boundaries, barriers that have to be moved. And indeed, the system of classificatory schemes is constituted as an objectified, institutionalized system of classification only when it has ceased to function as a sense of limits so that the guardians of the established order must enunciate, systematize and codify the principles of production of that order, both real and represented, so as to defend them against heresy; in short, they must constitute the doxa as orthodoxy.[23]

In Bourdieu's work, then, the commonsense world of doxa is the key to the most ineradicable adherence to the established order, while the questioning of doxa is one of the most fundamental and effective forms of struggle. To make the establishment come out on the side of one set of classifications and expectations against another (heretical) set of expectations is a major victory for those, in any particular context, who are dominated.

Bourdieu often makes the mistake of reducing "social" forces to "class" forces. Implicit in Bourdieu's work is the notion that doxa is created around class interests. In *Distinction* Bourdieu structures his argument around the "tastes" of the aristocracy, the middle class, and the working class. No mention is made of the ways in which doxa operates in relation to gender, ethnicity, age, sexuality, or place of residence. In short, Bourdieu's theorizations have too simplistic a notion of domination. By reducing the world to sets of dominant people (upper class) and dominated people (working class), he tells an incomplete story.

My purpose here is to examine some moments that Bourdieu refers to as crisis points in doxa—those times and places where the previously unquestioned becomes questioned and powerful groups seek to defend the "order of things" against the heresies of "deviant" groups. Unlike Bourdieu, I do not reduce the struggles to a class basis. In my view doxa serves a multitude of different but powerful groups in an array of sociocultural contexts. These moments of crisis in the flow of things are referred to here as transgressions.

Transgression, Resistance, and Deviance

Transgression is the final link in the chain of my argument and is important for several reasons. It is hard to tell what is considered normal without the example of something abnormal. Transgression, and the reaction to it, underlines those values that are considered correct and appropriate. By studying the margins of what is allowed we come to understand more about the center—the core—of what is considered right and proper. Transgression is also important in itself as an example of possible tactics for resistance to established norms. No hegemonic structure is ever complete, and it is always important to study the ways in which hegemonies are contested in everyday life. Perhaps most important for this project, transgression (literally, "crossing a boundary") is often defined in geographical terms. Geography, then, can tell us a lot about transgression, and transgression, conversely, provides valuable insights into the way places affect behavior and ideology.

Looking at transgression has methodological benefits. Describing and analyzing "common sense" could have been a time-consuming process involving years of fieldwork and questioning. Trying to get people to state what usually remains unformulated, however, would have been fraught with difficulty and subject to much misinterpretation on the part of the observer. By looking at events that upset the balance of common sense I let the events, themselves, become the questions. The occurrence of "out-of-place" phenomena leads people to question behavior and define what is and is not appropriate for a particular setting. The examination of common sense becomes a public issue in the speeches of politicians and the words of the media. The issues I examine become crisis points in the normal functioning of everyday expectations, and these expectations need to be made explicit. In many ways this work resembles the ethnomethodological studies of Harold Garfinkel.[24] As Garfinkel has shown, events that upset commonsense assumptions have the effect of annoying people, and this helps us discover the underlying taken-for-granted assumptions that help mold social action. Garfinkel's techniques became known as Garfinkeling. Unlike Garfinkel, I do not have to create situations in which expectations are not met. My "experiments" have already taken place. We can think of "out-of-place" events as "spatial Garfinkeling."

It may seem strange that I am studying relatively "exotic" events when my stated aim is to reveal something about commonsense geographies. This is explained by the methodology described above. The occurrence of unusual events is the catalyst for public reaction that seeks to defend common sense, and my examination is of these reactions. The French historian Georges Canguilhem argues that while the pathological may be logically secondary to the normal, it is existentially primary.[25] Likewise I am arguing that although "out of place" is logically secondary to "in place," it may come first existentially. That is to say, we may have to experience some geographical transgression before we realize that a boundary even existed.

This leads to the next issue concerning transgression — the distinction between transgression and resistance and the importance of reactions to transgressions versus the intentionality of the transgressor. There has been much talk in contemporary cultural theory about "resistance." Almost any activity from eating to walking to writing books and making films can, it seems, be construed as resistance. There is undoubtedly a degree of romanticization of the everyday going on in this talk. There is also a good deal of misguided optimism. I avoid talking (until the final chapter, at least) about resistance because of a number of theoretical problems I have with the term. The most prominent of these is the issue of *intentionality*. Resistance seems to imply intention — purposeful action directed against some disliked entity with the intention of changing it or lessening its effect. The resistance of an action therefore appears to be in the intention of the perpetrator, in the eagerness to overcome or change some obstacle. James Scott makes this clear in *Weapons of the Weak*:

At a first approximation, I might claim that class resistance includes any act(s) by member(s) of a subordinate class that is or are *intended* either to mitigate or deny claims made on that class by superordinate classes vis-à-vis those superordinate classes. While this definition ... is not without problems, it does have several advantages. It focuses on the material basis of class relations and class struggle. It allows for both individual and collective acts of resistance. It does not exclude those forms of ideological resistance that challenge the dominant definition of the situation and assert different standards of justice and equity. Finally it focuses on intentions rather than consequences, recognizing that many acts of resistance may fail to achieve their intended result.[26]

Transgression, in distinction to resistance, does not, by definition, rest on the intentions of actors but on the *results*—on the "being noticed" of a particular action. The question of intentionality remains an open one. Let me make the distinction clearer. Scott talks of the multiform actions of peasant laborers in Malaya that do not conform to the expectations of their masters. For these "everyday forms of peasant resistance" to work they depend on being "not noticed," as the object is to avoid retribution and to live as decent a life as possible. This resistance occurs behind the backs of those who are being resisted. In this project, the actions I study are analyzed in terms of the response of the "establishment" to certain actions—actions that are seen as being deviant or, more explicitly, "out of place." To have *transgressed* in this project means to have been judged to have crossed some line that was not meant to have been crossed. The crossing of the line may or may not have been intended. Transgression is judged by those who react to it, while resistance rests on the intentions of the actor(s).

Resistance and transgression are clearly not discrete sets. Some acts of resistance (although not the everyday ones Scott talks of) are judged as transgression. Similarly some actions judged as constituting transgression are intended by the actors and thus also constitute resistance. Since transgressive acts are the acts judged to be "out of place" by dominant institutions and actors (the press, the law, the government), they provide "potentials" for resistance. Intentional transgression is a form of resistance that creates a response from the establishment—an act that draws the lines on a battlefield and defines the terrain on which contestation occurs.

The illustrations in the second half of this book represent different levels of intentionality. The graffiti I study is generally not political in an intentional way. Graffiti artists may be expressing their existential alienation or simply having fun. The actions of the graffitists are certainly transgressive, but rarely resistant. The Stonehenge "hippies" were also attempting to "have fun," but they had a "spokesperson" who presented their actions as political opposition to the alienation of the modern urban world. The Greenham women were clearly not primarily out to have fun, and their actions were very intentionally and deliberately "resistant."

Finally there is the issue of "deviance." Deviance is commonly thought of as synonymous with "abnormal." The idea of deviance rests on the notion that there is something recognizably different about acts that break from established norms. Common definitions of deviance include the statistical definition—deviance as something that falls too far away from the "average." Under this definition it is deviant to be color-blind or left-handed. It is also deviant to have a Ph.D. Deviance can also be thought of as a pathological infliction. Often difference is "blamed" on some "problem" with the person undertaking the deviant act. Deviance in this sense is "unhealthy"—a disease. We shall see in the illustrations that follow that "out-of-place" acts are frequently described in terms of disease and contagion. Graffiti, for example, is often referred to as a contagion or a plague. The problem with this definition is agreeing on what constitutes "healthy" behavior. A similar problem arises when deviance is described as "dysfunctional" behavior—actions that fail to function in a way that leads to some goal. The question arises as to what appropriate goals might include. The delineation of appropriate goals is often a political act. Homophobic heterosexual people may define heterosexual family life as a desired goal and in doing so make homosexuality dysfunctional and thus deviant. Gay people, on the other hand, may have a very different set of goals.

A more effective definition of deviance is that developed by the Chicago sociologist Howard S. Becker:

> Social groups create deviance by making the rules whose infraction
> constitutes deviance, and by applying those rules to particular people
> and labeling them as outsiders. From this point of view deviance is not a
> quality of the act the person commits, but rather a consequence of the
> application by others of rules and sanctions to an "offender." The
> deviant is one to whom that label has successfully been applied; deviant
> behavior is behavior that people so label.[27]

Several points about this definition are worth amplifying for the purposes of this project. First, as with transgression, deviance is created through reactions—it is a consequence of responses to a person's (or group's) actions. When we concentrate on this aspect of deviance, the analysis of the process of labeling becomes more important than the characteristics of those who are so labeled. Nevertheless, the social characteristics of the labeled group and the labeling group do play a role. This is because the likelihood of behavior being considered deviant depends, to some degree, on who commits the act and who reacts to it. As Becker points out, a black man who has attacked a white woman is far more likely to be prosecuted (and executed) than a white man who has attacked a white woman or a black man who has attacked a black woman. The events at Central Park are a grotesque illustration of this.

The definition of acts and people as "deviant" clearly has a great deal to do with power. When looking at deviance it is important to consider who has the power to create the rules that result in the deviance label. As Becker points out, this is not a society with a simple set of agreed-upon rules. Rules vary with social groups. Different classes, ethnic groups, genders, ages, and sexualities recognize different rules. When these groups (with different rules) come into conflict, there is little consensus concerning what is or is not appropriate in a given context. One group, however, generally has the power to define the other as deviant.

Graffiti artists have a very strict set of rules regarding their art.[28] Beginners must undergo strict apprenticeships before they can leave their mark in certain places. The rules of New York City, however, do not recognize the rules of the graffiti artist. Because New York City government has the power to enforce its rules on the graffiti artists, it is the graffiti that is labeled deviant. In the same way the rich make rules for the poor, blacks' actions are defined by whites, and appropriate behavior for women is adjudicated by men. Power, in many ways, is the ability to make rules for others.

The term *rules* is perhaps too narrow for the purposes of this project. Rules imply some degree of formality. Law is the most obvious form of rules. The creation of deviance is not just related to the creation and breaking of the law. Rather we are talking about the looser term *norms*. It is not against the law to talk loudly to yourself as you walk down the street, but many observers will certainly regard you as "deviant."

It is my assertion that place plays a significant role in the creation of norms of behavior and thus in the creation of deviance. I have already argued that power is the ability to make rules for others. The ability to define what constitutes appropriate behavior in a particular place is one fundamental form of this power. Howard Becker does not emphasize place in his classic study of deviance. He does, however, refer to those labeled deviant as "outsiders." *Outsider* is commonly the term used to describe people new to a place or people who do not know the ways of a place. The use of the term *outsider* indicates that a person does not properly understand the behavior expected of people in a town, region, or nation. Outsiders are often despised and suspected of being trouble-makers. They are people "out of place."

One group of people referred to as outsiders are Gypsies. David Sibley's account of the government treatment of Gypsies in England is an example of the way deviance is created by the establishment of rules and norms and their transgression by a subordinate group with its own rules and norms.[29] Sibley draws our attention to the role of spatial arrangement in the creation of the Gypsies' "deviance." He describes a Gypsy camp as it would typically be organized. The camp would be arranged in a circular pattern with a single entrance. The windows of the caravans would face inward. The central area would be for play and socializing while the single entrance would be a deterrent to "Gorgios" (house-dwelling society). Planners, in their attempts to develop "acceptable" sites for the Gypsies, fenced them off from each other with fences and trees (the Gypsies prefer openness); they would separate home from work (despite the tradition of working at home among the Gypsies). In addition they would arrange the camps in straight lines as if they were generic housing estates.

The reaction of the planners points to the perception of traveling people as being "disordered." The rules and norms of the traveler culture has its own spatial expression (the circular camp, mobility, mingling of home and work), but this is misrecognized as disorder by the larger society, which labels the Gypsies as "deviant" and as "outsiders." The experience of the traveling culture illustrates the role of geography in creating rules, norms, and expectations. I have chosen to focus on transgression rather than deviance because transgression (and the term "out of place") implies inherent spatiality.

To conclude, transgression is important because it breaks from "normality" and causes a questioning of that which was previously considered "natural," "assumed," and "taken for granted." Transgressions appear to be "against nature"; they disrupt the patterns and processes of normality and offend the subtle myths of consensus. These deviations from the dominant ideological norms serve to confuse and disorientate. In doing so they temporarily reveal the historical and mutable nature of that which is usually considered "the way things are." The way the world is defined, categorized, segmented, and classified is rendered problematic. Such provocations result in highly charged attempts to diffuse the challenge presented by the transgressors. In his study of punk sub-cultures, Hebdige describes two major forms of incorporation; two ways in which the "order of things" is repaired and reinstated.[30] These are the conversion of transgressions into commodity forms (such as the transformation of the "sixties" counterculture into an "over-the-counter culture") and the labeling of groups as "deviant" by dominant groups such as the media, the police, and the judiciary. The remainder of this book is an examination of that labeling process in three specific instances. The majority of the analysis involves geographical interpretation of media representations of transgression. This is supplemented by discussion of the role of law and political institutions (local and national government).

Synthesis

My primary concern here is to describe the role of place in the construction of ideological beliefs concerning order, propriety, and "normality." I have chosen, for methodological and theoretical reasons, to study moments in which dominant ideological belief systems are challenged and disrupted. My suggestion is that the dominant reactions (of the media, the judicial system, and political figures) to such breaches of expectancies provide evidence of the relationship between place and ideology. My focus on media and government representations is based on the importance of such representations in the maintenance of ideology. These are particularly public reactions that reach a broad cross section of the "public." Critical media studies have firmly established the role of the media in reproducing "common sense."[31] Specifically, I outline the ways in which the language of these reactions utilizes metaphors and descriptive terms implying that the actions of certain marginal(ized) groups are "out of place." "Normality" is defined, to a significant degree, geographically, and deviance from this normality is also shot through with geographical assumptions concerning what and who belong where. There is, as Henri Lefebvre has argued, a spatial economy: "[Abstract space] implies a tacit agreement, a non-aggression pact, a contract, as it were, of non-violence. It imposes reciprocity, and a communality of use. In the street, each individual is supposed not to attack those he meets; anyone who transgresses this law is deemed guilty of a criminal act."[32] By tracing the disruption of this "spatial economy"—the internalized and naturalized boundaries that relate place to ideology—we can describe the geography of ideological expectations.

Part 2

Heretical Geographies

A Little Poem

We say that some are mad. In fact
if we have all the words and we
make madness mean the way they act
then they as all of us can see

are surely mad. And then again
if they have all the words and call
madness something else, well then—
well then, they are not mad at all.

—*Miller Williams, 1986*

Chapter 3

Heretical Geography 1:
The Crucial "Where" of Graffiti

The Graffiti Story

The scene is New York City as it enters the 1970s. This was to be a troubled decade for the world city. The city budget was steadily heading into a large deficit and the infrastructure was crumbling. The city was on the slippery slope leading to the famous fiscal crisis of 1976. Under Mayor John Lindsay and Mayor Abraham Beame increasingly severe "austerity measures" were imposed on the city, leading to a rapid and highly visible decline in its physical fabric. Fifty-one bridges faced collapse, and many of the city's six thousand miles of sewers threatened to do the same. Roads were crumbling and the subway was in a bad state of disrepair.[1] Payrolls for city workers were cut 15 to 25 percent. Park attendants, teachers, police, hospital workers, and firefighters all felt the effects of "austerity." The *Wall Street Journal* wrote:

> Basic city services, once the model for urban areas across the nation, have been slashed to the point of breakdown.... Evidence of the cutbacks is everywhere: the streets are blanketed with garbage. Robberies, to name but one crime, are at an all-time high. The subway system is near collapse, plagued by aging equipment, vandalism, the frequent breakdowns and derailments.[2]

Poor people were disproportionately affected by "austerity"—black people and Puerto Ricans especially so. In the two years following the fall of 1974 the city lost half of its Spanish-speaking workforce and two-fifths of its black employees.[3] These people were also the ones most affected by the breakdown in public services, for it was they who most used the public parks, transport system, and hospitals. A desperate city government looked toward the federal government for help. President Ford's lack of interest led the *New York Daily News* in October 1975 to print the headline "Ford to City: Drop Dead."

It was during this tense and strained period that graffiti began to appear with increasing frequency on New York's material fabric. In the early months of 1971 a young man named Demetrius traveled around parts of New York City with a broad-tipped felt marker and wrote the name TAKI 183 on select walls, doors, and hoardings. By the summer months his mark seemed to saturate areas of the city. The name appeared to signify nothing other than a made-up name — not so much an identity as a pseudoidentity. The appearance of the symbol marked the beginning of a protracted series of political engagements with the issue of graffiti in New York City, beginning in 1971 and extending through to the late 1980s.

The *New York Times* was made aware of TAKI's existence and decided to find the person behind the mark. They found Demetrius and dedicated a half page to his exploits.[4] They presented him as a modern-day folk hero — a colorful outlaw with an interesting hobby. Indeed the appearance of the article started a long series of exchanges in the New York media as to whether or not graffiti could be considered as a new folk art.

Just as TAKI received the attention of the media, his exploits were attracting a group of young admirers who quickly began to replicate TAKI's achievements. TAKI became a folk hero, and the appearance of graffiti throughout the city spread rapidly. At first the graffiti consisted of small-scale "tags," or pseudonyms with street numbers added. These were applied to public property everywhere. The target that gathered the most attention, though, was the New York subway system. By 1973 the "tags" had become more colorful. The graffitists had discovered the limitations of felt-tipped pens and the wonders of spray paint.[5] Gradually, large multicolored "masterpieces" became more common — decorating whole coaches of New York subway trains. The graphic designs were still centered around a single name, such as TOMCAT and KOOK. This was not the political graffiti of Europe or the football-fan style of England. Neither was it the "John loves Lucy" school-ground variety. It was rarely obscene. This graffiti was all style. The work would often take crews of graffitists all night in a dark and dangerous subway yard. The results were often breathtakingly striking.[6]

Graffiti groups and gangs began to form. "The Crew," "Challenge to Be Free," and "Fabulous Five" were notable examples. These small groups formed complicated and hierarchical communities with their own rules and ethics. The whole process from "racking up" (stealing paint) to "getting up" (producing graffiti) was highly organized. Beginners were called "toys," and the lucky ones got to be apprentices with the accomplished "kings." The graffiti itself existed in a hierarchy of achievement from "tags" (simple names inside of subway cars), through "throw-ups" (bigger names on the outside), to "pieces" (masterpieces — symbols, names, and messages often covering whole cars). The legendary "worm" (a whole train) was only painted twice[7] (see figures 3.1–3.3).

The appearance of the graffitists' colorful products on the subway system soon led to an increasingly strong set of reactions on the part of the media, the government, and the public. The *New York Times* was chastised for its "celebration" of TAKI 183 and blamed for the increasing popularity of graffiti. Its writers, in unison with the increasingly angry Mayor Lindsay, quickly turned against the city's graffitists. I shall examine these reactions later in the chapter.

The city government, fuming at the suggestion that graffiti should be considered "art," instituted a series of expensive, and largely fruitless, antigraffiti campaigns. These ranged from the use of guard dogs and barbed wire at subway yards, through the use of antigraffiti paint and acid washes, to the annual antigraffiti day in which good citizens (represented by Boy and Girl Scouts) cleaned up decorated subway trains and public buildings. The sale of spray paints to minors was banned, and people were banned from possessing spray paint in public places. Ten

Figure 3.1. Tags on the New York subway. (Photo by Lynn Forsdale, from Craig Castleman, *Getting Up: Subway Graffiti in New York,* copyright 1982 MIT Press, by permission.)

Figure 3.2. Throw-up by IOU One. (Photo by Ted Pearlman, from Craig Castleman, *Getting Up: Subway Graffiti in New York,* copyright 1982 MIT Press, by permission.)

Figure 3.3. A full-scale dedication to "Mom" by Lee. (Photo by Harry Chalfant, from Craig Castleman, *Getting Up: Subway Graffiti in New York,* copyright 1982 MIT Press, by permission.)

million dollars was spent in 1972 on attempts to halt graffiti, and 1,562 people were arrested on graffiti charges.[8] By 1975 Lindsay admitted that the struggle against graffiti was a losing proposition, and the *New York Times* was writing editorials suggesting that spending millions on graffiti was a waste of time and money.[9] There were, after all, more serious problems to deal with.

As graffiti was in the political spotlight it was also undergoing its strange transformation into art. In the early part of 1972 a group of street graffiti artists, under the guidance of a City College sociology student named Hugo Martinez, formed the United Graffiti Artists (UGA). Martinez wanted to find an outlet for the creative egos of Puerto Rican kids from deprived environments.[10] He regularly visited a corner of 188th Street and learned the codes and secrets of graffiti. He convinced some of the writers to give a demonstration of their talents at City College on a paper-covered ten-by-forty-foot wall. On 20 October 1972 the graffitists engaged in "legitimate art" for the first time.

By December the UGA was attracting the attention of the *New York Times*[11] and was paid six hundred dollars for performing in a ballet entitled Deuce Coupe. Their performance was reviewed in the *Wall Street Journal*:

> While the dancers performed to pop music, Co-Co and his friends [the UGA artists] sprayed their names and other embellishments to create a flamboyant and fascinating backdrop. As the graffiti writers took their bows, waving their cans of spray paint, the trendy, avant-garde Joffrey audience responded with loud applause and numerous enthusiastic bravos. "They're so real!" one young spectator exclaimed to his date.[12]

The UGA was granted a studio in Manhattan for rent of one dollar a year and quickly began to hold exhibitions in SoHo. Paintings sold for over a thousand dollars, and press reports were generally favorable. This was at the same time as reports of street graffiti were gradually becoming more frantic in their denunciations. One favorable review of graffiti made the connection between the gallery graffiti and its street cousin: "It would be well to keep in mind that there has often been something mildly anti-social in the practice of art and society has almost invariably profited from it in the long run. Well, that is for those of you who can't simply relax and enjoy the visual bonus that comes these days with the purchase of a subway token."[13] The author was pleased to report that the "respectable standing and the 'art' context [had] not cowed most of the UGA artists." The UGA members eventually disbanded. Two became professional artists.

Another, more democratic, graffiti organization that formed in the early seventies was the Nation of Graffiti Artists (NOGA). While UGA membership was limited to acknowledged "masters," NOGA was oriented toward getting kids off the streets and keeping them fed. They provided art materials and encouraged production of graffiti art, which sold for up to $300. At one point they offered to paint subway cars for $150 a piece. The Metropolitan Transit Authority rejected the plan.

Just a few years after TAKI 183 hit the streets and attracted followers and detractors, graffiti began to appear in the smart galleries of SoHo. SoHo had been a mixed neighborhood of low- to medium-rent housing and small businesses. By the mid-seventies businesses had moved out, and their premises were converted into "loft apartments" and artist studios. SoHo was becoming a hip place to live and be seen, and it was also becoming expensive. The former residents and workers could no longer afford to live and work there.[14] Mayor Lindsay, the sworn enemy of graffiti, encouraged the gentrification of SoHo and its art community in the conviction that there was an increasingly important "arts constituency" in the city. With this in mind, he was primarily responsible for significant increases in the state's involvement in art funding—particularly in the "bohemian" art world of SoHo, where the graffiti of UGA was being enthusiastically accepted as a new form of "primitive" art.

SAMO was a graffiti artist who had, like TAKI 183, spread his name widely throughout the city. He was "discovered" by SoHo art dealer Annina Nosei, who invited him to join her gallery. As Jean-Michel Basquiat, he worked in the basement of the gallery producing the work that was to make him a celebrity. Keith Haring had used chalk on black empty spaces for advertisements in subway stations around major art centers in Manhattan. Soon his work was inside the galleries rather than outside. These artists became the most distinguished graffiti artists, and their work appeared in the most prestigious galleries. Haring's work is now available in poster form, along with Renoirs, Dalis, and Picassos. His work even appeared atop Times Square flashing out across the city he had once "defaced." The influence of graffiti is clear in the work of contemporary artists such as Jenny Holzer, who produced official-looking plaques and posters with strange messages and plastered them around New York City. In her work *Truisms* (1977) she sought to "place in contradiction certain ideological structures that are usually kept apart."[15] At first these posters were placed on the street. They interrupted the flow of everyday thoughts with statements such as "A strong sense of duty imprisons you" and "Ambivalance can ruin your life." These posters later appeared in galleries and on flashing signs.

The New York City government still responded to graffiti negatively in well-known instances. Lou Reed wanted to be pictured spraying graffiti in the New York subway for an album cover. The city government persuaded his record company to change the cover. Other popular culture enterprises cashed in on graffiti. The Clash featured the graffiti artist Futura in a music video. Graffiti can now be seen in a deli in Madison, Wisconsin, symbolizing, no doubt, the New York authenticity of the store's bagels and cream cheese. Michael Jackson used a graffiti-covered backdrop of generic urban decay for his appropriately titled *Bad* video. An electric power company advertises itself in a national magazine with white graffiti pictured on a red brick wall. The graffiti says rebelliously, "Power to the People." Perhaps a fitting end to this story is the choice by DisneyWorld (the supreme court of representations) to represent New York City not with the Empire State Building or the Statue of Liberty but with a graffiti-covered subway train. Naturally the city government complained.

In the remainder of this chapter I step back into the story I have just told. I will concentrate on two parts of the story: the frantic responses to graffiti on the street that sought to portray it as deviant and the enthusiastic acceptance of it as art by the SoHo art community. As I will show, each of these responses (despite their apparent contradictions) reveals the power of place in the construction of "normality" and "deviance."

The Discourse of Disorder

The pages of the *New York Times* and other New York media, particularly in the 1970s, presented a discourse of disorder. In reaction to graffiti, the language and the rhetoric of the press, its readers, and government officials convey a deep fear of disorder in the landscape. This fear is prompted by the appearance in public spaces of people's names and pseudonyms. Reaction to graffiti describes it as a threat to order—as out of place—in two main ways: (1) by suggesting through a mass of metaphors and descriptive terms that graffiti does not belong in New York's public places and (2) by associating it with other places—other contexts—where either the order is different and more amenable to graffiti or disorder is more prevalent. In each case the geographical implications are powerful.

Throughout the 1970s graffiti is referred to variously as garbage, pollution, obscenity, an epidemic, a disease, a blight, a form of violence, dangerous, and a product of the mad, the ghetto, and the barbarian. An examination of these reactions reveals the role of implicit normative geographies in the ordering of "appropriate" behavior.

Dirt, Garbage, Pollution, Obscenity

One of the most prevalent terms used to describe graffiti is one form or another of dirt. I will give you a few of the many examples. A letter in the *New York Times* reads: "No civilized metropolis (Montreal, Mexico City, Moscow) would endure such garbage and its continuing proliferation in New York shocks many visitors and repulses untold numbers of local travelers."[16] City Council President Sanford Garelick is quoted in the *New York Times* of 21 May 1972 as saying, "Graffiti pollutes the eye and mind and may be one of the worst forms of pollution we have to combat."[17] Craig Castleman in his book *Getting Up* quotes Metropolitan Transit Authority Chairman Rich Ravitch as saying: "The subways in general are a mess, and the public sees graffiti as a form of defacement like garbage, noise, dirt, and broken doors."[18]

Dirt is something in the wrong place or wrong time. Dirt disgusts us because it appears where it shouldn't be — on the kitchen floor or under the bed. The very same objects (dust and grime) do not constitute dirt if they are in a different place. The meaning of dirt is dependent on its location. Because dirt appears where it shouldn't, it lies at the bottom of a hierarchical scale of values; dirt is valued by very few people. It annoys us in its persistence, in its audacity to keep turning up in places we thought were clean, pure, and pristine.

Mary Douglas, in her book *Purity and Danger,* examines the concept of dirt and pollution. She connects the dread of dirt to a fear of disorder. Removing dirt, on the other hand, is part of the establishment of an ordered environment. We make the environment conform to an idea, a sense of order. Dirt, she says, is "matter out of place," a definition that suggests simultaneously some form of order and a contravention of that order. Dirt, by its very definition, depends on the preexistence of a system, a mode of classification. Douglas makes this point well:

> Shoes are not dirty in themselves, but it is dirty to place them on the
> dining table; food is not dirty in itself, but it is dirty to leave cooking
> utensils in the bedroom, or food bespattered on clothing; similarly,
> bathroom equipment in the drawing room; clothing lying on chairs;
> out-door things in-doors; upstairs things downstairs; under clothing
> appearing where over-clothing should be, and so on.[19]

Dirt, then, is a mismatch of meanings — meanings that are erroneously positioned in relation to other things. Things that transgress become dirt—they are in the wrong place. If there was no "wrong place," there could be no transgression. Another way of putting it is that transgression represents a questioning of boundaries. Here we are not talking about the boundaries of a territory; no enforcement of access is implied. We are talking of symbolic boundaries. But still we return to geography, as these symbolic boundaries not only vary with place but are constituted by place. In all of the illustrations (graffiti, Stonehenge, and the Greenham women) we shall see the use of metaphors of dirt to describe and ridicule the transgressors. Douglas's discussion of "matter out of place" is relevant to all of them and provides a useful analytical tool for decoding the reactions to these transgressions. Beliefs about dirt and pollution relate to power relations in society as they delineate, in an ideological fashion, what is out of place. Those who can define what is out of place are those with the most power in society.

A note of caution is needed, however. First, Douglas's idea is devoid of any reference to the types of forces that are at play in the definition of "dirt." What counts as dirt varies widely across cultures. In each culture different types of pressures work to create these differences. Douglas fails to discuss the ways in which forces related to class, gender, and ethnicity, for instance, create notions of what is "out of place." Second, Douglas's analysis is entirely relative. We can safely assume that some things are almost universally out of place. Fatal diseases, for instance, are unlikely to be welcome anywhere. In the illustrations here, however, the objects of the word *dirt* are not out of place in any absolute sense. Graffiti, women at military camps, and young traveling festival-goers are not literally diseases. It is to some group's advantage to describe them as such for political, social, and cultural reasons.

Julia Kristeva builds on Douglas's insights in *The Powers of Horror*. Like Douglas she suggests that filth is a label that relates to a boundary. Filth to Kristeva is an object pushed beyond a boundary to its other side, its margin. The power of pollution is "proportional to the potency of the prohibition that founds it."[20] Kristeva's theorizations are more closely tied to power relations than are Douglas's. Kristeva is particularly concerned with gender relations, and her observations relate to the role of filth in those relations. Kristeva is more concerned with who it is that constructs prohibitions and boundaries and thus who becomes the margin. Symbolic orders are constructed through and by power, and filth represents the "objective frailty" of that order.[21] When graffiti is labeled as filth it is an acknowledgment of the threat that it poses to order.

A related reaction to graffiti is to label it obscene. A New York government committee on graffiti suggested that "the defacing of property and the use of foul language in many of the writings is harmful to the general public."[22] However, the vast majority of graffiti in public places, and particularly on the subway system, is essentially meaningless—usually a single word like Hurk or Sony. The *New York Times* itself frequently refers to the fact that graffiti is rarely obscene in content. For instance, a large article of June 1974 remarks that graffiti covering neighborhood walls usually consists of multicolored designs of simple names, with few obscenities.[23] Still public officials and the *New York Times* call graffiti obscene. What is obscene about a made-up name?

One suggestion is that criticism of graffiti as obscene is linked to the crucial *where* of appropriateness: "All display is a form of exposure and just as the spaces of reproduction in society are maintained through regulation, by means of taboo and legitimation, of places and times of sexuality, so, in this case, do writing and figuration in the wrong place and time fall into the category of 'obscenity.' "[24] Dirt and obscenity are linked by the importance of place in their very definition; they represent things out of order—in particular, out of place. Just as dirt is supposed to represent not just a spoiling of the surface, but a problem that lies much deeper (in terms of hygiene, for instance), graffiti as dirt is seen as a permanent despoiling of whole sets of meanings—neighborliness, order, property, and so on. Graffiti is linked to the dirty, animalistic, uncivilized, and profane.

Disease, Contagion, Madness

Less obviously connected to the idea of dirt is the idea that graffiti is linked to disease—graffiti as an epidemic or contagion. The *New York Times* refers to the "general graffiti epidemic."[25] A review of a graffiti art exhibition in 1973 notes that it will probably do little to "diffuse the graffiti epidemic."[26] The more poetic *New York Daily News* headlines a 1973 article "The Great Graffiti Plague."[27] An August 1974 headline from the same newspaper reads "The Trouble with Graffiti: It's a Catching Disease."[28] Elsewhere there are references to the recent "rash" of graffiti—a visible surface symptom of a deeper malaise. One official is quoted as saying, "Graffiti is the skin cancer of our civilization.... If it has value it is because it is a symptom of something rotten.... Turn your head because the stuff is bloody, bloodless brutality."[29] Disease has been connected to dirt; it has been seen as pollution of the body. Diseases are also referred to as disorders, the results of intrusions by alien objects that do not belong in a particular place—the body. The implication, of course, is that the body of the city is ill. Tuan notes that the city has served as a symbol of order and harmony, a visible symbol of a cosmic order, a stable society. Disease is one of the roots of fear; that is why lepers, for example, are separated from society. A disease in the city is a threat to order.[30] Implicit in the use of disease terms in the antigraffiti rhetoric is the idea of separation and confinement. The causes of disease need to be isolated; carriers need to be quarantined. Like dirt, a disease is a disorder with spatial implications. In the modern imagination, it seems, there is still a connection between environment and health. Felix Driver has described the relation between Victorian social science and environmentalism. Social science, he argues, was the "mapping of types of behavior to types of environment."[31] The distribution of health and, by implication, virtue, was said to depend on the influence of the moral and physical environment. Sanitary science, in particular, "examined the urban geography of disease, its relationship with local environmental conditions and the location, distribution and migration of the population."[32] Hence Foucault called doctors the "specialists of space." The theoretical structure behind this environmentalism was the idea of miasmas—invisible atmospheric substances created by the putrification of organic matter and the human body itself. The prime problem was then accumulation of filth. Moral conditions were linked to physical conditions. Crime was described as a "subtle, unseen but sure poison in the moral atmosphere of the neighborhood, as dangerous as is deadly miasma to the physical health."[33]

Although social science and medicine may have progressed since the nineteenth century, it seems that the rhetoric of journalists and politicians still link the moral, physical, and sanitary environments in similar ways. The point is this: the use of metaphors of disease and contagion implies disorder—the spread of pollution that causes the disease and also the moral disorder of people out of place. The moral geography of nineteenth-century sanitary science is replicated in the moral geography portrayed in the New York media. To use the term *disease* is to imply spatial transgressions and the possibility of spatial solutions to these problems. The implications of a plague or epidemic go further than this, though. Susan Sontag has traced the history of the use of the plague metaphor.[34] The word has its roots in the Latin *plaga* (stroke, wound) and has historically been used to describe extreme examples of calamity, usually with the implication of evil. As the use of the metaphor developed through the years it took on the implication of *coming from elsewhere*. Epidemics in Britain were often blamed on Germany and France, and later on the colonies, particularly Africa and Asia. Europe was constantly held to be a "pure" place threatened from elsewhere. This viewpoint has been inherited by the United States in its script for the rise of AIDS. AIDS is thought to have begun in "deepest" Africa and to have entered the healthy body of the United States through Haiti. The description of graffiti as a plague, then, implies foreign origin. As we shall see later, the metaphorical inscription of graffiti as dirt and disease are combined with a notion that graffiti comes from and belongs in the metaphorical "jungle" of the third world.

A particular type of medical metaphor that is frequently used is that of madness. This form of illness is singled out as apt for the description of graffiti and its writers. As Foucault has eloquently shown, madness is civilization's disturbing other—the ultimate disorder.[35] No less a figure than Mayor Lindsay is reported to have said it was "the Lindsay Theory that the rash of graffiti madness was related to mental health problems." For added effect, he went on to say that graffitists were "insecure cowards."[36] The metaphorical use of madness is backed up with the suggestion that graffitists are, in fact, insane. Some of the reactions to graffiti that appeared in the letters page of the *New York Times* also made the link to madness, describing the minds of graffiti artists as feeble and fragile.[37] The critic Roger Rosenblatt also linked graffiti to madness: "Most of the graffiti on the subways nowadays is indecipherable, which either means that the attack artist is an illiterate—frightening in itself—or that he is using some unknown cuneiform language or the jagged symbols of the mad."[38]

In his book *The Faith of Graffiti,* Norman Mailer discusses the horror felt by the "civilized office worker" when confronted with the inescapable image of graffiti. The office worker felt that if he or she were to write on public walls, all manner of filth would burst out all over. He writes: "My god, the feces to spread and the blood to spray, yes the good voting citizen of New York would know that the violent world of Bellevue was opening its door to him."[39] Here Mailer uses the images of dirt and insanity and suggests the link between them and graffiti. The compulsion to spread dirt and the potential to be placed in an asylum are a spatial action and a spatial reaction. Behavior out of place demands to be corrected by putting the perpetrator in her place.

Graffiti and the Place of the Other

Graffiti flagrantly disturbs notions of order. It represents a disregard for order and, it seems to those who see it, a love of disorder—of anarchy, of things out of place. In the journal *Public Interest,* in 1979, the well-known critic Nathan Glazer wrote: "[The commuter] is assaulted continuously, not only by the evidence that every subway car has been vandalized, but by the inescapable knowledge that the environment he must endure for an hour or more a day is uncontrolled and uncontrollable, and that anyone can invade it to do whatever damage and mischief the mind suggests."[40] Reactions to graffiti convey the link between graffiti and rampant anarchy by using other places—other contexts—as examples of where graffiti may be in place. Most frequently the places chosen are from the third world.

Graffiti is not just "out of place" because it is misplaced figuration; its "otherness" is also connected to its assumed source, the ethnic minorities of urban New York. We have already seen how the description of graffiti as plague implies the involvement of "outsiders." Dirt and madness, too, are often used metaphorically to describe the third world and its imagined inhabitants. The biographical characteristics do not always confirm the impression that graffiti is a product of traditional minorities,[41] but the general belief is that graffiti is a Puerto Rican or African American phenomenon rather than, say, Austrian, Swedish American, or, as in the case of TAKI 183, Greek. Once this assumption is made, the reactions to graffiti slip into a discourse that repeatedly makes reference to the "third world," which exists outside of the dominant value structure of the United States and the "West." The third world relation to the United States itself has a metaphorical similarity to the relation between white people and ethnic minorities in the urban United States. We do not have to make great leaps of interpretation to point to the assumed origins of graffiti; the most obvious references to the perceived ethnic characteristics of graffiti are those which directly refer to Latin America and Africa. One well-known positive reaction to graffiti serves as an example. The pop artist Claes Oldenburg wrote, "You're standing there in the station, everything is grey and gloomy and all of a sudden one of those graffiti trains slides in and brightens up the place like a big bouquet from Latin America."[42] Favorable and critical reviews of graffiti alike frequently refer to Latin America, the Caribbean, Africa, and even Russia. Along with the assumption that graffiti writers are probably from some distant place (some other context where graffiti is more appropriate), there is a heavy political question evident in seemingly pure aesthetic judgments. "Lady Pink," a graffiti artist, was referred to by one critic as a "paint-smeared Sandinista" (despite the fact that Pink was from Ecuador), suggesting that graffiti might be more appropriate "elsewhere," in a setting associated with violence and terrorism.

One particular example of this kind of comment deserves special attention. "TAKI 183," the seventeen-year-old Greek immigrant I discussed earlier, is widely acknowledged as the grandfather of U.S. metropolitan graffiti. His marks on subways were widely publicized and criticized in the early seventies through the pages of the *New York Times*. At first the coverage was positive, painting a picture of a folk hero with an interesting and creative hobby. This was in 1971. A year later TAKI was a vandal and a public nuisance and graffiti had become "one of the worst forms of pollution we have to combat." TAKI the folk hero became TAKI the vandal. A Greek immigrant in New York became the central symbol of filth and disorder.[43]

Many years earlier in Greece the then revolutionary poet Lord Byron scratched his name on the Temple of Poseidon. The critic Roger Rosenblatt, TAKI's fiercest critic, found this quite acceptable: "Even Lord Byron wrote his name on the Temple of Poseidon at Sounion in Greece — technically defacing a house of worship, but enhancing it too. Run your fingers along his signature now and you are touched by him who wrote: 'The hand that kindles cannot quench the flame.' "[44] To Rosenblatt, Byron's graffiti (although he does not use this term) is an enhancement of a beautiful Greek temple. TAKI's inscriptions on the decaying urban environment are sacrilege. The markings of the immigrant in "our city" are "defacements" (and sites of contestation within the contemporary dominant world power). Our inscriptions in other worlds (the signature of an author who rests squarely within the established canon) are the inscriptions of a former dominant imperialist world power on the place of the dominated. This story of a poor Greek immigrant and an established figure of world literature tells us of the role of geography in judgments of culture and aesthetics — in the interpretation of meaning.

Once we begin to see the (in some senses) obvious connections between graffiti and perceived ethnic difference, the more general labels of dirt, disease, and madness can be seen in a somewhat different light than I originally interpreted them. These appellations are all descriptive terms used at one time or another to describe "aliens" within the United States or, alternatively, the third world, particularly countries that in some way or another stand up against U.S. domination. "Dirty," for instance, is an appellation frequently applied to immigrants in cities, whether the Irish in London or the Chinese in Vancouver.[45] As Sophie Laws has suggested: "The idea that people with certain characteristics are dirty is very often found as part of the attitudes of a dominant group towards a less powerful one. It is a persistent feature of racism and anti-semitism as well as misogyny."[46]

David Ward, in his discussion of the connections between poverty and ethnicity in the North American slum, makes a similar point, connecting the arrival of immigrants in New York City during the nineteenth century with perceptions of disease, dirt, and anarchy. One commentator he discusses described immigrants as "the refuse of Europe [who] congregate in our great cities and send forth ... wretched progeny. Degraded in the deep degradation of their parents ... to be scavengers,

physical and moral, of our streets."[47] One inner city area in particular—
Five Points—became a national symbol for this immigrant slum deprav-
ity: "Every State in the Union, and every nation almost in the world,
have representatives in this foul and dangerous locality."[48] Interestingly,
Five Points was portrayed in engravings as an arena of disorderly street
life rather than a slumlike environment. An engraving from *Valentine's
Manual of Old New York* (1827) looks suspiciously like a Breughel
painting of carnival, with raucous buxom women and drunken men
scattered haphazardly along the streets. In the case of graffiti, the press
and the government choose to point to the chaotic and anarchic appearance of graffiti and suggest its ethnic dimensions while the urban infrastructure of New York was in a state of bankruptcy and disrepair. The
link between chaos (in the form of dirt, disease, and madness) and immigrants is not a new one in New York's history.[49]

Perhaps the best-known analysis of the "third world" in relation to
the themes of madness and dirt is Frantz Fanon's *The Wretched of the
Earth*.[50] He describes how the inhabitants of the third world have been
systematically violated through colonial oppression. Part of this violation includes the correlation of blackness with madness and dirt. Fanon
turns such arguments around, describing Europe (and the United States)
as insane and sunk in savagery. Any madness on the part of the third
world is, in his view, a direct result of colonial manipulation. He effectively turns the discourse of disorder around on the colonialists and
forces them (us) to look in the mirror.

Graffiti is continually portrayed (as I have already shown) as the chaotic, untamed voice of the irrational. As such it is both resisted and condemned. Graffiti is rebellious, irrational, dirty, and irreducibly "other."
In these senses it is connected to the third world and to immigrants—
themselves described as rebellious and irrational. The "West," particularly the Western city, is (at least ideally) the product of reason and the
inevitable progress of history. The graffiti artist (like the rebellious third
world) is the insane spoiler who resists reason and introduces chaos.[51]

Another context in which graffiti is frequently placed is that of the
European Communist world. Recently the *New York Times* featured a
picture of the Berlin Wall as it was symbolically falling down. The picture included some bright new graffiti. The punch line was that this was
the east side of the wall—another sign of newfound freedom springing
up next to McDonald's and the polling booth. The implication, of course,
is that graffiti, in this case, represents desired disorder—disorder in a
context that we are used to thinking of as overly authoritarian and orderly. In this context graffiti is associated with freedom and democracy—the Westernization of Eastern Europe, and, inevitably, the end of

Communism. How different from reactions to graffiti in New York! In one context graffiti is seen as a symptom of the end of civilization, of anarchy and decaying moral values, and in another it is a sign of a free spirit closing the curtain on the stifling bureaucracy of Communist authoritarianism.

It is clear that the question of whose world is being written over—the crucial "where" of appropriateness—is never a purely aesthetic judgment. The question of geographical hegemony—the taken-for-granted moral order—inevitably imposes itself on the politics of aesthetic and moral evaluation.

The Image of the City

The reactions of government figures and the media to graffiti point overwhelmingly to one fact. It is only superficially the material defacement of public property that is at stake; the real issue is the image of New York City. It is not that spray paint has been applied to the side of a subway train but that the act of graffiti creates an illusion of disorder. This notion of disorder is tightly woven into a set of ideas about "proper places." The use of terms like "dirt," "madness," and "disease" underline a fear of spatial disorder; the implication that graffiti belongs in other places—in the third world or the ghetto—suggests a fear of rampant anarchy in New York City.

The fight against graffiti is a fight against all perceived forces of disorder and a conflict over the proper place to one's meaning—over different notions of dirt. To a figure such as Mayor Lindsay, graffiti is a massive and continuing defacement destroying the proper significance (meanings) of the carefully controlled facades of the urban environment. New York itself is threatened. Mayor Lindsay, when opening the Prospect Park Boathouse in 1972, remarked on the graffiti that was bound to appear on it and pleaded "for heaven's sake, New Yorkers, come to the aid of your great city—defend it, support it and protect it."[52] I would suggest that it is not the material culture—the buildings of New York—that the mayor was worried about, so much as New York as a symbol of control, order, and harmony.

It is not surprising that one analysis of graffiti argues that in some senses graffiti is the ideal crime for a marginalized culture. Its criminality lies in its refusal to comply with its context: it does not respect the laws of place that tell us what is and what is not appropriate. Graffiti is a crime because it subverts the authority of urban space and asserts the triumph (however fleeting) of the individual over the monuments of authority, "the name over the nameless."⁵³ Graffiti can be described as a "tactic" of the dispossessed—a mobile and temporary set of meanings that insert themselves into the interstices of the formal spatial structure (roads, doors, walls, subways, and so on) of the city.

Graffiti also challenges the dominant dichotomy between public and private space. It interrupts the familiar boundaries of the public and the private by declaring the public private and the private public. Graffiti appears on the streets, the facades, the exteriors, and the interiors that construct and articulate the meanings of the city. To the graffiti writer, everywhere is free space. The presence of graffiti denies the dominant divisions of meaning. The practice of graffiti by dominated groups makes claims upon the meanings of spaces; it utilizes the open, free quality of spaces that are not officially free or open. As Susan Stewart suggests, graffiti attempts a "utopian and limited dissolution of the boundaries of property" reflecting an older, Latin sense of the street as a "room by agreement" and extends it to include "the street as playground, ballfield, and billboard by agreement—or by conflict, subterfuge, and the exercise of power and privilege."⁵⁴

As private space is made public, public space is made private, individualized, stylized. The style of graffiti—its fluid characters and colors—symbolizes the fluid and mobile nature of those who practice it (the kings). The transit lines become mobile billboards—moving sets of colorful names that get out and go places. It is this mobile billboard that transects the fixed, static urban environment of sanctioned meanings created by the dominant notions of property and place. To these spaces, the monumental buildings of height and anonymity, the graffitist adds personal marks on a scale perceptible to the individual. The street, in some sense, is "appropriated" by those who live in it, reclaimed from the enormous condescension of those who own it. The graffitist opposes the static, monumental politics of the dominant with the mobile, personal tags of the dominated.

The urban environment is constructed around a set of "appropriate" places, areas imbued with sets of meanings deemed correct by dominant groups in society. There are places to play, pray, sleep, eat, make love, and an infinite number of other activities. The associations between the place and its meanings are powerful and often public and communicable. The built environment materializes meanings—sets them in concrete and stone. In the process of making meaning material, these images become open to question and challenge. Social groups are capable of creating their own sense of place and contesting the constructs of others. Once meaning finds its geographical expression it is no longer personal; it is there—visible, material, solid, and shared. Once it is known what type of behavior is appropriate for which place, it is simultaneously obvious which things are inappropriate and unacceptable and thus challenging to the guardians of the established order.

While it has been argued that graffiti is a form of existential self-affirmation to the graffiti writer, it is also the case that graffiti means something very different from the perspective of the unsympathetic viewer. Indeed graffiti seems to threaten the existence of those who do not relate to this obscure idiom. One harsh critic of graffiti, Rosenblatt, suggests this view:

> Graffiti makes you scared [because] we do not ever see who writes HURK and SONY. The artist is a sneak thief, and just as he attacks his canvas suddenly, his work attacks you.... [T]hese names (scary in their very loudness) are yelling to you in public places, where you wish to preserve your own name.[55]

Rosenblatt suggests in this passage a complicated connection between wishing to remain private in public and the idea that graffiti represents a symbolically violent attack on an equally symbolic category of property. The graffiti writer is a "thief." This view of graffiti is underlined by other voices of authority who clearly see graffiti as a threat to considerably more than the surface on which it is written. A Philadelphia city ordinance banned the sale of spray paint to minors, stating that "graffiti contributes to the blight and degradation of neighborhoods and *even discourages the formation of business.*" Similarly in Los Angeles a leading police official stated that "*graffiti decreases property value* and signed buildings on block after block convey the impression that the city government has lost control, that the neighborhood is sliding towards anarchy."[56] Here we see how graffiti is seen in relation to a context that includes property values and local business in its perception of order but excludes the spray-painted mark of an individual who lies outside of the property and business relations that get to define that context.

In the case of reactions to New York graffiti we have seen a determined effort to express, in the language of common sense, a spatial ordering of types of behavior and the moral implications thereof. The landscape of New York can be seen as a normative landscape of "proper" places—that is to say, experienced contexts in which people behave themselves and act according to expectations that are, in part, spatially distributed and determined: art belongs in art school, the streets are for driving, and so on. Graffiti comes along and upsets this assumed, seemingly natural world, and the moral landscape has to be outlined and stated as orthodoxy, as the right way to do things. It is at this point—when the expectations about place and behavior are upset—that the formally assumed normative geography has to be underlined and reinforced, made explicit in the discourse of reaction in the press and city government. The link between spatial context and behavior is crucially changed from an *assumed, natural, common-sense, and unquestioned* relationship to a *demanded, normal, and established* relationship that has been questioned. In the first instance the appropriate behavior is defined as the *only* form of behavior; in the second it is defined in relation to an *"other"*—a heretical geography. The appropriate is defined by the inappropriate.

In reactions to graffiti there is a constant linking of geographical and moral disorder; a perceived disorder in space caused by graffiti is linked to a moral disorder, a particular inappropriateness. In reacting to the perceived transgression of graffiti, the New York media affects the meaning of New York and places within it. The powerful voice of the media defends particular meanings and derides others. In addition it is important that the always already existing meanings of places affect the nature of the discourse—for example, the assumed meaning of the ghetto, of New York, of Latin America ...

The meaning of both acts and places is historically variable. The same place (or the same act) may have opposite meanings at different times. Graffiti is not inherently or essentially "abnormal," "dirty," "disorderly," or "sick." Graffiti is not naturally "out of place." In fact, the New York media discourse of normality and its implied meanings for place (the subway system, public buildings, the city itself) can be and have been presented in other terms—sickness as health, disease (disintegration) as creativity, disorder as art. Consider the graffiti-covered subway train that was chosen as a representative symbol of New York for a Disney exhibition. A characteristic of Disney World as a place is that it chooses positive images—images of creativity, health, exuberance, liveliness. It would be extremely unlikely that graffiti was chosen because it represented disorder, disease, madness, and obscenity. Disney has no place for such things. A sounder hypothesis is that graffiti was chosen as a symbol of creativity and participation (democracy)—a representation of a vibrant, colorful, creative New York City.

Additionally the very same characteristics of graffiti that make it repugnant to Mayor Lindsay make it appealing to segments of the art world. Again crime becomes creativity, madness becomes insight, dirt becomes something to hang over the fireplace. Just as the reactions of the press to graffiti tell us about the role of place in the construction of order and thus of deviance, so does the more positive reaction of the art establishment.

The Paradox of Graffiti as Art

Paradoxically (it seems), at the same time as graffiti was painted as a wild, anarchic threat to society by one dominant group (the "authorities"), it was taken off the streets and placed in galleries by another dominant group (official culture):[57]

> The movement of graffiti to canvas and gallery space continues the process of substitution by which historical contingency is mythologized; mediating figures such as art students become the new graffiti artists … social workers and photographers become spokespersons and publicists for graffiti writers; acceptable, readable and apprehensible in scale, graffiti painting is enclosed within a proper space and time and delimited for consumption as a singular artifact.[58]

As Paul Hagopian has commented, the entry of graffiti into the gallery presented a paradox:[59] the affirmation of graffiti's "status" as an art vitiated the lawlessness on which its "appeal" was based. We can construct a table of oppositions between graffiti-as-crime and graffiti-as-art.

Crime	Graffiti Art
Outside	Inside
Temporary	Permanent
Wild	Tame
Nonartifact	Artifact
Large	Small
Illegible	Readable
Noncommodity	Commodity
Unexpected	Expected

Most of the attributes of graffiti that make it appealing as crime are nullified by the act of placing it in the gallery, making it into art. In effect, the art world has transformed and commodified graffiti by displacing it. As Atlanta and Alexander have argued:

> The art-world promised a way out of the ghetto only to confine the work of the graffiti painters to the more restricted code of the art-world. . . .

In the process of gallery consumption little of the specific meaning of the graffiti art was communicated, or even survived the threshold of the gallery itself.[60]

As graffiti underwent its metamorphosis from crime to art it suffered a displacement from the street to the gallery. Graffiti in the gallery is graffiti in its "proper" place. It is no longer the tactic of the marginalized but part of the strategy of the establishment, conforming to the codes of the "proper place."

The meaning of graffiti was subsumed within a lineage defined by art critics and gallery owners. Whereas graffitists take their inspiration from the signs and styles of advertising, the art world begins to place graffiti in a different tradition of "pop art" and the "primitive." One art show catalog read, "Urban-bred, the graffiti artist continues the tradition of pop-art which he admires."[61] That particular exhibition was titled *Post-Graffiti,* announcing the death of "real" graffiti and the rebirth of the pop art tradition. Long "histories" of the graffiti tradition were invoked, ranging from cave paintings to Arabic traditions of place-marking. The movement of graffiti from the street to the gallery involved a simultaneous insertion of graffiti into a tradition, a history outside of which it had previously existed. Graffiti was now legitimated by its place inside the gallery and by its place in the history of art.

The appellation "primitive" was frequently applied to graffiti as art. Graffiti's appeal to the art world lay in its apparent wildness and spontaneity (which was at least partly a result of its refusal to obey the rules of place). Graffiti was romanticized as a folk art. This was despite the remarkable sophistication of graffiti techniques, the rigid apprenticeship system that graffiti artists worked through (from "toys" to "kings"), and the continued practice of different forms by the graffiti artists in their "black books." The assumption that graffiti is somehow primitive is linked to the frequent assertion that graffitists are from "the jungle" in the form of Latin America or Africa. Oldenburg's description of the subway car from "Latin America" and Norman Mailer's description of graffiti as "the impulse of the jungle"[62] reflect the assumed primitive and "natural" aspects of graffiti. There is clearly a question of race and "Orientalism" in the assumptions of graffiti's promoters. I have already suggested that this assumption of the ethnic status of graffitists often appears in media accounts of street graffiti in negative ways. In the art world these third world associations are given a positive twist and are associated with unrestrained creativity. The association of graffiti with nature, the primitive, and the crazy is applauded in its new context.

So as graffiti is reconstituted as art, desecration becomes a matter of taste and consumption. Graffiti as crime (and dirt) was often painted on a subway car sixty feet long and twelve feet high that moved through the city with all its delineated territories. The graffiti would remain only a few days before being scrubbed off by the "buffer"—a machine that removed graffiti with various acids. Graffiti was mobile and temporary. The graffiti writer, working in the train yard, would never see the whole thing until the train moved out of the yard. The whole process was quick and fluid, allowing no possibility of perspective or a distant view: "The transience of the painting means that the cultural meaning is involved with the process of doing, of pulling it off. The scale and speed of the transformation is an important part of appreciation of the painting."[63] In the gallery graffiti is a product of contemplation and permanence. The artist can remove herself from the artwork, contemplate it from afar, and revise it. Graffiti's almost constant motion and ephemerality becomes ossified into a static and "permanent" object.

By the secular magic of displacement, graffiti is transformed from the wild, criminal, reviled, and despised product of the insane and deviant into the creative, inspired, and aesthetically pleasing product of the artist. In the process of the movement from the street and subway to the SoHo gallery, the "meaning" of graffiti and the moral judgment of it are changed dramatically. It is surely paradoxical that the same act (painting a stylized logo) can be at once reviled and admired, removed and preserved. In one area money is spent to remove graffiti and in the other it is spent to buy it and add daring and "local color" to some wealthy patron's living room. At the same time that Michael Stewart, a young graffiti artist, died by strangulation at the hands of twelve transit cops, graffiti art was selling for thousands of dollars in Manhattan galleries. Graffiti is simultaneously repressed and commodified.

At least part of the explanation for this apparent schizophrenia can be found in Peter Stallybrass and Allon White's book *The Politics and Poetics of Transgression*. The authors suggest that there are complex cultural processes "whereby the human body, psychic forms, geographical space and the social formations are all constructed with interrelating and dependent hierarchies of high and low."[64] The book is particularly involved with the diverse ways in which the "high" in culture is troubled by and attracted to the "low" in culture. In each of their arenas (human body, psychic forms, geographical space, and social formations) the opposition between high and low is seen as a fundamental basis for ordering and sense making in European cultures. Transgression of the high/low divide in any of the four arenas affects the division in the other three. In other words, the transgression of boundaries between high and low space is reflected in social boundaries. In addition, the authors show how "high" discourses, "with their lofty style, exalted aims and sublime ends, are structured in relation to the debasements and degradations of low discourse. [They] tried to show how each extremity structures the other, depends upon and invades the other in certain historical moments to carry political charges through aesthetic and moral polarities."[65] By "high" and "low" the authors mean the divisions recognized by the higher socioeconomic groups that exist at the centers of cultural prestige and power. Although other groups also have "high" and "low" designations, they do not generally have the authority to generalize their classifications across society. An art critic, a gallery owner, or the mayor of New York is better able to define what counts as "high" than is a graffiti artist. Clearly the discourse of "art" is a "high" discourse in society, one associated with the head and the mind, with specialized spaces and the generally educated classes. The contention of Stallybrass and White is that a "high" discourse generally defines itself in relation to a "low" discourse in order to confirm its own position as "high." We begin to see the logic of the relationship between graffiti as art and as dirt. As the authors note, this is the logic of "Orientalism" as developed by Edward Said.[66]

In his well-known formulation, Said talks about the "low" (in this case the cultural and geographical construction of the Orient) as a site of contradictions between mutually incompatible representations: one marked by the imperative to reject and debase and the other by desire and intrigue. The "Orient" in Western discourse is at once the inferior "other" and an "underground self." This paradoxical construction of the "other" is an oxymoronic formulation of power and desire for the "low."

Said's discussion of colonial and neocolonial representations of the Middle East is certainly not the only documented example of this ambiguous relation between the "high" and the "low." Stallybrass and White themselves observe the ambivalence surrounding the slums of the nineteenth century. They describe the combination of loathing and fascination with which "social reformers" approached the slums of England. While reformers such as Chadwick and Mayhew described the slums, the poor, the prostitutes, and the filth of vagabond life, their work showed an obsessive desire for the world beyond the boundaries of bourgeois respectability. It is telling that Chadwick's report, *An Inquiry into the Sanitary Conditions of the Labouring Population of Great Britain* (1842), was a bestseller, while in excess of ten thousand copies were given away. "As the bourgeoisie produced new forms of regulation and prohibition governing their own bodies, they wrote even more loquaciously of the body of the other—of the city's 'slums.' "[67] Again we see the ambivalence with which the "high" relates to the "low." Stallybrass and White analyze the recurrent pattern of the "high" attempting to reject the "low" for a number of reasons and discovering that it is dependent on that low "other," but also

> that the top *includes* that low symbolically, as a primary eroticized constituent of its own fantasy life. The result is a mobile, conflictual fusion of power, fear and desire in the construction of subjectivity; a psychological dependence upon precisely those Others which are being rigorously opposed and excluded at the social level. It is for this reason that what is *socially* peripheral is so frequently *symbolically* central ... The low-Other is despised and derided at the level of political organization and social being whilst it is instrumentally constitutive of the shared imaging repertoires of the dominant culture.[68]

This formulation provides a fruitful framework for thinking about the relationship between graffiti as crime and graffiti as art.

The space of the art gallery is clearly a specialized space in the culture of New York, a space separated from all those "everyday" spaces outside. It is a space associated with high culture, with the mind rather than the body, with patrons high in economic, cultural, and social capital. It is a central part of the geocultural construction of "high." The world of the inner city and the subway, of "everyday" space, is a bodily space, a space of action, a space with unspecialized and "commonplace" activities. Remember that graffiti was also continually represented in terms of the third world. These spaces, even if imaginary, are also constituted as "low" in the established discourses, peopled by the ubiquitous "man on the street." They are spaces of unreason, lacking rationality and order. An area of deviance and dirt, remarkably like the slums described in Stallybrass and White and the Orient in Said, is constructed out of the description of graffiti and its place.

The relationship between dominant groups and graffiti flips between the "low" designations and its appropriation into "art." We can think of this as the rarified spaces of high culture *including* the "low" within it as an "eroticized constituent of its own fantasy life."[69] By incorporating graffiti into its own spaces, the "high" turns graffiti into a tamed representation of the more fascinating elements of the "low." Graffiti serves as a metonym for the wild, chaotic everyday space outside. In a sense graffiti as art is a representation of itself outside just as a stuffed animal in a museum is a representation of itself in the wild. Seen this way it is quite understandable that dominant socioeconomic groups can both revile and preserve graffiti as an example, a symbol, of the non-high, of the geographical, social, and cultural other. While graffiti and its writers are excluded at the social level, while the forces of the media, law, and politics are leveled against the "great graffiti plague" and a young graffitist like Michael Stewart is killed, graffiti remains symbolically central in the identification of the high and the proper. The "civilized" has to negotiate its position in relation to the "primitive." Established powers can simultaneously call for an end to graffiti and sell it, at high prices, to the residents of SoHo and Greenwich Village.

Legitimate Creativity and Specialized Space

The displacement of graffiti from everyday space to specialized "art" space is one reaction to graffiti that tells us something about the power of place in relation to ideological values. It is a reaction that seeks to insert graffiti into a "proper place" and rob it of its denaturalizing powers. It is "natural," after all, for art to be in galleries—if it is not in a gallery it is not "art." In addition, by absorbing graffiti, the art world assured it an economic value; it could be bought. Graffiti in the streets was associated with devaluing property values. The ordination of graffiti as art, consciously or not, subverted the subversive.

The entrapment of graffiti in the art gallery in some ways is a mirror image of the efforts of artists to break out of the specialized art space. The history of art is one of the gradual removal of artistic products from everyday life (in the form of "craft") to the specialized and removed object of intellectualized appreciation. Once an artist would have made intricately carved window frames or instruments to be used in sacred rituals. Now the artist makes "useless" products to be framed and admired. Creativity once was a part of everyday life and now it is reduced to "proper places." Galleries are "sites of *legitimate* creativity in a society which conceives of this phenomenon as the specialized practice of the artist."[70] This removal of legitimate creativity from everyday life is connected to the rise of capitalism:

> In the wake of the generalization of the social relations of commodity production during the course of the nineteenth century, this theoretical specification of the "aesthetic" became the intellectual basis for the institutionalization of art as a specific, and very special kind of, commodity: namely, a commodity the exchange-value of which derives,

paradoxically, not from its usefulness as such (its direct social utility), but rather from the specific form of its uselessness: its capacity to sustain "disinterested" or "aesthetic" contemplation.[71]

So as art developed as a commodity it was gradually removed to specialized spaces and made the object of individual aesthetic response. Graffiti, outside the gallery in everyday space, was out of place and therefore did not count as legitimate creativity.

Modern artistic endeavor has begun to challenge this separation of art from the everyday. Alistair Bonnett discusses the efforts of the Dadaists, the Surrealists, and the Situationists to transgress the art/everyday barrier. Dadaism, for instance, attempted to move art out of the formal space of galleries and into clubs and public halls where they would hold anarchic "cabarets." Marcel Duchamp, a prominent exponent of Dada, is well known for taking a mass-produced urinal, calling it "fountain," and placing it in a gallery. The point of the urinal was to ask the question, "What counts as art?" and relate that to the space of the gallery. That is to say, the urinal revealed the way that the gallery as a specialized setting magically turned something into art. It highlighted the magic by which the "ordinary" could become something intellectually exciting by being placed in art space.

Another example of artists questioning the art/everyday barrier is the *If You Lived Here* project by Martha Rosla.[72] The Dia Art Foundation took a SoHo studio and presented within it an artistic statement about homelessness. The walls were covered with pictures of the homeless and about the homeless, interlaced with pieces of text such as a quotation from Mayor Koch that read, "If you can't afford to live here, mo-o-ve." Homelessness does not fit into the established subject matter for aesthetic appreciation. The exhibition succeeded in drawing connections between the art space and the space outside. SoHo is a major area of gentrification in New York, and one of the main gentrifiers is the arts community. Gentrification, among other factors, has been responsible for the removal of low-cost housing and the increase in homelessness. So here were a group of artists using a gallery to raise awareness about homelessness. The title *If You Lived Here* included a certain amount of irony about the effect of art on the homeless in SoHo. The title made viewers highly aware of the connection of the gallery to the particular area in which it was located. The exhibition deliberately showed the way art galleries are not free-standing, pure spaces of aesthetic contemplation but spaces that are connected to the economics and brutality of everyday life. Whereas the established art gallery is supposed to be apart from the humdrum world, the Dia Art Gallery sketched out the naïveté of such a belief.

The prime directive of the graffiti artists in the subway is to reproduce the "tag" as frequently as possible (sometimes as many as ten thousand times). This massive reproduction of the sign is impossible to restrict to a few areas of high culture, where the emphasis is placed on uniqueness and originality (in the sense that the "original" is valued and reproductions are not "authentic"). The street graffiti elevation of reproduction to the highest value stands in contradistinction to the art world's elevation of the singular piece of art that one person can buy and own exclusively. There is simply no room in the gallery for all those people writing all those tags. Graffiti resists its absorption and continues its transgression of proper spaces and places.

Graffiti in a Contested Landscape

The system of dominant, "appropriate" meanings in the urban fabric can be referred to as a "hegemonic" landscape: a landscape with a set of structurally "agreed-upon" signifiers, which, rather than being imposed in a deterministic fashion on the landscape, are constantly contested and negotiated. A hegemonic landscape is one that is never static and fixed but always, sometimes minutely, changing as a result of the continuing struggle between dominant and subordinate cultural groups. Culture is seen as a "signifying system through which, necessarily (though among other means), a social order is communicated, reproduced, experienced and explored."[73] This view of culture combines (1) an anthropological view, which sees culture as a whole and distinct way of life, and (2) the more specialized sense of "aesthetic and intellectual activities," extended to include all signifying practices from philosophy to graffiti. Such a culture is an arena of contest — a contested terrain:

> The reality of any hegemony, in the extended political and cultural sense, is that while by definition it is always dominant, it is never either total or exclusive. At any time, forms of alternative or directly oppositional politics and culture exist as significant elements in society.... [A]lternative political and cultural emphases, and the many forces of opposition and struggle, are important not only in themselves but as indicative features of what the hegemonic process has in practice had to control.[74]

In what Bourdieu calls the "symbolic struggle over common sense," dominant and subordinate sociocultural groups use geography as a weapon in domination and resistance. Geography is also used to assimilate, in a hegemonic way, the resistant elements. Just as the graffiti writer challenges the codes of the orthodox through inappropriate geographical behavior, the orthodox retaliate with the forces of geo-orthodoxy.

One form of "solution" for the "graffiti problem" has been to demand that the writers, when caught, erase or paint over their original handiwork. Another is to demand that the graffitists become art students working in orthodox ways with orthodox methods in established places "where art belongs." Susan Stewart describes a typical case of this punishment: "The director of the Philadelphia Anti-Graffiti Task Force has announced that graffiti writers will be asked to go to vacant housing projects and paint venetian blinds, flowers, or human figures on boarded-up windows."[75] Magically, the graffitist, whose project is to destroy the facade of the dominant environment, is made to recreate it and to hide rather than point out the decay he or she is forced to live in. Graffiti writers are told that they have declared their meanings in the "wrong place" and that it will be reassigned to the "right place" through disciplinary measures.

This official form of punishment is really the most obvious and least insidious attempt to assimilate, geographically, the graffitist's energy. Far more devious is the way in which the formal spaces of art galleries exploit the "illegitimate" meanings and spaces of graffiti. Again a kind of geomagic is performed by the simple act of taking graffiti off the streets and (dis)placing it in the gallery—out of the unofficial spaces and into the sanctioned and revered domains of established and commercial art. Crime, with a flick of the wrist, becomes art; the valueless is turned into price-tagged and packaged art ready for your living-room wall. Much of the meaning of graffiti lies in its subversion of the authority of urban spaces. This is also the source of its criminality. Graffiti is not a crime that actually harms anyone. Graffiti writers reject the claims of "vandalism": "Here is a thing that doesn't hurt you. When a train comes out of the darkness, voom!, all it does is excite your heart, make your eyes follow it. It doesn't take your wallet."[76] The criminality of graffiti, unlike most crimes, lies in its being seen, in its transgression of official appearances. To take this and put it in a gallery negates its criminality as well as its meaning.

As graffiti is assimilated into the geographical mainstream, the proper spaces, it is given new meanings. It is no longer crime, it is a commodity—a simple piece of work you can buy and take home. As a painting it serves as a symbol—a metonym—for all the public spaces so resemanticized in the great "outside." It is like one of the exhibits at a freak show that some great and brave white explorer has retrieved from one of the far corners of the earth, which can serve as a simulation for all the other "wild things" that exist out there. Not only has graffiti been removed from the public spaces, but it has also been made static by the frame of the picture and the space of the gallery or living room.

Conclusions

A suggestion here is that places are the result of tensions between different meanings and that they are also active players in these tensions. Places have more than one meaning. Some meanings are complementary and fit neatly on top of each other. Other meanings seem to be incompatible—to be awkward and displaced—if they are located with other meanings. The incompatibility is not natural or inevitable (we need only realize that some places have different meanings at different times—meanings that may have once seemed heretical). Rather meanings are *said* to be incompatible by someone whose interests lie in preserving a particular set of meanings.

Concerning the issue of analyzing the "creation of places," we can see that it is possible to look at the form of a place as the creation of a given "culture" and interpret it as meaning such and such. This has been the strategy of much of cultural geography. Another method, however, is to look at the way meanings are constructed by the active and continuing conflict of meanings and geographies produced by different groups of people. To do this I have looked at the *discourse* of those attempting to define a favored meaning for places, in this case places in New York City.

Within a particular discourse (say the discourse about graffiti in the New York press), a network or web of meanings is created. These meanings are created by direct reference (the meaning of Central Park is X, the appropriate behavior in the subway system is Z) or, more frequently, by metaphors and descriptive terms applied to perpetrators of transgressions against the favored meaning of places (dirt, madness, disease, obscenity, and so on). The discourse creates a set of associations with its subject (disorder with graffiti).

The object of the discourse—that which is being interpreted—is an alleged transgression, an activity that is deemed "out of place." Along with this transgression is an alleged transformation (or threatened transformation) of the meaning of a place (New York). Put another way, the transgression threatens to bring about a meaning for place that is not favored by those involved in creating the discourse of reaction.

The claims made by the discourse in reaction to perceived transgression seem to be as follows:

1. Something is out of place.
2. Some act is out of place.
3. Some act is incompatible with the *proper* meaning of place.

The implications of these changes are as follows:

1. If the transgression continues, the meaning of the place will change.
2. If the meaning of the place changes, the place itself will change.
3. The new meaning will be *their* meaning (the meaning of the other).
4. The place in question will become *their* place (the place of the other).

Place, then, has no determinate meaning, no natural and transcendent meaning. The meaning of a place is the subject of particular discourses of *power,* which express themselves as discourses of *normality.* In other words, there are certain realms of discourse with more power than others (such as the media). These powerful discourses ascribe meanings to place in the language of common sense, of normality. No discourse is neutral or unchanging. Discourses are ideological insofar as they attempt to define what is good and true, what exists, and what is possible (the limits to change) and insofar as they serve the interests of powerful groups.

It is (in part) through these ideological discourses that meaning is created, including the meaning of places. The question of who controls the discourse (the media, for instance) is an important one for geographers because it says something about who gets to participate in the construction and dissemination of meanings for places and thus places themselves. The meaning of place, then, is (in part) created through a discourse that sets up a process of differentiation (between us and them). This operation, though, is a reflexive one, as meaning, in turn, is created in place, in context—in association with a web of meanings particular to places.

The meaning of an act (graffiti) is framed within a discourse of metaphorical association (dirt, obscenity, and so on). In addition, the meaning of an act is categorized in terms of its geographical context, the place in which it occurs (New York). The meaning of graffiti in the Bronx is different from that of graffiti on Wall Street. The presence of graffiti on the subway is annoying to the authorities because the trains travel through the city to areas not commonly associated with graffiti. The meaning of graffiti is clearly changed by placing it in the art gallery. The assessment of the meaning of an act is thus associated with place. The place of an act determines (as much as it is determined by) the reaction to the act and the meanings accorded to it. Just as the meaning of an act is associated with a particular place, the meaning of a place is associated with appropriate acts (or at least the absence of inappropriate acts). The question then is not, "What does a place (New York) mean?" or "What is the meaning of a particular action (graffiti)?" Rather the question becomes, "How do places (and actions in them) get the meanings they do? Who gets to say that certain meanings are appropriate?" And, eventually, "Whose world is it?"

Chapter 4

Heretical Geography 2:
The Sacred and the Profane —
Stonehenge and the Hippy Convoy

In the midsummer of 1992 the newspapers of Britain were awash with grim stories of thousands of (mostly young) people referred to as "new-age-travellers."[1] They were meeting in Wales for festivals, traveling in cars, caravans, and buses. The *Daily Mail*, a solidly right-wing British tabloid, had sent an undercover reporter to explain this phenomenon. The reporter stayed with the travelers in the county of Powys. His report, which appeared on 28 July, was headed, "Once it was a verdant hillside, now an army of 20th century no-hopers has turned it into a mire of nihilism." Under this, in still bigger letters, read "Mud, Drugs and a Vision of Hell."[2] The two-page report recounts the reporter's experience of "hell." It concentrates on the use of drugs, the mud and filth, and the "run-down" vehicles. Two days later, on the editorial page, the same paper featured a piece entitled "Feeding A New Generation of Vagabonds." It began: "Yesterday was a triumph for the forces of madness, it started with a university professor telling Radio 4 that there was nothing wrong with the moral code adopted by the hordes of travellers who had descended on Wales."[3] The writer continued, in the spirit of rationality no doubt, by nostalgically looking back at the times of poorhouses and the "practical distinction" between the "genuinely needy" and the "sturdy vagabonds."

The moral panic of midsummer has, in fact, been an annual affair since (at least) the early 1980s. This seemingly ritualistic confrontation between traveling people and the "authorities" has a lot to tell us about the geographical ordering of "normality." Let us return, then, to the "Stonehenge festival" and the adventures of the "hippy convoy." To fully understand the story we have to begin with the larger context of Britain in the 1980s and the recent history of "moral panics."[4]

The 1970s in Britain was a time of economic decay marked by long and hard-fought battles between government and unions. Edward Heath, the prime minister through the early seventies, sought to fight world recession by imposing wage restraint on workers. This resulted in a long series of strikes by miners. Heath attempted to implicate the miners in a plot with Arabs who were, at the time, increasing oil prices. He argued that the miners were acting against the "national interest." Simultaneously the mainstream press began to talk of "creeping communism" in unions and in the Labour Party. More and more "totalitarian Marxists" were discovered in the political Left. The miners continued to strike and Heath called an election in February 1974, which he lost in a clear class confrontation.

The second government of the seventies was the Labour Party of James Callaghan. Callaghan's government was a centrist "social democratic" government. The world recession deepened during the late seventies and was marked with extreme rates of inflation (greater than 20 percent) and a weakening currency. Living standards fell and working-class interests continued to be subordinated to those of capital. The Labour government was based on "the social contract," which involved a stronger voice for the unions in return for an agreement not to ask for too much money. This commitment to the unions was enough to allow the press to label the government "irresponsible leftists" but not enough to ensure the prioritization of working-class interests. As the world recession deepened it became apparent that the British economy was one of Europe's weakest. The government had to struggle to prevent capital from taking flight overseas and it placed the majority of the economic burden on labor. In the end labor resisted and strikes ensued, leading to the "winter of discontent" in which miners, garbage collectors, transport workers, and many others went on strike, resulting in scenes of chaos such as the sight of London parks full of garbage and the army acting as strike breakers. It was against this backdrop of a country in chaos that Margaret Thatcher was elected prime minister, a post she would hold throughout the 1980s. Throughout her "reign" she reminded the voters of the "chaos" induced by the confrontation between the Labour government and the unions.

The almost continual state of crisis from 1972 to 1979 set the stage for the ideological hegemony of "Thatcherism"[5] — a set of values that rested on the foundations of the idea of "consensus" and "order." People were obviously upset by the ongoing condition of chaos and conflict. Words like "consensus" and "order" were very appealing. As Stuart Hall has shown, the British public became fixated on the idea of a "conspiracy" against the "British way of life." This conspiracy is the "necessary and required form in which dissent, opposition or conflict had to be represented in a society which is, in fact, mesmerized by *consensus*."[6]

Society came to be defined as one of harmonious unity with a lack of structured class, gender, or ethnic conflict. Conflict, seen against this background of harmony and "common interest," can only be understood as the product of the deviant minority of subversive people who willfully conspire to destroy the "harmony" by force. Conversely, the state became the embodiment of consensus—the legitimate—as opposed to the evidently illegitimate individuals and groups who sought to "make life difficult."

The press was instrumental in broadcasting this view. The *Daily Telegraph* became the semiofficial voice of the Right, running special issues on the evils of Communism. "Moral panics" were created in order to illustrate the evil of the Left; for example, education was said to be in the hands of irresponsible "reds," and thus standards were declining, unions were ruled by outrageous "loony lefties," and the Labour Party was under the wing of the Kremlin. Magazines were increasingly censured for "conspiring to corrupt public morals." Teachers were accused of "promoting homosexuality" and Communist politics; women were chastised for going to work and leaving children at home. Conspirators were everywhere, as Lord Chancellor Hailsham explained:

> The war in Bangladesh, Cyprus, the Middle East, Black September, Black power, The Angry Brigade, the Kennedy murders, Northern Ireland, bombs in Whitehall and the Old Bailey, the Welsh Language Society, the massacre in Sudan, the mugging on the tube, gas strikes, hospital strikes, go-slows, sit-ins, The Icelandic Cod war [are all] standing on or seeking to stand on different parts of the same slippery slope.[7]

The breadth of the alleged conspiracy against the British way of life was astounding. Welfare mothers, teenage pregnancies, child abuse, drunkenness, football hooliganism, decaying educational standards, and divorce rates were all blamed on the leftist subversives and the welfare state. To replace drunkenness, child abuse, and so on, the new Right proposed patriotism, family values, and hard honest work. The choice was obvious—common sense.

The new government of Margaret Thatcher spoke of new "old" values of the Victorians. It proposed a free market completely devoid of "government interference," together with the values of the small businessman, middle-class respectability, self-reliance, and family snugness. The press played an important part in spreading the new word. The *Daily Telegraph,* the *Daily Express,* the *Daily Mail,* the *Sun,* and others consistently reminded the readers of the "old days" of disorder when the government would rise or fall according to the whim of militant unions. A new picture of an ordered Britain was built from the ruins of seventies chaos.

Thatcher's new England was a world of extraordinary authoritarianism but not the direct repression of brute force (although this has played a role). Rather, Thatcherism's authority rested on a powerful populism — many people in England *believed* her and accepted the new moral order as common sense. Based on this populism, Thatcher instituted what Stuart Hall calls a "law and order society." People were portrayed as generally "sensible" and "moderate." The government portrayed itself as the protector of moderate people. In order to do this it had to control the few — "the mindless minority." It became a legitimate function of the state to police the new "extremes" (that is, not moderate or sensible) in order to protect common sense.

A key strategy in the reinforcement of "common sense" was the creation of "folk devils." Problems were raised that created alarm and anxiety among the public. Campaigns were mounted to "solve" each problem temporarily. Examples include "youth" (promiscuity, long hair, vandalism), "race," education, and so on. People experienced social crisis as a series of these panics.

Eventually these panics were linked so that the illusion was created of a single many-faceted enemy that Conservative Members of Parliament (MPs) referred to as "the permissive society": "The sale of drugs, pornography, the growth of the women's movement and the critique of the family are experienced and signified as the thin edge of that larger wedge: the threat to the state, the breakdown of social life itself, the coming of chaos, the onset of anarchy."[8] The folk devils were portrayed as brothers and sisters in one huge subversive family that lurked everywhere. With this shift to a conspiracy mentality came the law-and-order society:

> The state has won the right, and indeed inherited the duty to move
> swiftly, to stamp fast and hard, to listen in, discreetly to survey, to
> saturate and swamp, to charge or to hold without charge, to act on
> suspicion, and to hustle and shoulder, in order to keep society on the
> straight and narrow. Democracy, the last back-stop against arbitrary
> power, is in retreat. It is suspended. The times are exceptional. The crisis
> is real. We are inside the "law and order" state.[9]

So a central feature of Thatcher's new common sense was the rule of law and order. The world under this view was (and still is) clearly divided up into the majority of moderate people and the tiny fringe minority of "extremists"; it is divided into good and evil, civilized and uncivilized, order and chaos. This is the story that was being told. These divisions touched on people's very real concerns of threats to bodies and property in a time of rising crime. Since social conditions were never presented as a reason for this, increased law and order was the obvious solution — the commonsense measure. It would be too easy to write it all off as "false consciousness," but the law-and-order society spoke to people's real interests in direct and comforting ways.

This law-and-order solution was thrown at every facet of the "permissive society" during the 1980s. Homosexuality, drugs, and the position of women were all subjected to one form or another of law and order in order to reinstate moral respectability, in an attempt to restore the family as the spine of a respectable society. It is in this context that the Stonehenge convoy (and the Greenham Common Women's Peace Camp, the subject of chapter 5) needs to be understood. Let's go back to 1974.

It was in that year that a free peace festival at Stonehenge became a regular feature of the alternative events calendar in Britain. In 1974 the pirate radio station — Radio Caroline — urged people to go to a celebration of peace and love at Stonehenge during late June. Subsequently posters would appear throughout England each year stating that there was a "rumor" that another festival was being held over the solstice period. By the late 1970s the festival was attracting crowds of up to five thousand people. Every year it was held in the time leading up to the summer solstice, with some people arriving as early as late May. The people who attended the festival were a mixed group of mainly young white people. Some were travelers and Gypsies who moved from one festival to another throughout the year, sleeping in an assortment of vehicles, from horse-drawn wagons to large old double-decker buses. Others were young people from the cities who came for the music and atmosphere. These people joined the convoy for the spring and summer months only. Many of them were unemployed and others were homeless. The period between the midseventies and mideighties was notable for its high levels of unemployment, particularly among young people. They wished to escape the boredom of the dole queue or, alternatively, of low-paying repetitive jobs. The travelers and young city dwellers both believed in broadly "new-age" mystic spirituality; both wished to escape "materialism, comfort and social status for a simple life in the hills and fields of rural Britain."[10]. Both groups were united by the fact that the media referred to them as "hippies."[11]

Throughout the 1970s the festival aroused little interest. It rarely happened at the actual site of Stonehenge but somewhere from which it was visible. A stubble field adjacent to the tourist's parking lot was the usual site. The festival-goers camped there, traded in food and ethnic crafts, and listened to music. The festival was called a "model free festival" by the Festival Welfare Services (funded by the government) in 1979. It was generally organized with help from the police. The police offered advice to the participants on ways to avoid disturbing people who lived nearby. Local government authorities provided garbage bags and carts to move the refuse away. Voluntary drug care associations and welfare services usually provided support for the festival.

All this changed in 1985 when the National Trust and English Heritage (government bodies responsible for the management of monuments and landscapes of national significance) obtained a court injunction banning eighty-three named individuals from the site. On 1 June 1985 on the Wiltshire-Hampshire border (nine miles from Stonehenge), the convoy of festival-goers was stopped at a roadblock by police in riot gear. Five hundred arrests were subsequently made in the so-called battle of the beanfield (see Figure 4.1). The battle involved an unusual degree of violence by the police in front of TV cameras. The coverage of the event surprised even the owner of the beanfield—the Earl of Cardigan—who condemned the action in an interview in the *Daily Telegraph*:

> Vehicles were their homes and obviously you do find women and children in homes. Assuming the police knew this, it was surprising that they should break in the windows of every single vehicle, covering the women and children inside with broken glass.... Seeing in a Hampshire field, not Northern Ireland or Lebanon, on that summer's afternoon pregnant women screaming hysterically and babies lying in broken glass, for whatever reason, really cut me up as a father of a six month old baby.... It was like using a sledgehammer to crack a nut.[12]

In dealing with the "hippies" the police used tactics developed to deal with the miners involved in the strike of 1984–85 (the mother of all moral panics),[13] which even if appropriate for the miner's strike was certainly not appropriate for dealing with people traveling to a "festival of peace and light." The action was defended as a successful solution to a "public order problem."

The following year history repeated itself. On 20 May 1986 another injunction was granted to English Heritage banning forty-six named individuals from within four miles of Stonehenge. One hundred people were already camped near the monument. The police convinced them to move westward into the county of Somerset, where they camped in an unplowed field of a farm near the village of Somerton. The farmer, Les Atwell, who suffered from angina, on seeing the convoy arrive, collapsed; he quickly became the symbol of the violated property owner cruelly

Figure 4.1. Arrest at the battle of the beanfield. (Photograph of unknown origin.)

destroyed by the malicious "hippy" convoy. The members of the conservative National Union of Farmers (NUF) and the government began to discuss changes in the law concerning trespass. On 29 May the convoy was asked to move on, and they headed south to Dorset. As the vehicles moved along a road outside of Poole the leading vehicle was rammed by police vehicles, and twelve arrests were made by police refusing to show any form of identification. So the convoy, prevented from stopping in three counties, reached Stoney Cross in the New Forest on 2 June.

The Home Secretary, Douglas Hurd, met with Conservative MPs from the area and discussed changing the trespass laws to make it a criminal rather than a civil offense. The next day the "hippies" were discussed in the House of Commons, and on 5 June a special cabinet meeting was devoted to a discussion of the "hippy" problem. Thatcher set up a special committee to discuss changes in the trespass law. When the government was granted a possession order for Stoney Cross by the High Court, the judge in the case pleaded that the "hippies" be given a chance to fix their vehicles and be removed slowly (presumably to avoid a repeat of the "battle of the beanfield"). On 8 June the convoy requested forty-eight hours to repair their vehicles; as evidence of their intent to leave they took down a large marquee tent. The next morning at 4:50 A.M. 440 police officers from five counties cleared the camp in two hours in a sweep known as Operation Daybreak. Forty-two people were arrested and 129 vehicles were impounded. Travel warrants were issued to allow the travelers to take trains "home." At a cost of half a million pounds the police succeeded in neutralizing the convoy. Again the festival at Stonehenge did not take place. This seemingly ritualistic attempt by the travelers to reach Stonehenge has been repeated every year since, and each time a massive police presence has prevented the festival from happening. In 1991 the travelers held their festival fifteen miles away and left the hundreds of armored police to stand around Stonehenge and watch the Druids go through their ritual as the sun came up on Midsummer's Day. The *Times* reported the event as follows:

> The confrontation at Stonehenge between police and kamikaze hippies has become a hardy perennial for the media. It used to look like the final 20 seconds of the Sixties: the last of the drop-outs who had dropped down too far to come back. Now reinforcements from the New Age seem to have given the circus a second wind. Once again, the Age of Aquarius is taking hold and creating a cult of unreason. But the Druid roots of this mystic pilgrimage are all but lost, and all that the solstice jamboree represents now is a set-piece battle between anarchy and order.[14]

By 1992, with the British economy still marginal in the European context, the travelers were mixed with the latest moral panic—"ravers," followers of the new postindustrial funk, "acid-house." As Stonehenge was off-limits, they headed for central and south Wales, where they were described by the *Daily Mail* in poetic terms.

The remainder of this illustration is divided into three sections that describe the geography of a moral panic. The first deals with the conflict between the "hippies" and the "authorities" over the proper use and meaning of Stonehenge, the second with the issue of the traveler's mobile lifestyle, and the third with the theme of property and trespass. My aim, as with the previous and following chapter, is to delineate the role of space and place in perceptions of transgression.

The Meanings of Stonehenge

> *Stonehenge and the hippies are both relics of past eras. Both have their places so long as they do not meet.*
> —Daily Telegraph, *5 June 1985*

> *Guarding Heritage from the Masses*
> —Headline in the Times, *21 June 1991*

The disputes over the alleged "deviance" of the "hippies" followed from the confrontation that arose in response to the banning of festival-goers from the area immediately surrounding Stonehenge in 1984. Stonehenge is in the center of Wiltshire, thirty miles north of the south coast and eighty miles west of London. The landscape around it is one of rolling chalk downs, known as Salisbury Plain. The nearest town is Amesbury; two and a half miles to the east and eight miles to the south is the cathedral city of Salisbury. Stonehenge itself consists of large stone blocks (monoliths) arranged in a circular pattern. The outer ring is made of sarsen, an extremely hard form of sandstone. The blocks are about thirteen feet high with horizontal blocks made of the same material placed across their tops to form a ring of doorwaylike structures. The inner circle is made of an igneous rock called bluestone and stands about six feet high. Inside the inner circle is a horseshoe of more sarsen stones about twenty-four feet high, and inside those is another horseshoe of bluestones between six and eight feet high. In the middle is a single fallen and broken "altar stone" made of another type of sandstone.

To properly understand the struggle over the meaning of these mysterious stones it is important to outline the background to the conflicting sets of ideas about the meaning of Stonehenge. Behind the contemporary arguments over the use of Stonehenge is a history of Stonehenge as an important site in the construction of English cultural identity. The arguments of English Heritage (as the guardians of the "official" view) are based on this construction of the monument as "heritage"—as *the* site of national importance.

Stonehenge is one of the few human structures predating the Roman conquest that still stands. It is this sense of purely English antiquity that makes its preservation so crucial. The first written mention of Stonehenge is from a history of England requested by the Bishop of Blois in the early twelfth century. The history was written by Henry of Huntingdon in 1130. He wrote: "Stanenges, where stones of wonderful size have been erected after the manner of doorways, so that doorway appears to have been raised upon doorway; and no-one can [imagine how] such great stones have been so raised aloft, or why they were built there."[15] In this history of England Stonehenge was one of three English "marvels," along with the "Devil's Arse" (a cave in the Peak District) and Cheddar Gorge. In stories told in early British histories, Stonehenge featured in the mythopoetic tales of Arthurian legend. The story that was accepted from the twelfth century through to the sixteenth century went as follows. A Saxon king named Hengist killed 460 British lords by a cunning trick on Salisbury Plain. The rightful British king, Aurelius Ambrosius, returned from exile in Brittany and defeated the Saxons. Aurelius called upon the magician Merlin to get the "Giant's Circle" from Ireland in order to build a monument to the lords who had been killed. Urtherpendragon took 15,000 men to Ireland, defeated the Irish army, and tried to remove the stones but failed because of the size and weight of the stones. Merlin found this amusing and eventually moved them himself to Salisbury Plain and built Stonehenge. When Aurelius died he was buried there and was succeeded by Urtherpendragon, who in turn was buried at Stonehenge and succeeded by Arthur Pendragon. This story was best told by Geoffrey of Monmouth, a well-known historian who also insisted that the ancient Britons had sacked Rome. The whole story was resoundingly patriotic in its glorification of the Britons and the mythical King Arthur — perhaps the central figure to this day in "pure" English mythology. Indeed it is Arthur who is expected to rise from the dead sometime in the future and save England in its hour of need.

Stonehenge, as a place integral to this story, was placed at the center of English cultural identity. The story went through many changes but was more or less accepted by most historians for several centuries. Caxton, the inventor of the printing press, was ordered to print a history of England in 1480 and faithfully replicated Geoffrey of Monmouth's account. The pro-British flavor of the story was not lost on the Italian historian Polydore Vergil (1543), who wrote that Geoffrey had extolled the British "above the noblenesse of Romains and Macedonians, enhauncinge them with moste impudent lyeing."[16]

The story of Merlin and Stonehenge was perpetuated through many cultural products. A similar story is told in Spencer's *The Faerie Queene*, for example. Between 1590 and 1620 many plays were performed based on the myth. By the mid–sixteenth century more curious minds were examining Stonehenge anew. Although the Merlin story was largely discredited, Stonehenge remained an object of intrigue and a symbol of the nation. Stonehenge's central place in English iconography led many of the country's most important writers and painters to observe the monument. The first paintings of Stonehenge appeared in the 1560s and 1570s. Jonathon Swift and Daniel Defoe described Stonehenge. Charles II apparently hid there while retreating from the Parliamentarians in the civil war. James I considered it interesting enough to commission Inigo Jones to do an architectural study of the monument; in it Jones insisted that the stones were built by the Romans. By the eighteenth century the gothic charm of the place was inspiring the Romantics with their fanciful tales of druids and northern European superiority over classical influences. William Wordsworth wrote:

> Pile of Stone-henge! so proud to hint yet keep
> Thy secrets, thou that lov'st to stand and hear
> The Plain resounding to the whirlwind's sweep
> Inmate of lonesome Nature's endless year.[17]

Romantic painters of the British landscape flocked to Stonehenge. Foremost among them were Constable and Turner, who painted scenes of sublime terror featuring the stones and fearsome weather. Turner's painting has lightning striking the center of the stones while Constable's has huge clouds and a double rainbow (see Figure 4.2). William Blake also painted Stonehenge as part of an illustration for *Jerusalem* (see Figure 4.3). An illustration by James Berry for an edition of Shakespeare's *King Lear* shows Lear weeping over the dead Cordelia at Stonehenge.

Stonehenge has also been a dramatic setting in novels. Most famous, perhaps, is the tragic finale to Thomas Hardy's *Tess of the d'Urbervilles*. After killing her husband, Tess takes flight with her lover Angel across Salisbury Plain until they come across the stones in the dark. There Tess lies down on the "altar" stone, refusing to continue. "Now I am home," she says as she falls asleep. In the morning, just as the sun rises, the police capture the two lovers, and Tess gives in happily to meet her execution. Here Stonehenge is Tess's home because it is pagan and predates organized religion. Tess descended from Pagan d'Urbaville, and throughout the novel represents the idyllic and the pastoral against a background of modernization, agricultural machinery, and "new ways." Hardy, an author constantly aware of the changes in rural life in eighteenth-century England, uses Stonehenge as a symbol of preindustrial Britain — roots and "home" in a changing and rootless world.

Despite the interest shown in Stonehenge by the cultural elite, it was not given much attention by the general public before the beginning of

Figure 4.2. *Stonehenge*. John Constable, 1836. (By courtesy of the Board of Trustees of the Victoria & Albert Museum, London.)

Figure 4.3. *Jerusalem*, William Blake, copy E, plate 100. 1804–20. (Courtesy the Yale Center for British Art, Paul Mellon Collection.)

this century. Although the modern popularity of Stonehenge has its roots in the interest of King James I in the monument and his visits to it, the imagination of the general public was not seized until the very last day of 1900, when two stones fell over and the *Times* directed people's attention to the mysteries that surround Stonehenge.

One group of people who were attracted to the monument were the "druids." The Ancient Order of Druids—a kind of freemason group—was founded in 1781 in secrecy. The "Grand Lodge" of this society visited Stonehenge in August 1905 for a mass initiation to which well-known people were invited. A large tent with lots of food and drink was set up. After a banquet, initiates were blindfolded and the druids changed into ceremonial white robes and large white beards. The initiates were then marched into the circle and the oath was administered. The druids continued to use Stonehenge at midsummer and they feature in the contemporary story of the "hippies" that follows. Often the visitations of the druids were against the wishes of the owner, Sir Edmund Aritrolus, who charged for admission to the stones. The druids claimed that they could not be charged for admission to their own temple. The druids challenged Sir Edmund to have them arrested. He did not and the ceremonies continued. Arguments raged over the rights of Sir Edmund as a property owner. In 1913 the Ancient Monuments Act protected Stonehenge from demolition or export. Sir Edmund, however, still owned it.

During the years around World War I the military began to change the landscape around the stones. The Royal Artillery set up camp to the north and airplanes began to fly over the area as an airfield was established nearby. The Royal Flying Corps even requested the demolition of Stonehenge as it was a danger to low-flying aircraft. The roads in the area were filled with military vehicles, including the first tanks, which passed within yards of the stones. The stones often trembled due to shock waves from nearby explosions.

Both Sir Edmund and his heir died in the war and the estate went up for sale. It was sold on 21 September 1915 at auction. It was bought for £6,600 by Cecil Chubb, a local landowner. In 1918 Chubb offered Stonehenge to the nation and the government accepted, giving Chubb a knighthood. The government straightened the stones and laid concrete foundations beneath them. They encouraged scientific study, which continued to reveal nothing and only served to deepen the mysterious nature of the stones and enhance its appeal to visitors. The tourist problem became more and more acute. In the 1920s, 20,000 visitors visited in a year. In 1951 the figure was 124,000; in 1961, 337,000; and in 1971, half a million.[18] In the 1980s, over 800,000 tourists annually visited the monument.

It wasn't until March 1978 that the harmful stress of tourism was acknowledged and a fence was constructed around the stones. This was not without controversy; the original deed of gift made when Stonehenge was presented to the nation in 1918 by Chubb states that there must be "free access to all." The fact that nearly a million visitors walked through the stones in 1977 made the new fence the easiest way to control tourists and prevent erosion and damage. Although the tourists did little damage to the hard stone, they eroded the chalk underneath and around the stones, resulting in construction of the fence.

The attraction of Stonehenge has not been limited to tourists. The solstice celebrations of the druids have continued. Between the wars the celebrations at the site included a resident jazz band. By the 1960s the "festival" had become more varied, with fair sideshows and Morris dancers: "A howling mass of people, old, young, children jumping the prostrate stones, teenagers running madly chasing each other and shouting, others sleeping on the ground wrapped in rugs, picnic parties, litter and bottles lying around."[19]

In 1962 temporary barbed wire fences were introduced during the solstice period and only the druids were allowed into the stones, but by 1969 this proved fruitless. Meanwhile more facilities, including a car park, café, and bookstore, were introduced at Stonehenge. By 1974 the festival was attracting "alternative society" for the first time, and it soon established itself as an annual event leading to the ban in 1984 and the conflicts that followed. The contemporary struggle over the appropriate use of Stonehenge is thus the latest in a line of "problems," including the visitation rights of druids and the destruction caused by tourists.

An Alternative View

One side of the struggle during the 1980s was represented by the National Trust and English Heritage with support from the Department of the Environment. English Heritage, which manages the site, exists to preserve sites of historical importance to "the nation." This importance for Stonehenge is based on its history as a site that represents the nation. It is English Heritage that obtained the court injunction against the "hippies." Such "authorities" believed that Stonehenge must be protected against "improper" uses. This argument is opposed by the travelers who insist that Stonehenge belongs to the people and that no person can morally be prevented from entering the site. Many also believe that Stonehenge is a holy site of power and mysticism.

The traveler's case is made in a letter to the *Times* (20 June 1978) in which the participants talked of their feelings for the monument: "We come to Stonehenge because in an unstable world it is proper that the people should look for stability from the past in order to learn for the future." They go on to contrast their treatment of the site with the official treatment of the site. They argue that the site is, in reality, endangered by its established uses:

> Exceedingly large tracts of land are covered by military camps and tank ranges. One military exercise does more damage to the landscape than we could possibly do in 20 years.... We would not run a road through Stonehenge, and given our way it would soon be removed. A very important part of the monument is now a tarmac car park, ugly to behold. We would not surround it with barbed wire and arc lamps. As for the rest of the land making a natural setting, it is nothing but field after field surrounded by barbed wire fences long before we came. The Director-General well knows that he and he alone is all that stands between the festival as it is at present and what he would call a legal festival. Holy land is holy land and our right to be upon it cannot be denied.

The conflict over Stonehenge is one between the view held by the travelers that Stonehenge is a spiritual center made to be *used* rather than looked at and the view of English Heritage that Stonehenge is a monument that needs to be *preserved* for the nation. The argument centers on the meaning of "national heritage" and people's rights of access to places that are considered part of that heritage. English Heritage, with the exclusionary powers of the state behind it, seeks to make Stonehenge a museum, an exhibit, and a scene for tourists to gaze at from removed observation points. Like any other museum piece it would display the sign "Do not touch." In the process of defining Stonehenge thus, English Heritage turned Stonehenge into a fortress defended against the "hippies" — a situation described as the Stonehenge Gulag by one historian.[20] The "hippies" denied that Stonehenge had ever been intended as a museum or exhibit. They say that Stonehenge was built to be used:

> The current policy of the authorities prevents the release of the full spiritual power of Stonehenge. It seeks to impose a narrow set of standards regarding normal leisure practice in ancient places upon everyone. It robs the site of its use value and turns it into an exhibition. Stonehenge ... only comes to life when it is used as a living spiritual and leisure resource.[21]

Pierre Bourdieu, in his book *Distinction*, gives us a theoretical tool that aids us in the quest to explain these different perceptions of Stonehenge. He describes, with reference to art, food, music, and many other facets of a broadly defined culture, the division between *function* and *form*, which corresponds to the aesthetics of the working class and the bourgeoisie. Intellectuals and those with high cultural capital (usually approximately analogous to those with economic capital) tend to place value on the *form* of an object, while the working classes value things for their function. For instance Bourdieu finds that people with little cultural capital who look at a photograph of an old woman's gnarly hands will remark on the ugliness and deformity of the hands, imagining what it might be like to have them and use them, while the cultural elite react with a distanced reference to other art it reminds them of. Often they find the photograph beautiful, presumably because of its composition. The "pure gaze" of the educated, Bourdieu argues, represents a break from the "ordinary attitude" to the world—the attitude that emphasizes function and survival. The aesthetics of the bourgeoisie creates a division between "legitimate" culture and the rest of life, between "pure" pleasure and "facile" pleasure, between such things as "art" and "food." "Pure" pleasure, Bourdieu argues, "is predisposed to become a symbol of moral excellence and a measure of the capacity for sublimation which defines the truly human man."[22]

The culture that results from the separation of pure aesthetics and mundane activities such as eating and dressing is a sacred culture:

> The denial of the lower, coarse, vulgar, venal, servile—in a word natural—enjoyment, which constitutes the sacred sphere of culture, implies an affirmation of the superiority of those who can be satisfied with the sublimated, refined, disinterested, gratuitous, distinguished pleasures forever closed to the profane. That is why art and cultural consumption are predisposed, consciously and deliberately or not, to fulfil a social function of legitimating social differences.[23]

The separation of "aesthetic objects" from everyday life makes the object sacred. Distinction involves geographical separation of special realms from "everyday" realms. Art is made sacred by its location in the gallery. Take the museum as an example. In a museum objects from all over the world and from a variety of different time periods are placed together and juxtaposed in a way that says nothing of the object's original context. Although originally intended for a variety of functions, both sacred (a crucifix) and profane (an eating implement), by their very presence in the museum the objects become sacred objects separated from *use* and venerated for their *form*.

The alternative view of Stonehenge is that it is not a "monument" as such. The travelers and festival-goers believe that the spatial separation of the stones from people is a denial of the spiritual function of Stonehenge. Just as in a museum, the stones are denied their proper context and appear as removed, abstracted, disinterested symbols. The festival-goers upset the categorization of Stonehenge in two ways: by insisting on its use value and by refusing its separation from everyday space.

Another perspective on the Stonehenge debate is to see the festival in terms of the "carnivalesque." Bakhtin's theorization of popular culture in the work of Rabelais suggests the resistant and subversive power of popular cultural forms.[24] Such things as carnivals, fairs, and everyday language, he argues, are a powerful set of tools for subordinated culture that constantly undermine the presumptions of elite culture. The inversion of symbolic domains of "high" and "low," for instance, pokes fun at the establishment and irritates the agents of dominant culture. The carnivalesque celebrates use value, profanity, and incompleteness and temporarily dethrones the sacred, the complete, and the distinguished. In the case of Stonehenge the transgressors were people attempting to hold a noisy, joyous festival in a place established by the National Trust as a place of observation and reverence. The "profane" nature of the festival upset the perspective of Stonehenge as sacred—as bounded, finished, and monumental. The festivities of the "masses" must have annoyed those who sought to portray the stones as a monument to be preserved. Indeed, if Bakhtin is to be believed, the festive behavior of the "hippies" will have undermined the "narrow-minded seriousness" and "pomposity" of the "official view" and revealed the relativity of established "truth."

Finally the travelers' intention to use Stonehenge as a festival site disturbs assumptions about "normal leisure."[25] The way in which the National Trust manages Stonehenge emphasizes it as a place to visit—a tourist attraction for people who normally work. One reason for the "hippies" being barred from the site is their transgression of work/leisure distinctions. Leisure, among other things, is a reward for productive labor, a realm of freedom away from work, an activity that involves participation in consumer culture and that occurs in leisure spaces. The travelers appear to ignore or deliberately transgress so many of these assumptions about leisure that they are considered a "high-risk group." The druids hold a ceremony at Stonehenge that has been allowed to continue, yet the druids have no more claim to authenticity than the "hippies" do, being essentially an invention of the late nineteenth century. Nevertheless the druids have continued to receive the cooperation of the authorities. The "hippies" are not trusted because they do not behave in "normal" ways in both work and leisure.

A "normal" adult is propertied and is in paid employment or is supported by someone in paid employment. In addition the leisure activities of a "normal" person are financed by their participation in the formal economy. A "normal" person deserves leisure because they have worked to earn it:

> Lifestyles among the propertyless which are built around the deliberate withdrawal from the formal economy, ... non-work and welfare support are denounced as unhealthy for the individual and debilitating for society. The propertyless who emphasize "fun", "spontaneity" and "pleasure" over "discipline", "sobriety", and "obligation" are dismissed as little more than parasites.[26]

Leisure is often distinguished from "what has to be done." It is a realm of freedom and autonomy away from work. It is both subordinated to and separated from work. Work is considered a public activity while leisure is private. Such distinctions, although dominant today, are relatively recent. Before the Industrial Revolution work and leisure were difficult to distinguish spatially or culturally. The Industrial Revolution in Europe created distinct times and places for work and leisure. Work was established as the primary activity and leisure was restricted to "useful" pursuits.

The creation of work and leisure as separate spheres had a peculiar social geography to it. The bourgeoisie perceived the "free" time of the working class to be a threat, as the workers were not thought to be civilized enough to engage in constructive leisure pursuits. In fact, from the bourgeois perspective, the workers were "sunk in bestiality, improvident, intemperate and sexually rampant.... They did not attend church and appeared to have few morals. They were the very negation of the bourgeoisie."[27] So the bourgeoisie set about regulating the "free" time and space of the mass of people. The social geography of leisure was one in which the propertied classes had an abundance of space at home for leisure activities. For the bourgeoisie leisure was very much a private activity. The workers, however, did not have the space for private leisure and utilized public space for such pursuits. Bars, sports stadia, carnivals, and the streets were the sites for workers at play. Each of these seemed to threaten the norms and morals of the middle class and each, in turn, was regulated and licensed. The net result was a reduction in truly public leisure space—a gradual privatization of space. By the twentieth century street life, a characteristic realm of play throughout history, was all but abolished.

This brief history is intended to illustrate the "licensed" nature of leisure. The word "leisure" comes from the Latin *licere*—"to be allowed," a definition that implies both freedom and permission. Someone is doing the allowing, the licensing. Leisure, then, is more than a realm of freedom from necessity; it is also a sphere that is controlled: "Leisure relations are relations of permissible behaviour. What is considered appropriate and inappropriate behaviour in leisure time articulates power relations as succinctly as do the rules governing work."[28] The "hippies" in the convoy were leading a life that transgressed the spatial assumptions of both work and leisure. The social geography of leisure that has existed in England since the Industrial Revolution demanded private, regulated leisure and formal paid employment at the workplace. The "hippies" did not separate work and leisure and engaged in both in public and unregulated ways.

Druids may celebrate Stonehenge, but when they have finished they return to their predominantly middle-class jobs and families. The "hippies," however, appear to have no job and return to a caravan or tent. The "deviance" of their lifestyle results in the foreclosure of their right to have any say in the management of "national heritage":

> The situation is compounded by the political challenge of the hippies. The hippies do not simply want to widen access to the site, they also maintain that the official management has contributed to the disenchantment of Stonehenge. In criticizing the form of official administration, the hippies emphasize that the official administration is just that, *a form* among many other possible forms. It is not natural, inevitable, normal or timeless. Rather it springs from a specific conjunction of historical and material factors which can be changed through concrete action.[29]

The action of the "hippies" reveals the historical nature of the "normal." The media and government reactions interpreted here represent an attempt to restore "normality" and "healthy" leisure activity.

The denial of the hippies' evaluation of Stonehenge, then, is related, in some measure, to their lifestyle—a lifestyle that involves mobility, lack of property, and a lack of participation in the formal economy. In terms of the actual chain of events surrounding the Stonehenge phenomenon, the critique of the hippy lifestyle according to geographic norms of property and rootedness followed and sprang from the arguments over the proper use of Stonehenge. The following sections, then, are connected to Stonehenge in two ways. First, as I have suggested above, the judgment of the alternative view of Stonehenge as inappropriate was linked to other geographical features of the hippies' lifestyle, and second, once the hippies were prevented from reaching the monument, the actual chain of events moved away from the stones and involved a more direct reaction to the geographical transgression of the hippies' everyday lifestyle.

The Convoy of Pollution: Mobility and Deviance

The law of the normal presents itself as permanently beleaguered. In the name of the "average citizen" it defies "the human cess pit" of "abnormal" leisure and the onslaught of "the violent permissive society". Metaphorically speaking, the normal presents itself as the bastion of health and reason, while deviant leisure is reviled as a disease to the social organism, the ever threatening "convoy of pollution".

—*Chris Rojek*

They deface the fields and the roadside with their junk.... They live in squalor and proclaim it as their right to do so. They are shiftless and irresponsible. They descend upon communities and contribute nothing to them.... They are pests and only those who don't see this would defend them.

—*Daily Mirror, 30 May 1986*

It is no consolation for the villagers to be told by the hippies that while they may be smelly outside, they are clean at heart.

—*Daily Telegraph, 5 June 1986*

We have already seen that there was a conflict over the meaning of Stonehenge and behavior appropriate to that place. Much of the conflict, however, occurred once the travelers were stopped from reaching their original objective. Indeed, as I mentioned at the beginning of this chapter, the conflict is still going on. The focus moved away from the meaning of a particular place and more toward the general behavior of the people traveling through and camping in the countryside. Two geographical themes stand out in the reporting of the "hippy" lifestyle: the connection of deviance to mobility and the moral value of property.

As in the previous illustration (of graffiti) an important part of the labeling process in the construction of deviance is the use of descriptive terms like dirt, disease, and smell. Again, as in the previous case, this does not appear to be a precise "objective" description but rather a refusal of difference—a recognition of disorder in the unfamiliar. Metaphors of dirt are associated with place; something is where it shouldn't be.

At social security offices where the "hippies" were expected to claim benefits, protective screens were raised due to the fear of hepatitis, despite the fact that the disease is only spread through blood contact.[30] The *Sun* provided a colorful description of the "hippy" camp:

> The camp is squalid. Piles of litter are building up, scrap metal is being accumulated. Dogs and goats are eating off the same plates as people.... The insides of their cars and vans are filthy. Cooking rings are thick with grease, bits of carpet are matted with dirt, stinking bedding is scattered everywhere.[31]

A *Daily Telegraph* article referred to the group as "being in quarantine" from society.[32] References to disease went to some bizarre extremes. The *Daily Mail* suggested that the "hippies" were spreading ringworm, tapeworms, and several viruses through their diseased dogs, cats, and goats.[33] Les Atwell is reported as saying that the "hippies" would "poison" his land. The field, he said, "will be disease ridden ... for at least two years."[34] As if to sum things up the chief constable of Hampshire referred to the travelers as "a convoy of pollution."[35]

The task at hand here is not to discover if, in fact, the travelers had hepatitis but to see what it is about their lifestyle that led people to speak in these terms. Since the use of terms such as *dirt, odor,* and *disease* implies a geographical transgression, the analysis suggests some ways the travelers ignored or deliberately transgressed assumed, "commonsense" geographical orderings.

In the House of Commons on 3 June 1986, the Home Secretary, Douglas Hurd, declared that the travelers were "nothing more than a bunch of medieval brigands with no respect for the law or the rights of others" (Parliamentary Debates, 1986). This description raises the issue of mobility as a lifestyle and the way in which it is viewed. Below I examine this issue of mobile lifestyles as deviant. The travelers were often referred to as "vagabonds": "The convoy is a group of people who have no respect for law and order. They are vicious to deal with in any situation. They are vagabonds."[36] Here the Wiltshire police chief constable, Donald Smith, attempts to convey the impression that the travelers are dangerous. In the end he resorts to simply saying "they are vagabonds," as if the implications of that are self-explanatory. A *Daily Telegraph* article frequently refers to the travelers as "vagabonds" and "itinerants."[37] The *Daily Mail* calls them an "outlaw wandering army."[38] In the Commons David Heathcoat-Amory referred to them as "travelling gangs" and Tony Marlow called them "marauding anarchists" in the middle of an unrelated debate on pension schemes.

A distinction arises in media reports between the quiet settled countryside of southwest England and the noisy "invasion" of the travelers:

"The hamlet of Lytes Cary has never seen anything like it. A scatter of houses along a lane of head-high cow parsley, it is normally a quiet place near Somerton, home to about 30 quiet people. Somerton is pretty quiet too."[39] The description of a small village near the convoy is typical of the way the "west country" is portrayed. As well as the quiet, news reports emphasized beauty: "The fair face of this unique area is being disfigured and fouled. The New Forest is recognized internationally as of prime ecological importance and as a place of quiet recreation for our people."[40] "The situation at the moment is that these anarchists are soiling this beauty spot and harassing both residents and holiday makers."[41] Here the travelers are "soiling" an area and annoying both "residents" and "holiday makers." The residents are homeowners and settled, and the holiday makers are engaging in legitimate forms of travel and will eventually return to a home and job. The "hippies," however, are clearly "deviant" in their nonsettled lifestyle, and thus they soil normality.

In distinction to the rustic images of the countryside, the "hippies" are portrayed in a series of military metaphors, as in the description of "the Wiltshire farmer whose land has suffered a massive invasion from hippies who are camping there on route for their annual pagan pilgrimage to Stonehenge,"[42] and in the headline that read, "Row over the 'Outlaw' Wandering Army."[43] Terms like "invasion," "army," and "gang" are supported by words that suggest massive numbers ready to overtake the countryside: "The hippies who are massing for a banned festival at Stonehenge, mobbed Mr. Gummer."[44] The contrast between the settled quietness of the countryside and the noisy marauding army of mobile vandals is ideologically effective, as it draws on geographical assumptions about the value of the quiet, natural countryside so important to British mythology and contrasts it with the assumptions of deviance and anarchy implicit in the propertyless lifestyle of the travelers.

Many of the festival-goers were people who traveled as a way of life. During the year they would travel around the country in their buses, caravans, and trucks, camping out, staying in Gypsy camps, and working in scrap metal or other "informal" types of labor. These separate groups would meet together in spring and form convoys to reach Stonehenge. Through most of the summer months they attended a variety of free music and arts festivals. Other festival-goers were predominantly young people from urban areas who were unemployed and/or homeless and chose to travel during the festival season. Just as the "hippies" had a different idea of what Stonehenge meant and how to use it, they also had a different lifestyle from the majority of citizens. This was noted with some sympathy in the *Guardian*. In an article headlined "Travelling Tribe of

300 Individuals Tries to Leave 'Rubbish Society' Behind," Tony, a traveler, is allowed to speak: "I think we are people who have seen society for what it is. It takes a lot of courage to make the move, to give up everything you know."[45]

Traveling as a way of life has historically met with violent, symbolic, and legal resistance. Hitler's persecution of the Jews and Gypsies before and during World War II was perhaps the most famous case of negative portrayals and treatment of people perceived as "rootless." The murder of six million Jews and half a million Gypsies was, to some extent, based on an ideology of rootedness. Prior to and during the 1930s academics and intellectuals in Germany succeeded in creating a German mythology centered in the "roots" of Germany.[46] Authors such as Martin Heidegger and Herman Hesse described the value of the forest, with its lush green trees and deep rich soil. Heidegger idealized the life in the forest to counter what he saw as the increasing alienation and rootlessness of city life. The emphasis was on the deep roots of the German character. Jews and Gypsies, on the other hand, were symbolized by desert snakes winding around the German roots seeking to destroy them. Jews were also associated with both the desert (with its lack of soil) and the city (the modern cause of alienation and inauthenticity). The intentions of those who created this mythology remain uncertain, but we do know that Hitler was able to use these notions in his doctrine of genocide for Jews and Gypsies.

Britain also has a long history of discrimination against and persecution of people associated with seemingly aimless traveling. An Elizabethan "Acte for the Punishment of Vacabondes" defined all wanderers as "rogues."[47] The Vagrancy Act of 1824 made it an offense to be in the open or under a tent, coach, or wagon without any visible means of subsistence and unable to give a good account of oneself.[48] An act of 1882 decreed that all persons "purporting to be gypsies" were to be treated as rogues and vagabonds. The 1959 Highways Act made it an offense for a Gypsy to camp beside a road. A 1967 court case defined a Gypsy as a person "who has a nomadic life."

David Sibley's book *Outsiders in Urban Society*, in which these and other ordinances are cited, is an excellent example of an analysis of people considered "out of place." He shows how society simultaneously romanticizes Gypsies and labels them deviant. They are romanticized because they supposedly are in touch with nature, leading a traditional existence in brightly colored caravans pulled by horses. Gypsies are reported to have mysterious powers, and Gypsy women are portrayed as objects of desire. These romantic images, however, exist only in books and poems. When Gypsies actually camp near a settlement or in an urban area, they are generally shunned. Government agencies mistreat and misunderstand the life of the traveler. Part of the problem is that the Gypsies do not conform to the romantic ideal. They do not wear exotic clothes and they travel in cars and buses:

> The contrast between the manifest deviance of the group and the muted part of the culture that is romanticized clearly reinforces the image of deviance, since to appear to have abandoned a noble existence, in harmony with nature, for one that conflicts with mainstream conceptions of order and harmony is an indication of degeneracy.[49]

In order to understand the phenomena of "deviance," we must look at dominant society as an active partner in its production. Peter Archard has indicated that literature on vagrancy has tended to separate the "problem" from the society in which it is located.[50] Rarely is a connection made between the supposed deviance of travelers and the unequal distribution of political, economic, and social power. Often the "offenders" are simply blamed for their own deviance, without any attempt to explain the way in which the deviant category is defined by the dynamic relationships between subordinate and dominant groups in society. Clearly the definition of mobility as deviance is rooted in the positive valuation of roots in a place-bound, property-owning society.

Judith Okely's analysis of Gypsy-travelers has attempted to relate the "deviant" status of the traveling lifestyle to wider societal and cultural forces. She acknowledges that "larger society's way of treating and identifying gypsies are fundamental constraints of the gypsy's actions."[51] In particular she identifies the avoidance of wage labor, the need for intermittent access to land, and the status of "no fixed abode" as representing symbolic and ideological disorder to house-dwelling society.

It becomes clear from reading Sibley's and Okely's accounts of the Gypsy/house-dwelling relationship that ideas about geography play a central role in the construction of normality and thus of deviance. In a society with geographic norms of property ownership and the separation of home and work, a traveling lifestyle is highly abnormal. From the viewpoint of the dominant mode of living, the traveling lifestyle appears to be disordered, dirty, and irresponsible. A lifestyle that is perceived as disorder is really, as Sibley and Okely both show, a different kind of order, a different set of priorities and expectations. The planning of "sites" for Gypsies in England is instructive. The sites are planned much like an ordinary housing estate, with straight lines in fenced-off areas with separate work space. This disregards the preference of Gypsies for open space, circular camps, and spaces that serve as both domestic and work environments. The sites can be interpreted as geographical correctives for the perceived disorder of the Gypsy lifestyle. The Gypsies have to be "straightened out."

A self-organized Gypsy camp is circular with a single entrance. The main windows of all the caravans face inward. Every trailer and the occupants can be seen by everyone. Curtains are rarely used. The central area is for play, work, and socializing, while the single entrance deters intrusion. Dominant "house-dwelling" lifestyles emphasize separation between houses and families, privacy, and strong demarcations of home and work.

> Once travellers feel security of tenure or access, rubbish is cleared, and the spatial boundary extended to the edge of their plots or the camp itself. Rubbish may be pushed over the hedge or fence or the outer rim of the circle. The toilet places will also be sought outside. The inner/outer boundary of dirt and cleanliness is thus completed in territorial space. Hedges are symbolic as well as physical boundaries. A gypsy accused of having illicit sex is said to have gone behind the hedge.[52]

The notion of travelers as disorderly and dirty is ill founded. The order is as strict as any order. There is an emphasis on family groups, inside/outside divisions, physical proximity, and segmented, hierarchical space within caravans: "The concern with spatial order and the domestic environment, however, does not extend beyond the trailer because, with a tradition of nomadism, people do not feel an attachment to a particular piece of land and so do not feel the urge to put boundaries round it and defend it."[53] Travelers have their own geographical order and their own sense of cleanliness. As most people in society do not see or understand this, they simply perceive it as disordered and dirty. To the Gypsies it makes much more sense, for instance, to defecate outside their camp in the hedges than to defecate inside their homes, close to their kitchens.

The relationship between Gypsies and house dwellers is an instructive one to bear in mind when considering reactions to the Stonehenge convoy. Many of the same themes arise. Indeed, many of the convoy members were Gypsy-travelers. Like the Gypsies, the convoy members led a life that had an order dramatically and visibly different from the majority of society. This different order was perceived as disorder.

One story that gained particular attention was the story of Emma, a young child who came to symbolize all the traveling children. Often the media would concentrate on the apparent dirtiness and lack of discipline among the children, who were evidently "deprived." The travelers, a *Sun* editorial claimed, made up "an evil society where dope is king and where little children are treated no better than animals."[54] The *Daily Telegraph* called the travelers "misguided Huckleberry Finn-type characters and children deprived of a normal family environment."[55] In an article entitled "The Convoy Kids" we are told of children with "their faces streaked with mud, wearing tattered denims and even bovver boots."[56] Emotive photographs appeared of a sad-looking young child and her long-haired father as they were moved from camp to camp. The *Daily Mirror* featured a two-page spread with the title "So Where Does He Go Now?" with a photograph of a small child who later turned out to be a girl called Emma.[57] On 11 June the story was followed up by the news of the "lost" hippy child finding a "refuge," as a local farmer provided clothes and food. The interest in the Emma story was such that the paper included a feature on "Emma, the Kid from Nowhere," in which a reporter interviewed Emma's father.[58] Emma, it seems, is "never short of cuddles, clothes or food" and "regular bathing." This story is contradicted by the *Sun,* which claimed that Emma was "not toilet trained at four."[59]

The interest in the children reflects the theme of mobility, as children are closely associated with a "normal" family environment. Nothing raises emotions more than deprived children, and here we have children "deprived" of a "normal" home. Emma is the "kid from nowhere" who, we are reminded, has "no say in the way she lives."[60] Gypsy children have similarly been the object of such interest, as they appear to freely wander away from their parents, do not go to school, and seem to be "dirty." The unusual communal arrangements for child care are not seen as different; they are perceived as "wrong." The social and cultural geographic norms of home, family, and privacy are obviously and visibly transgressed.

Any landscape is a representation of order. The land is divided up and segmented into territories and places, each of which correlate to types of behavior. It is possible in any one of these places to act "out of place" (such as holding a festival at Stonehenge). Mobility, though, appears to be a kind of superdeviance. It is not just "out of place," but disturbs the whole notion that the world can be segmented into clearly defined places. Because the easiest way to establish order is through the division of space, mobility becomes a basic form of disorder and chaos — constantly defined as transgression and trespass. It is no accident, then, that the control of mobility is foremost in the minds of those who have an interest in maintaining their own definition of order. The pass laws in South Africa were designed to achieve such an end because the biggest threat to segregation was, and still is, movement.

A mobile lifestyle is also connected to other territorial expectations, the most important of which is the division and the rootedness of home and work. People are expected to live in a "fixed abode" ("no fixed abode" is a highly suspicious characteristic) and to go to a place of work. All the apparatus of state bureaucracy has depended on this arrangement for centuries. Taxes are paid according to location. Social security claimants cannot easily move without risking the loss of their benefits. Even voting rights are typically tied to particular places. Traveling people upset all these expectations; they do not have a "fixed abode," and as they do not go to a place of work, they do not appear to work at all. In fact home and work occur together and move with each other. Gypsies typically earn money by dealing in scrap metal, which is often seen surrounding their parked caravans and is perceived as "dirt." The convoy travelers also worked informally, making crafts and ethnic goods that were sold at fairs in the summer. Mobility, then, poses a big threat to those unaccustomed to that lifestyle. As most of society is defined by territories and the expectations that go with them, mobile people cannot help but offend such expectations. As almost every activity in the modern Western world has its place, mobility is the ultimate kind of geographical deviance.

Private Property and Trespass

A central story in the convoy controversy was the collapse of Les Atwell, a west country farmer, as the travelers moved into an unused field of his. The anger of the press, farmers, government, and local residents was directed against the travelers after this event: "The law is an ass, a rampant ass.... [T]respass by 300 hippies with vehicles is exactly the same as trespass by a little old lady out on a country walk.... The law can't see the difference but everybody else can."[61] A *Daily Telegraph* editorial titled "Forgiving Trespass" expressed sympathy with Atwell and referred to the "massive invasion" of the "hippies."[62] Another editorial in the same paper referred to the "hippies" as a "threat to private property and a public nuisance" and asked if our "social obligations towards the unfortunate extend to those who wish to have no part in that society?"[63] As suggestions for a criminal trespass law emerged there was increasing concern for the "innocent" trespasser, such as the hiker or birdwatcher, involved in "normal" leisure activities. In the House of Commons the Home Secretary declared that "we must search for a way of distinguishing between ... [ramblers, youth hostelers, and the landowners association] and the undoubted mischiefs" (Parliamentary Debates, 1986). The *Sun* talks of the possible change in the trespass law so that trespass with intent to reside would be made illegal. "The rights of ramblers," it assures us, "would be protected."[64]

A debate quickly took shape around the issue of trespass. Much of the outrage in the media was directed against the law that made trespass of private property a civic, rather than a criminal, offense. Thus the need for a criminal trespass law was raised in Parliament. The National Union of Farmers, landowners associations, and conservative MPs from the southwest pressured the government to change the law. A special ministerial committee was formed to discuss such changes and Prime Minister Thatcher, addressing the House of Commons, declared that she was "only too delighted to do anything I can to make life difficult for such things as hippy convoys" (Parliamentary Debates, 1986). She added that if it took new trespass laws to deal with the convoy, they would be introduced.

The trespass of the Stonehenge convoy was the latest in a series of threats to private property in the 1970s and 1980s that attracted national attention, including the possession of empty buildings by squatters, sit-ins by university students and unionized labor, and the actions of the Greenham Women. Trespass had been one of the few effective "weapons of the weak" in sociopolitical struggle. A redefined trespass law would thus be an effective move against such resistance.

Ancient laws, formulated in a society that preceded capitalism, had been designed to deal with the nebulous issue of *preserving the peace.* Offenses included "violently entering or keeping possession of lands or tenements with menaces, force and arms."[65] The protection of private property was not the major focus of these laws and was only tangential to the aim of preserving the peace. The outcome was that a trespasser *could* enter a house or land so long as it was entered peacefully (that is, if the door was unlocked or a window open). Equally a person who owned the property *could not* enter by force without committing an offense. Squatters, for instance, would enter empty buildings and put locks on the doors to prevent their forceful ejection. Landlords found themselves restrained by the law as much as they were helped by it.

As the trespass law became more and more threatened, it became a "terrain of contestation" because of the appeal, as Peter Vincent-Jones puts it, "of the greater possessors to the legal basis of their exclusive control in the *right to exclude* squatters from their private property."[66] But the trespass law was not the whole story. Along with the attempts to change the law went a whole series of representations of trespassers as offenders against commonsense.

Common-Sense Representations and Changes in the Law

The legal remedy for being "out of possession" (trespassed against) was common-law action. A "judgment of possession" that would declare someone the legal possessor of property had to be obtained from the county or high court. A writ of possession needed to enforce removal could not be issued without every trespasser having been given notice, by name, of the proceedings. In addition fourteen days had to pass between a judgment and the granting of the writ. The possession, therefore, relied on a *right to exclude,* the legal form of expressing the economic power of exclusive control.

This right to exclude is a major pillar of capitalism, guaranteeing and legitimating private property in both the domestic and industrial spheres. Home owners and managers had exclusive rights to property. Workers had temporary rights to use property to fulfill their contracts, and squatters had no rights at all. Given this, it is no surprise that the property owners sought to strike back against infringements by increasing the effectiveness of their legal remedies.

In 1970, following several industrial sit-ins, several changes were made to the trespass laws. Trespassers no longer had to be individually identified in a court action (an often lengthy process), and the fourteen-day waiting period between summons and writ was reduced to five. The effectiveness of these changes is evidenced by an increase in the number of trespass charges from 776 in 1973 to 5,683 in 1980.[67] The laws effectively buttressed the rights to exclusive possession.

Changes in the law, as this example illustrates, require a public display of support for the institution of private property. One way this is achieved is through media representations like those of the travelers. Vincent-Jones hints at a relationship between constructions of "common sense" and the more formal functions of law. He describes how squatting in the 1970s, for instance, was "constructed" as a serious danger to society by the media. If the media was to be believed, the squatters were a danger to *all* domestic premises; they prevented more deserving people on waiting lists from getting a home; they were "freeloaders and layabouts," probably foreign, and wantonly destructive; and they generally presented a fundamental threat to civilized society.[68] Two quotations amply illustrate the similarity between media reactions to squatting and to the convoy:

> It is not merely that they deprive those who have been waiting in the queue for a home patiently. The havoc they cause is unbelievable to those who have not seen it. To describe their living habits like those of pigs is unfair to pigs who are generally of a kindly disposition, not given to wanton destruction, and react reasonably favourably to clean living conditions. The GLC handed out pictures of devastation caused in a block of new flats at Paddington, but they could have taken similar pictures almost anywhere in inner London. Baths piled high with

rubbish, ceilings collapsed from rubbish piled above, mindless slogans scrawled on doors and decorative panels, posters and newspaper articles hammered to the walls and kitchens piled high with the debris of feeding habits that would disgrace a chimpanzee's tea party.[69]

Of the many strange and frightening features of contemporary British life, none carries a more obvious and direct threat to society's survival than the growing phenomenon of squatting. Innumerable houses up and down the country are now in illegal occupation by organized gangs of thugs, layabouts and revolutionary fanatics. Costly and irrecoverable damage is continually being done to private property from sheer malice.... In reality the motive for most of the squatting is either political—a settled purpose of subverting public order—or simple greed and aggression.[70]

The media representations of the Stonehenge convoy also portrayed the "hippies" as a threat to everybody, as wantonly destructive, as cynically motivated (unlike the homeless and the unemployed), and as living like animals. Both the squatters and the convoy represented particular types of crisis in "normality," and normality had to be defended, in particular the sanctity of property. The media mythology of the invading squatter and hippy prepared the (spurious) grounds on which people might accept the need for criminal measures. Representations of deviance are effective and credible because they make some kind of ideological sense out of an apparent crisis; they appeal to people's "common sense." In both cases the threat to private property was immersed in a sea of signification—in a highly emotive discourse of disorder that included images of degeneracy (drug taking, promiscuity, dirtiness, disease), violence, and animality. A distinct division was created between the deviant marauding bands and the ordinary person:

At one pole was presented the image of the ordinary Englishman, defending his "castle" or waiting patiently in the council housing queue, perhaps suffering from some disability, weakness or old age, or already the victim of some terrible disaster. At the other pole were ranged the squatters, live-for-nothing intruders "taking over" in organised bands, spreading rapidly and causing havoc, disrespectful of your home and its contents, living surrounded by debris like animals.[71]

One frequent request made of the convoy members was that they "get a job." The conservative agriculture minister is reported to have visited the camp and told the people there "for a start you can get off other people's property and find some jobs."[72] Similar advice came from a local MP, Patrick McNair-Wilson.[73] The travelers were frequently contrasted to "normal" citizens:

The layabout army, dragging around with their pathetic children with no future, come thumbing their noses at hard-working people who pay for their idleness.[74]

They despise work themselves but make life a purgatory for those who do labour to earn their own living. They descend like a plague of locusts on land which is not their own.... The whole of law-abiding, tax-paying, job-doing and job-seeking society is being taken for a ride every time one of these hippy convoys trundles on its sponging way.[75]

Many of the strategies suggested to deal with the "hippy problem" involved reabsorption into the "normal" working life. One plan was to deprive the travelers of welfare services if they hadn't "worked" for six months. The suggestion was to make the "hippies" work on public projects for their unemployment money.[76] It is striking how similar the reactions to squatters and the reactions to the "hippies" are. Not only are the descriptions of the "deviants" the same (dirty, violent, and so on), but so are the descriptions of "normality." In the quotations above we are presented with a person (usually a man) who has a job (at a time when over 10 percent of working-age people were unemployed) and a house. Les Atwell, the farmer who collapsed at the sight of the "hippies" on his field, is portrayed as just such a person: "This is not a rich landowner pushing homeless people off his land but a smallholder who is having his livelihood ruined by common criminals."[77] Here the farmer is changed from a privileged landowner to a "normal" person, and the travelers are changed from underprivileged people to reckless criminals. The insinuation is that *any* normal person might be the victim of these malicious deviants. John Gummer's speech diverts any sympathy we may have for the travelers toward the figure of Les Atwell. With regard to the media representations of squatters, Vincent-Jones writes:

The danger was clear: everyone was threatened by squatting, therefore all were expected to participate in condemning the violation of exclusive rights, even if this celebration of private property involved a little dramatic license. This is how the squatter, a modern folk demon, provided the pretext for reaffirming and celebrating the institution of private property, and then for redrawing the boundaries of exclusive right through a further legal transformation.[78]

The Stonehenge convoy became another folk devil through similar representational strategies. Again the representations were followed by changes in the law.

The introduction of criminal proceedings regarding trespass followed the media reaction to squatters. In 1977, the introduction of the Criminal Law Bill affected the legal position of all trespassers by conferring the power of entry on the police in order to search for and arrest people suspected of being guilty of one of several new offenses. The debate over this bill included many references to the "squatting problem" that reflected the mythical representations that had been created in the media. Sir Michael Havers, MP, expressed the belief that squatting was unfair because "it occupies accommodation either being used or about to be used by a new occupier."[79] It was suggested that many people on council house waiting lists were being displaced by the undeserving squatters, "thousands of whom are nothing short of freeloaders who live off the backs of the homeless and ratepayers."[80] Thus some key elements of the squatter mythology built through representations in the media were mobilized to justify the changes in the law. The changes were pushed through at a time when people were convinced that criminal measures were necessary to protect "normal" people. Thus "common sense" was mobilized to legitimate law.

The 1977 changes followed on the heels of negative media representations of squatting. The representations of the hippy convoy were followed by a similar debate about the necessity of changes in the law. Again a small and powerful group of actors (NUF, landowners associations, Conservative MPs) sought to defend property by arguing for the criminalization of trespass. As in the case of the "squatting menace," the "threat" was experienced by the reader of newspapers as a threat to themselves by the creation of a moral panic affecting all "normal" and "decent" people. Lord Mellors in the House of Lords referred directly to the media representations when he asked if the minister was aware that "most British people who have seen the scenes on television have been absolutely sickened ... [by] ... this crowd of scruffy people, who do not pay taxes, nor send their children to school, nor look for work, nor do anything that is proper and decent."[81] Again the values of private property were strengthened through representations of a vulnerable minority as "deviant."

One way to look at the hippy convoy, and indeed all of the illustrations here, would be in terms of property and trespass and the legal definitions thereof. Such an analysis, I believe, would miss the point that property, as well as being a formal legal concept, plays a central role in the geography of common sense. In this illustration I have linked property to ideas such as rootedness and the established meaning of Stonehenge in order to argue that they all play a role in forming our normative expectations. Such normative expectations are buttressed by legal sanctions, but, more often than not, these sanctions are not necessary because people behave according to what is "normal." The original "trespass" against Stonehenge and the subsequent trespasses on private land can be seen as a matter of the law and its enforcement. All of these trespasses, moreover, challenge the rights of officials to determine the use value of a site and thus to delineate the geography of normality. Property is, after all, connected to words such as *proper* and *appropriate,* words that feature prominently throughout this book and are used to express assumptions about common sense. The "hippies" were more than just trespassers; they were "out of place." They were not just "illegal"; they were "abnormal."

Defining the Geography of Normality

In a "normal" and "decent" society people work for a living, pay taxes, and obey laws. There is a geography to this normality, as well. The transgressions of the "hippy" convoy serve to reveal a number of related assumptions concerning the implicit connections between geography and normality. The discourse of the media and government in reaction to the activities of festival-goers was one that spoke out in defense of the "normal" and the "decent" against the "deviance" of the "hippies." The story started with arguments over the proper meaning of Stonehenge. The banning of the previously uncontroversial festival in 1984 was based on the idea of protecting national heritage from the "masses." Stonehenge has, after all, been a central site of English culture — the very "heart of England" — in an array of English representations from old myth through landscape paintings to the novels of Hardy and Forster. It was this idea of Stonehenge as a symbol of the nation that English Heritage was obliged to defend. Against this was the view of the festival-goers that Stonehenge was not an abstract exhibit but a living site to be used at the solstice for its originally intended purpose. On one side of the argument was the idea of preservation and removal from the people — an idea that Bourdieu insists represents a split between legitimate and "facile" pleasure, a split that is predisposed to affirm the superiority of those "satisfied with the sublimated, refined, disinterested, gratuitous, distinguished pleasures forever closed to the profane."[82] On the other side is the idea that Stonehenge is part of life — linked to, not separated from, everyday enjoyment. Some members of the convoy believed that the site was spiritual and should be *used* as such. Others just thought that it was a place to have fun, a carnivalesque idea that snubs its nose at the refined distinction of separation. English Heritage had the force of the state (legal remedies and hundreds of riot-gear-clad policemen) on its side and "won" the conflict. The question remains, however, as to why the hippies were prevented from using the site while the druids were given permission to continue.

One answer is that the mobile lifestyle of the travelers marked them as a low-trust group in the eyes of the authorities. In the second half of this chapter I considered the geographical characteristics of the "hippies" that contributed to the perception of them as a group not worthy of trust. Mobility as a way of life involves being permanently out of place. Mobility resists forces of discipline imposed by boundaries and territories. More particularly the mobile lifestyle of the travelers ignores taken-for-granted spatial norms of British society. It involves the mixing, for instance, of work and leisure. Since the "hippies" had no obvious workplace they were considered to be leeches on society offending "law-abiding, tax-paying, job-doing ... society."[83] Conversely, although they are considered as not working, neither are they seen as involved in "healthy" leisure. Since they appear to have no home place to return to, their actions must be distinguished from the "innocent" trespassers— the ramblers and bird-watchers. Druids, although strange, are respectable middle-class freemasons who return to their homes and well-paid jobs after their solstice celebration. The lives of the druids conform to the geographical definitions of normality. Finally, the mobile world of the travelers involved trespass—a deviation that forced the authorities to delineate the linkage between the word *property* and the word *proper.*

If the representations of the "hippies" are any indicator, a geography of normality in England includes people with fixed abodes, people who own property, and people who enjoy seeing ancient monuments but not using them. By acting "out of place," the travelers, deliberately and by accident, forced the media and the government to categorically define expectations of normality and to underline the manifest "deviance" of the travelers. This definition process spoke not only to people's social presuppositions in a general sense but to their explicitly geographical sense of appropriateness. Not only did the travelers "avoid work," but they also lived in moving vehicles; not only did they indulge in "reckless violence," but they also "invaded" other people's property; not only were they "dirty," but they also held festivals at national monuments.

In each of the three major sections of this illustration I have shown how the travelers deviated from sociocultural-geographic norms. In each case powerful actors in society defended established, "common-sense" doxic geographies against the alternatives presented by the "hippies." We can think of the dominant geographies as sacred. The idea of Stonehenge as a "national heritage" to be "defended from the masses," the valuation of rootedness, and the sanctity of property are all parts of an established system of geographical values. The transgression of these norms by the "hippies" provoked reactions that define the geographical orthodoxy—the geography of normality. The actions of the "hippies" are offenses against the "sacred" geography; they are represented as a "profane" geography of the debased and deviant.

The link between the conflict over the use and meaning of Stonehenge and issues of mobility and trespass are linked by the sequence of events that took place in the mid-1980s. The issues of the "hippy" lifestyle might never have been raised in the national media if the festival had not been banned. The conflict around the solstice in the years since has involved hundreds of policemen in riot gear, tens of court appearances, and millions of pounds. It would have been significantly cheaper to provide the "hippies" with a site for the festival, give them water and festival services, and let them disperse after the solstice. It says something about the importance of upholding the meaning of a place like Stonehenge and the geographical order of things in general that the authorities were willing to go to such great lengths to uphold them.

It is a central point of this illustration, and the others included here, that the delineation of the profane defines the sacred, the underlining of "deviance" outlines the "normal," and reactions to transgression define orthodoxy. These definition processes mobilize common-sense understandings of space and place as powerful ideological tools.

Chapter 5

Heretical Geography 3:
Putting Women in Their Place —
Greenham Common

> *How much has the perception of Greenham women as*
> *dangerous, threatening and dirty to do with the fact that in*
> *western life cups are not supposed to be on the ground, and*
> *women are supposed to wear nice clothes and be at home*
> *with husbands?*
>
> — *Lynne Jones*

Deep in the heart of England there lies a town called Newbury. It is a town in the "home counties" — an area extending west of London across the south Midlands. It is an area often represented in caricatures of rolling hills and grazing sheep, a green landscape dotted with small English towns and villages worn by history. Old weathered stone pubs and churches surround village centers and flat green cricket grounds, which are decorated with white-linen-clad players every weekend. It is a bucolic scene that attracts tourists and home buyers alike. Narrow roads wind through the fields flanked by hedgerows, trees, and ancient stone walls that no one remembers how to build or fix.

This area is also one of enormous wealth. Within commuting distance of London, it attracts yuppies who wish to escape the city's tentacles and enjoy the country life. It is an area haunted by the aristocracy, frequented by lords and ladies attending the regatta at Henley or a local hunt. Wealthy people retire here — to the comfort of old England and walks in the (not too backbreaking) hills. Less represented is the extremely productive mechanized agriculture and the wealthy corporate farmers who benefit from it. It is the area of Britain least devastated by economic recessions. It has been almost entirely conservative in its voting habits — a huge blue blotch on the political map.

In addition, the home counties (along with East Anglia) area has the most military air bases operated by the Royal Air Force and the United

States Air Force. Many of these air bases have been the sites of nuclear weaponry and bases for long-range F-111 bombers. It is from this area that U.S. bombers flew missions to bomb Tripoli. It is from here that attacks would have been launched against the Soviet Union. Consequently it is also the area that would have been most highly devastated in a Soviet reprisal. Beside one of these bases, in the middle of the home counties, is Newbury, Berkshire. Affluent people live there in large Victorian houses with driveways lined with ancient oaks and the shells of disease-ridden elms. The gardens are perfectly manicured. Pubs and churches abound. It is a town with a cricket team and a local hunt. Newbury is also the site of one of Britain's more famous horse race tracks. Around Newbury thoroughbred horses are raised and trained.

Within sight of some of the Newbury homes is the huge U.S. air base of Greenham Common, once the home of ninety-six cruise missiles and their nuclear warheads. The air base is a vast expanse of concrete, barbed wire, and secretive bunkers made of tons of reinforced concrete designed to resist penetration by nuclear warheads. Huge U.S. C-5 "Galaxy" transport planes land on the runway frequently, shattering the peace of the countryside. In the years 1983–87 they were bringing weapons of mass destruction.

Around the base since 1981 the Greenham Common peace women have camped in a series of higgledy-piggledy camps of lowly polythene structures known as "benders": "Everything was right on top of everything else at Greenham Common, the peace women were right on top of the military, and the expensive houses and the Newbury golf club and the race course were right on top of the peace camp."[1] The site of the air base and the protest camps in the heart of the English countryside is partly responsible for the remarkable impact of this protest on people's consciousness. The place of Greenham Common connects the local and seemingly mundane with the global scale of superpowers:

> On the one hand this patch of English countryside is a small link in a
> vast system, the means of destroying millions of people (and land and
> buildings) in a faraway place, controlled from another place equally far
> away. On the other hand the superpower has to come down to the local
> scale, to face to face confrontations over a piece of fence, to the
> irritations of local bye-laws and so on.[2]

The fact that all this occurs in the countryside also differentiates this protest from the normal "demonstration" that takes place in the city, where the places of power are more wrapped up in the tangle of comfortable streets and buildings. Nuclear installations in the countryside stand out sharply from their bucolic surroundings. The viewer is confronted with a sharply delineated air base surrounded by expanses of fields, woods, and hills. This juxtaposition reveals the naïveté of ideas of "rural peace." The beauty of the countryside is threatened by the contents of the base. These contradictions lie under the sheen of normality. Most passersby probably do not see the contradictions but simply walk or drive by. Without reflection the base in the country attracts no special attention. It is this "normality" — this "common sense" — that the establishment seeks to preserve. The Greenham women, by breaking with the "normality" of their own lives — by leaving homes and families and deciding to live "rough" for months on end — sought to expose the contradictions of weapons of mass destruction in the English countryside.

The name Greenham Common immediately invokes two powerful images in the minds of most English men and women. One is the image of a U.S. air base — the home of cruise missiles controlled in the United States and aimed at Eastern Europe from their sinister bunkers. The "other" is the image of a group of women camped outside the base in makeshift tents protesting the presence of the cruise missiles. This place means both things, and the mind constantly shifts between them.

The story I am about to relate concerns a set of conflicts about what (and who) belongs where and about what (and who) is out of place. The main part of the story is a tale of the popular press reaction to the presence of the women at Greenham. The story is also about the reaction of the residents of Newbury to the women.

> I had not realized that the women's protest camps were so vulnerably situated. They were sandwiched between two hostile territories inhabited by powerful groups who loathed them for different reasons. On one side they had the grey teeming world of the Cruise missile base with its values of the police and the military. On the other side they had the prosperous world of Newbury, with its English gardens and thoroughbreds and its values of the wealthy shopkeeper, and the racehorse owner. I soon discovered that both these worlds had an obsessive horror of the peace women.[3]

Both the press and the Newbury residents considered the women "out of place" and did their best to speed the removal of the women. But why were the women there at all? The answer is that they considered the base and the missiles to be "out of place" — on the earth and particularly in England, in the green rolling meadows of the "home" counties. What constitutes a defilement? This is the ideologically charged geographical argument that takes place in "deepest England."

In this illustration I approach the question from several different perspectives. I show how the women are seen as out of place due to their desertion of *home*. Through the early part of the 1980s it was suggested, directly and metaphorically, that the women have abandoned, neglected, and betrayed "home." Home, though, is a signifier without a fixed referent. Often the home is the home in Newbury or elsewhere; the home with husband, wife, kids, and pets; the home with a kitchen. At other times the home is England, and the English countryside itself is metonymic for the "free" world—the "open" society. The transgressions of the women rest on geographical bases. The women are "out of place." They are not being "proper" women since they are not at "home."

The women's perceived displacement from home is not the whole story, however. The women are not only away from their "natural" realm but they are also *in* a particularly unfeminine place—on the perimeter of the masculine world of the military base. The presence of the chaotic, unhierarchical peace camps alongside the hierarchical, ordered air base on the one hand and the neatly ordered English rural landscape on the other constitutes an offense to the hegemonic-geographical order. Using literature on carnival and the carnivalesque I argue that the peace camp exhibits "grotesque realism," which contrasts radically with the "classical body" of the air base and the tidiness of the farmland. In addition I present a brief analysis of the masculinity of the military and suggest that the peace women upset assumed female roles in the military establishment. The air base then is both a "classical" place and a "masculine" place. The women, by being on the perimeter, are doubly out of place. Finally I present some alternative stories about the Greenham women in order to take the ideological prop of truth away from the mainstream press reports. I show how different groups take the same "facts" and come to profoundly different conclusions about the actions of the peace women. Before any of this, however, it is helpful to present a brief history of the camp.

A History

The Greenham Common Women's Peace Camp has been called by one commentator a political icon for the eighties.[4] Indeed the events at Greenham Common and the stories that have been told about the women there illustrate many of the key tensions in contemporary political activism. Unlike graffitists and the "convoy," the Greenham women were engaged in deliberate political protest. Many of the transgressions at Greenham were intentional strategies to direct attention to the first British home for U.S. cruise missiles.

The peace camp is the result of the conversations of a group of women in south Wales during 1981. Calling themselves "women for life on earth," they marched from Cardiff, Wales, to the U.S. Air Force Base Greenham Common in Berkshire, England. Greenham was to be the first base for the new U.S. cruise missiles and their nuclear warheads. The women wanted to draw attention to this. Ten years later Greenham has become imprinted on the British people's minds as a symbol of the peace movement and of resistance against the logic and practice of nuclear diplomacy. Greenham also became associated with feminist political strategy. Throughout the early eighties the British (and world) media reported on the presence of women at the air base, from as few as twenty to as many as thirty thousand. The press story, though, is not the whole story. The media showed very little interest in the original march from Cardiff and continued to ignore the women for over a year when they decided to camp out by the gates to the air base. Similarly, media interest in the camp died, while the camp exists to this day.

The original march from Cardiff to Greenham was inspired by a march from Copenhagen to Paris earlier in 1981. The women's march to Greenham was not an isolated case in the United Kingdom, either. The major antinuclear group in the U.K. was and still is the Campaign for Nuclear Disarmament (CND), which was experiencing a resurgence of interest at the time with a membership of some fifty thousand (as opposed to three thousand in the mid-1970s). In addition, many local peace groups were forming, such as Scientists against Nuclear Arms (SANA) and Women Oppose the Nuclear Threat (WONT). The wider context was one in which Margaret Thatcher had been in power for two years, the cold war was still icy, and U.S. cruise missiles were to be based in the United Kingdom. The Thatcher government was a firm advocate of the "deterrence" argument, and CND was advocating unilateral nuclear disarmament on moral, political, and economic grounds. The march to Greenham coincided with the beginning of a vigorous confrontation between the government and the supporters of CND. The opposition Labour Party was soon to take up the cause of unilateral disarmament as part of its election manifesto in 1983.

When the women arrived at Greenham they delivered a note to the base commander which read:

> We will not be victims in a war which is not of our making. We wish neither to be the initiators not the targets of a nuclear holocaust.... We are implacably opposed to the siting of U.S. cruise missiles in the country. We represent thousands of ordinary people who are opposed to these weapons and we will use all our resources to prevent the siting of these missiles here.[5]

The women offered to take part in public debates. The offers were refused. Support from unions and individuals, in addition to the arrival of people from other parts of the country, encouraged them to stay so they set up camp in September 1981. Still the media showed little interest in the women's protest. When the press did concern themselves with the protest the coverage was ambivalent ("as few stereotypes as the average bus queue").[6]

In February 1982 the group decided to make the camp for women only. Some men had been present since the end of the march. The decision was made for political and practical reasons. It was believed that it would be a strong and affirmative message to build a minisociety of only women on a nonhierarchical model. It was also believed that the presence of men would inevitably prompt violence between the police and the protestors. The absence of men, they surmised, would discourage the police from violent tactics. The men left angrily, some destroying shelters they had made. It was now the Greenham Common Women's Peace Camp.

In March 1982, 250 women blocked the main entrance to the base. They continued to block the entrances at random and unannounced times for the next few months. In May the women suffered the first of many evictions from common land and they moved to land belonging to the Ministry of Transport. In August a group of women "occupied" the sentry box at the main gate and were eventually arrested. Their trials in November resulted in the first extensive media coverage of the Greenham women and encouraged massive support for the women, which culminated in 30,000 people "embracing" the base on 12 December 1982. The perimeter fence was completely surrounded and decorated with personal objects such as balloons, diapers, recipes, webs of string (symbolizing the "web of life"), and a bottle of nail-biting lotion that bore the words "cruise makes me nervous." The purpose of the protest was to transform the fence from a negative obstruction to a positive form of expression—an art gallery. The women brought with them personal objects that signified "life" to them. The Greenham fence has been seen as a piece of art expressing the anxieties of the people. Guy Brett describes how "many surprising and eloquent new meanings come about by the chance juxtaposition of people's contributions." The women created, unselfconsciously, a collage on which mass-produced objects and images were placed in an unexpected context and became powerful signs. "Taking a teddy bear from a child's room and placing it in view of the silos of nuclear missiles is as eloquent as writing a poem."[7] This was just one of many ways in which the Greenham women played with and upset the rules of place and context.

The next year, 1983, was the year of Greenham. The media paid almost constant attention to the women camping outside the gates and the regular mass protests around the base. That was also the year of the general election and the year of the arrival of cruise missiles at the base. Nuclear disarmament had become the main issue in the political campaigns, and the government went all out to discredit the CND and the Greenham women. With the help of an obliging press, they succeeded. Throughout the year the women creatively called attention to the cause by removing fences (see Figure 5.1), dancing on top of silos, blockading entrances, holding picnics inside the base dressed up as Easter bunnies, and decorating the fences with webs.

By the end of 1984, and particularly after 1987, the media interest in Greenham ended, with the exception of a few stories in the "quality" press (*Guardian*, the *Times*, the *Observer*). The majority of my analysis, therefore, concerns press coverage between the end of 1982 and the end of 1984. Most of the data is from 1983. This period is one of intense propaganda battles between the CND, the Labour Party, and the Greenham women, on one side,[8] and the conservative government and the right-wing press, on the other. It was a period of struggle over hearts and minds concerning nuclear weapons. Early in 1983 polls showed that a majority of people in the United Kingdom opposed the presence of U.S. cruise missiles on British soil. Many cited the Greenham women as influential

Figure 5.1. Breaking the fence at Greenham, October 1983. (Photo by Paula Allen, from Guy Brett, *Through Our Own Eyes* [London: New Society Press, 1986]. By permission.)

in their decision. The government, in response, appointed Michael Heseltine as minister of defense in January 1983.

Heseltine's mandate was to counter the growing popularity of the peace movement and to make a case for "deterrents." The media coverage during these years is intimately connected to the government's wish to discredit the antinuclear movement. The *Daily Mail,* the *Daily Express,* the *Sun,* the *Daily Telegraph,* and the *Times* were all pro-Thatcher to one degree or another, while the *Daily Mirror* and the *Guardian* largely opposed the government.

In general the press echoed the government's arguments, put forward at elaborate press conferences. The degree of slavishness with which the press agreed with the government is exemplified by two "coincidences" regarding terminology. In January 1983 ministers were told not to refer to "unilateral disarmament" but to replace it with "one-sided disarmament." Almost immediately the press started using the words "one-sided disarmament."[9] The other "coincidence" is that at roughly the same time (early 1983) the press began to put quotation marks around the word *peace* whenever it was referred to in conjunction with the women. It became the Greenham Common Women's "Peace" Camp. The word the women chose for themselves is here turned against them to question their motives and effectiveness. These discursive terms exist in a broader context of a shift from press interest in the women to outright hatred and disgust.

Cruise missiles eventually left Greenham in 1987 as part of the treaty between the United States and the Soviet Union. Some women are still there. In addition, the camp inspired similar camps elsewhere in the world (Seneca Falls, New York, and Puget Sound, Washington, in the United States, and Pine Gap, Australia) and in England (Molesworth).[10] Greenham became a model for peace politics. It focused media attention on the presence of a nuclear arsenal and a significant opposition to that presence. This media attention is the object of study in this chapter. The media coverage of Greenham is a kind of discursive site for excavation, which begs analysis. With the exceptions of Alison Young's *Femininity in Dissent* (1990) and Lynne Jones's essay on perceptions of peace women (1987),[11] surprisingly little analysis of this excavation site exists.

The general theme of this book is that transgressive events prompt responses that defend and seek to reproduce established geographies. The Greenham protest as an all-women, antinuclear, permanent encampment outside a missile base forced such a defense. An analysis of the media response reveals the boundaries of assumed, normative geographies. The divisions of mad/sane, good/evil, criminal/law-abiding, and normal/abnormal that appear so frequently in the press discourse all have geographical foundations in the assumed displacement of women from the home and the family to the all-women environment of the camp.

The Discourse of Displacement

The women at Greenham are described as out of place by the mainstream press and others. This displacement has two obvious sides to it: the women are not where they are supposed to be (home) and they are where they're not supposed to be (Greenham). The following section is an analysis of the ways in which the press indicated that the women belonged at home, in the private arena. My technique here (as with my other illustrations) is to look at metaphors and descriptive terms used by the press and to suggest their links to place and space. The metaphors and descriptive terms are dirt, smell, food, clothes, children, sexuality, hysteria, and rats and moles.

Dirt and Smell

As with graffiti and the convoy, the press frequently refers to this particular transgression using prose saturated with a plethora of references to dirt and pollution. You will recall that Mary Douglas has referred to dirt as essentially "matter out of place." At first glance it seems strange that the press should spend so much energy describing the "squalor" of the peace camp when the issue appears to be nuclear weapons and disarmament, but the pollution references have to be read as part of a wider discourse underlining the idea that displacement is involved at Greenham — the women of the peace camp are out of place and the references to pollution are symptomatic of that geographical-ideological judgment of the women and their actions.

> Mud splashed halfway up their legs. It oozed a raw onion smell and spread like brown paste over a chunk of Berkshire. Peace was a dirty business.[12]

> Yards of stinking rubbish spilling out of black plastic bags and donated refuse containers hit the eye and the nostrils at the entrance to camp, which oozes with thick, wet, mud.[13]

> The area in and around the site on either side of the access road is littered with rubbish, rags of old carpet, parts of broken fences and bags of refuse.... [T]he whole site is ugly, an environmental eyesore.[14]

The media discourse consistently referred to the garbage bags, muddy conditions, blackened teapots, and various smells. Speeches in Parliament also referred to the "eyesore" of the peace camp. Indeed, the *Daily Express* suggested that the "best way of judging" the peace camp is not by its effect on people's beliefs about nuclear weapons but by "the filth, muck and squalor they have left behind."[15] At one point Monsignor Kent, a Catholic priest and Campaign for Nuclear Disarmament (CND) activist, wrote to the Newbury newspaper complimenting the women on their courageous stand. In reply a Newbury citizen wrote a letter that read: "If cleanliness is next to godliness Mr Kent should look at the state of the 'ladies' at Newbury police courts to realize how far from God his flock has strayed."[16]

The use of dirt in media discourse about Greenham Common goes beyond a general indication of "out-of-placeness." Although dirt does connote "matter out of place," it takes on a more specific significance when it is used in connection with women. In all kinds of ways, women in Western society are associated (more so than men) with dirt and its removal. Women are the housewives, domestics, and maids of the world. They are expected to keep the house clean. In addition they are supposed to be the epitome of cleanliness themselves. They are the ones who do the cleaning *and* they are the ones who must keep clean. The images of dirt at the peace camp, therefore, indicate a double transgression. Cleanliness/dirtiness is one of the more powerful ways in which women are differentiated from men. Advertisements and magazine articles consistently point to the need for women to keep their environment and themselves "pure," odorless, and clean. Millions of dollars are spent selling soaps, detergents, and perfumes to women. Soap opera became a popular television format based on the premise that it would appeal to women and sell the sponsors' soap brands. The Greenham women do not fit the ideal of the ever clean and fragrant woman. In their "negligence" they have failed as women. I have already mentioned some of the general dirt metaphors. One that deserves special attention is that of "smell."

In December 1983 the *Daily Express* suggested ominously that "the final solution" to the Greenham "problem" was Chanel No. 5.[17] This statement was just one comment embedded in a larger fascination with the women's alleged unsanitary conditions. The lack of hygiene associated with the women represents a deeper questioning of the women as moral beings, or simply as "real women." The *Daily Mail* article titled "Dirty Work on the Thin Blue Line" reports that some policemen, after removing Greenham women, "can't bear to touch food or sit down with the family until [after] a long soak in the bath."[18] The same newspaper had reported earlier in the year that the police who removed Greenham

Common trespassers did so in "atrocious conditions" and that some of the officers had to have their uniforms destroyed because they had become so dirty.[19]

Again and again the press returns to images of malodorous waste—particularly defecation and menstrual blood. The *Guardian* tells the story of confrontation between peace campers and the residents of Newbury. It reports the leader of the Newbury protesters as referring to a "tide of human excrement" at the camp. She goes on to say, "All I know is that there is excrement around the camp—people have told me. I've never been there." Finally she speaks of the "filth, smell and immorality,"[20] linking the dirt and odor with a deeper sense of the campers' perceived "immorality." The *Daily Mail* reports on interviews with guards who work at the base: "There is no good will here. Why? At first every policeman seemed reluctant to say. What they dread and find unforgivable is being ordered to lay hands on women who often deliberately and calculatingly *stink*."[21] A *Daily Telegraph* article describes the women's alleged odor-producing behavior in some depth: "Almost the entire area within several hundred yards of the perimeter fence of R.A.F. Greenham Common is in constant use as a lavatory—including the gardens of local residents. Soiled sanitary towels are used to 'decorate' the fences and surrounding areas."[22] The fascination with odor and dirt in the women's peace camp is endless. Undoubtedly the conditions in which the women lived (and some still do) were not those of the ideal sanitized household, with all its deodorants and detergents, but to say that the women deliberately stink is probably the same as saying that they neglected their feminine duty—the duty to be clean. One must question whether the same fascination would have occurred if the peace camp were not all women. The fact that it is women who have allegedly committed olfactory transgressions has special significance.

Alison Young, in *Femininity in Dissent*, provides a thought-provoking analysis of this obsession with the "feminine odor." She argues (following Freud) that the privileging of sight and the visual over other senses relates to the construction of difference between men and women. There was a time, the story goes, when sight was not as privileged and the menstrual odors, or "*odor di femina*," deeply affected the male psyche—producing anxiety with its immediate intensity. This anxiety, she argues, threatens the "male psychic economy," which privileges sight. The smell of women, therefore, is odious to the dominant order as it threatens to undo the oppression of women through its celebration of womanliness. It is important to repress smell, to describe it as "waste" or "pollution," and to prescribe perfume and douches—the final solution!

This suggestion is supported by Alain Corbin's analysis of odor in the French social imagination.[23] His history details the gradual elimination of odor in both public and private space. He charts a series of medical and architectural "advances" that defined odor and eliminated it. Whereas once women were instructed not to bathe too often and the men's *aura seminalis* was considered a powerful sexual stimulant, by the end of the eighteenth century smells of all kinds were being associated with disease and disorder. Public spaces (through sewage systems, for example) and then private spaces (the separation of rooms according to bodily function) were progressively sanitized. In terms of the individual body, men and particularly women were instructed to use perfume, to douche, and to wear clothes in bed in order to control the threat of smell.

We do not have to agree with the details of Young's or Corbin's analyses to realize that women who smell bad would not be part of the everyday experience of the air base guards or the residents of Newbury. It is true that men, too, are supposed to be clean and odor-free, particularly in Western society, but there are many situations in which body odor would seem acceptable for men (when associated with physical "manly" endeavors). Women, on the other hand, are almost constantly reminded of their obligation to be clean, pure-smelling, and wholesome. Odor, especially that related to menstruation, also has its "proper place" — it has been constructed as a private phenomenon, a phenomenon of the home or, in extreme cases, the menstruation hut. Sanitary technologies consistently attempt to make menstruation disappear. Ads for sanitary towels tend to emphasize how product X will make sure that no one notices! Menstruation is supposed to be a big secret. Public knowledge of menstruation is most definitely taboo and out of place. Julia Kristeva, working out of a psychoanalytic tradition, has argued that menstrual blood "stands for danger issuing from within the identity (social or sexual); it threatens the relationship between the sexes within a social aggregate and, through internalization, the identity of each sex in the face of sexual difference."[24] As a bodily secretion the blood stands for the transgression of boundaries.

Several recent studies of menstruation underline the sociocultural construction of menstruation as a private, hidden phenomenon.[25] Sophie Laws studied menstruation from the perspective of men through a series of individual and group interviews and an analysis of textbooks. Her argument is that, in general, ideas about menstruation create an understanding from men's perspective and exclude women. One very powerful idea about menstruation is that it should be hidden away. Along with this idea is the notion that menstruation is a "dirty" process and should therefore be kept private. Laws critiques the belief that menstrual blood is inherently dirty and that it is "natural" to be repulsed by it. This is the argument that etiquette surrounding menstruation springs from the essence of the phenomenon—that menstruation is just disgusting. If this were true, menstruation would be hidden everywhere. Evidence (even from predominantly male anthropologists who do not often consider menstruation a subject worthy of attention) suggests that this is not the case. Congo Pygmies associate menstruation with life and encourage intercourse during the period; Australian aborigines paint themselves red so that everyone knows when they are menstruating. So even when there are rituals surrounding menstruation, they do not automatically imply hiding and separation. Even when there are taboos, they are so varied that it is hard to reduce them to a general statement. In line with this thought Mary Douglas stated that she could "not think of any physical function of which the ritual treatment is constant across the globe."[26]

Rather than concentrating on the nature of menstruation, Laws believes that it is a physical function that separates men from women and as such is used by men in a patriarchal society to put women in their place. Her series of interviews led her to the conclusion that "knowledge of a woman's menstruation becomes ... something specially reserved for the heterosexual relationship: it must be kept carefully hidden from all other men including one's father and sons. Thus the experience of menstruation is reconstructed in such a way as to emphasise an image of women's lives as constructed by men's gaze."[27] Menstrual blood is treated as polluted and dirty by the men in Laws's interviews, who often distinguished it from "real" blood. The judgment of menstrual blood as dirt is a wider judgment of the place of menstruating women. Laws concluded that "one cannot isolate 'meanings' of menstruation in our culture apart from the idea that it is something which must be hidden."[28] Men consistently reported being shocked when they first came across sanitary napkins or heard women discussing their periods: "One of the big surprises of adult life, was going into people's houses and finding things openly displayed in places. I didn't believe it, because at home these things had always been hidden away, and it was like a real shock to me, because it was all like something that was not mentioned, never spoken about."[29] Laws's interpretation of the expressions of shock by men concerning exposure to menstruation is that the women had done nothing to actively cause this reaction. Rather they had failed to "take the trouble to observe the etiquette which the males had come to expect would be observed in regard of themselves as males."[30]

Emily Martin examined representations of menstruation and menstruating women from another angle. She looked at metaphors used to describe menstruation in biology and anatomy textbooks and compared them with words used to describe processes in the male body and women's own views of menstruation. The overwhelming view of menstruation in textbooks was one of failure. Words such as "degenerate," "decline," "withdrawn," "lack," "leak," "deteriorate," and "dying" were common in Martin's study. Menstruation is seen as a failure of production—yet another month without pregnancy.[31] As Martin points out: "Menstruation could just as well be regarded as the making of life substance that marks us off as women, or heralds our nonpregnant state, rather than as the casting off of the debris of endometrial decay or as the hemorrhage of necrotic blood vessels."[32] Linking this research into representations of menstruation back into the story of Greenham Common, we can make some interpretations concerning the geographical implications of the reactions to the visibility of menstruating women at the camp. Most important, menstruation in our culture is predominantly perceived as a private phenomenon best kept at home. As with other themes in the media, the concentration on the sanitary napkins of the women implies an unsavory displacement. Menstruating women belong at home. In addition, menstruation is commonly portrayed as "failed production"—the opposite of pregnancy. While pregnancy is to be displayed proudly for all to see, menstruation, as its inverse, is to be kept secret and hidden. Again the visibility of the women's menstruating upset this ideological-geographic categorization of appropriate behavior. To the women, the use of sanitary pads and menstrual blood in their fence decoration symbolized the affirmation of life. As Emily Martin has argued, menstruation can symbolize many things other than failed production.

Caroline Blackwood was so disturbed by the images of foul-smelling women that she decided to visit the camp herself. Her story is a very different one: "Enemies of the Greenham women always accused them of smelling. I was always waiting for the famous smell of the peace women, but I never once detected it on any of the camps. The camps smelt of wood smoke, but that was quite pleasant. The tanks that the women used as lavatories were deep in the woods and far away from the benders."[33] Blackwood surmises that strangers are often accused of smelling. New children at school are called "smellies." Foreigners of all types are accused of being unsanitary and smelly.[34] Perhaps the women were called smelly because they were newcomers in a tight community—people out of place.

In a broader sense the allegations of bad hygiene and dirt can be seen as a response to the way in which the women transgressed so many boundaries that are perceived as normal. Not only were they away from home but they also confused public and private space. The women, for instance, appealed to the ancient custom that the common belonged to everyone and that they could not be evicted from land that nobody owned. Local residents and the press saw the women's presence in terms of the narrower concept of "property." The presence of the women affected property values. The residents of Newbury, then, saw the issue in terms of "tidiness" and "hygiene" and attempted to reverse the rights to common land.

The decoration of the Greenham fence by the women also deviated from expected behavior and familiar boundaries of place. "Art" has remained a rarified category in Western society, with its own places. Just as graffiti on the subway could not be valued as art, the collage of personal, life-affirming objects on the fence around Greenham could not be art. The Greenham women saw things differently once they understood objects in relation to a different set of values:

> The doom-laden myth that in a consumer society people can only relate to things by buying and discarding them, and are incapable of treasuring anything, proves to be untrue at a deeper level that Greenham brought into the open. Art postcards are in fact a good example of cheap, mass-produced objects which are treasured as an intimate part of a person's identity and individuality. It is the same attitude which brings to light beauty or hidden meanings in the bits of plastic, packaging, discarded imagery and other waste which has been pronounced "dead" by the profit system. Revealingly the groups of local residents, police and MOD personnel who came to rip the decorations off the fence ... saw everything, including familiar things they have in their own houses, as "rubbish."[35]

The media continually refers to decorations on the fence in terms of rubbish and garbage, particularly if the decorations happen to be tampons and diapers (both of which are seen as "life-affirming" symbols by the women). It would have been hard for them to see these objects as "art," as one art critic did:

> Each person contributes to a spirit of equality, and there is no privileged viewpoint from which to see the work, or an ideal observer for whose eye a dramatic effect is built up. And yet the whole does have an impact far greater than any part. The really astonishing thing is the aggregate; and its implied meaning, that people's creativity, once released, is endless. This work of art was *nine miles,* not long, but *round.*[36]

John Berger has shown how art has evolved to support ideas like property and power.[37] The use of oils or the perspective technique give the illusion of control and ownership of the painted objects. Art has traditionally involved an "author" and a "viewer." The Greenham fence breaks these informal rules. The effect cannot be owned or, indeed, comprehended by the perspective of a single viewer. There is no author. It only remains for the objects on the fence to be considered "matter out of place" and consigned to the trash heap.

Food and the Kitchen

The issue of dirt is most clearly related to the perceived displaced nature of the women when it is connected to the makeshift nature of the Greenham kitchen and the expectation that women enjoy and are good at preparing and cooking food. Particularly remarkable is the multitude of references to "blackened" teapots and kettles. Any medium to long article on Greenham mentioned this symbol of women's displacement from the English hearth. The *Times* referred to the "smoke-blackened teapot which may eventually yield tea." The *Sunday Telegraph* described "the pitiful sight of badly dressed women grouped together around a tiny fire cooking baked beans in pitch black pots." The *International Herald Tribune* talked of the "battered, charred teakettle."[38] Almost every other newspaper, at some time or another, finds space to mention the blackened cookware. This stands in stark contrast to the model image of the shining, antiseptic kitchen of advertisements in which idealized women patiently wait for their husbands' compliments on return from work or, alternatively, in which career women happily use prepackaged instant microwave dinners with no mess.

The image of the blackened kettle is implicated in a set of references to food, all set against the perfect kitchen. The *Times* talked of "dark bean-filled soup" that turns out to be rancid and "a large chunk of cheese, several loaves of bread, dustbins with cereal and dry food and cartons of aging apples [that] lie scattered, rain-soaked and haphazard on makeshift tables." Inevitably they had to mention the "blackened pots," which "hang on a large board propped up against a tree."[39] At the other end of the quality spectrum we get a remarkably similar picture in the *Sun*: "The cooking pot on the fire has a mixture of vegetables and pasta burning on to it. The kettle is black. And all around is dirty crockery."[40] The left-wing tabloid, the *Daily Mirror,* added to the general impression when discussing the experiences of some newcomers:

> Gingerly, they helped in the filthy rat-infested kitchen which was littered with discarded food scraps and dirty pots and pans. One of the camp's four stray cats licked the remains of a bowl of custard as one of the students bravely tried to wash up in an old cauldron with cold, grey, greasy water."[41]

Finally the *Daily Mail* remarked that "the table on which the women prepare food has half empty boxes of margarine with a dirty knife still left in one."[42] The kitchen is metonymic for domesticity in general. The woman at home cooks and cleans in the kitchen. It is a model of order and hygiene. In the pictures we are given of Greenham Common we see chaotic culinary disorder. Cutlery is left dirty and rats wander around. Any food that is mentioned is almost always referred to with some distaste—words like *rancid* and *burnt* are used frequently. Not only do the women refuse to conform to the accepted standards of cleanliness, they cannot cook anything but beans and lukewarm tea.

Clothes

Another signifier of the women's displaced character is their clothing. The newspapers frequently return to the dress of the "ladies" in order to compare them with "normal" women. The *Daily Mirror* described the "shaved heads, combat clothes and bover boots of the grimy-faced women who inhabit the most famous peace camp in the world."[43] The press takes time to mention the combat fatigues, the dirty boots, and the tattered jackets that mark these women off from the women at home. One story that received great attention was the case of a woman (Mrs. Johns) who left her husband and family for the camp and later got divorced. The *Daily Mail* describes Mr. Johns's first visit to the base to see his wife:

"In among the shanty-like straggle of tents and sleeping bags he found a woman dressed in a kaftan and beads and wearing no make-up. It was his wife." Only a moment's thought is necessary for one to realize that the lack of makeup on Mrs. Johns is hardly surprising, given the camplike condition of her life. Similarly, combat clothes are the ideal dress for living in the open. That is what they are designed for. The *Mail*, however, takes the clothes and lack of makeup to signify the change from "an apolitical housewife into a fervent feminist and anti-nuclear campaigner."[44] The same housewife/feminist-campaigner, home/Greenham dualism is set up in a piece in the *Daily Mirror*. Again the women's practical clothes are used as signifiers of this distinction: "It's hard to identify with a gang of women dressed in army fatigues who don't look as if they've ever changed a nappy, nursed a case of measles or dreamed of blowing the family allowance for a party dress."[45] Here the "gang of women" are clearly out of place. The fact that they are a "gang" (women together without men) and are wearing fatigues highlights their difference and displaced nature. The potential in-place is given by the second part of the sentence. Women who change nappies, nurse children back to health, or spend their family allowance (probably their only money) on a party dress are at home. The party dress—a dress that is frivolous and only used on one or two occasions—is sharply opposed to the cheap functionality of the combat fatigues.

Caroline Blackwood's visits to the peace camps revealed to her another perspective on the issue of clothing. "One of the most liberating feelings in the eccentric little community," she said, "was the realization that no one gave a damn how you looked." Blackwood was constantly amazed at the repetitious references to the women's unfeminine clothing in the press and among Newbury residents. One old man in a pub said, "But if only they could dress better and wash more. A woman who doesn't dress nicely dishonours herself, don't you think?" Blackwood points out: "Wading around in the deep, freezing mud and snow like soldiers in the trenches of the first world war, if the women were to wear the flowing chiffon and the sables their critics appear to demand, it would be inappropriate to the point of lunacy."[46]

Children

The use of signifiers like dirt, clothing, and misplaced kitchen equipment serves to compare the Greenham women with the "normal" woman— the woman who is in place. In place usually means at home with husband and children. This distinction between home-family-children and Greenham is made again and again in less metaphorical and more direct terms. One frequently asked question is "What about their children?" The *Daily Express* asked, "Can these women explain exactly what is happening to their *children* while they are away from home for months on end?" A report in the *Daily Mail* said, "They are anxious to be considered as martyrs. But the real martyrs are their neglected children." The former mayor of Newbury—Councillor Brian Philpott—was reported in the *Daily Telegraph* as saying, "On the one hand they attack the state on cruise missiles and on the other they expect taxpayers all over the country to pay their dole money and look after their families whom they have in some cases totally abandoned."[47]

Alternatively the press decides to deride the women's attempts to raise children in the camp rather than at home. The *Daily Mail* discussed the birth of a child, Jay, at the peace camp. Greenham, they said, is a "squalid sort of place, not the sort of place where you would expect people in a so-called civilized society to have young babies living."[48] In an editorial entitled "It's Time to Go Home," the *Sun* commented on the removal of Jay from the camp by social service workers: "Until a couple of days ago Jay's home was in that mixture of filthy disease-ridden tents that is called the Greenham Common peace camp." The *Daily Express* asked,

"What sort of women expose themselves to conditions like they are living in and subject their children to the same sort of thing?" A resident of Newbury, when protesting against the peace camp, is quoted by the *Guardian* as saying, "The behaviour of these women, particularly the way they let their children roam around in the mud, is a health hazard and a disgrace." There were further complaints about the "filth, smell and immorality" of the women and of how they mistreated their children.[49]

The perception of the women's relation to children is clearly marked by assumed notions of "proper place." It is not right for women to be at the camp away from their children, who are left, presumably unattended, at home. Equally it is inappropriate for women to have children with them at the camp because that is seen as mistreatment. The only alternative left to the women is to be at home with their children. One of the organizers of a protest in which twenty thousand women encircled the base, Joan Ruddock, explained the protest in the following way: "This is an action where women want to be in the frontline, with men in the support role. This is a place men are not used to occupying—supporting women, looking after the kids at home. That's where my husband is today."[50] The protest's theme was "For centuries women have watched men go off to war. Now women have left for peace."

One of the more curious sides of the reaction related to children is the presupposition of children itself. One observer noted, "Last week I met just one married woman, a mother of one, at the camp. The peace campers were principally young students, who had dropped out of courses, girls on the dole, artists and teachers."[51] The probability is that most of the women at the camp had nothing to do with children. The assumption made by the media is that any adult woman should have a husband and children. The extension of the accusation that the women mistreat their children (by not being at home or by having them at the camp) is that the women are especially abnormal as they do not even have children and do not plan to have any. This theme, the theme of deviant sexuality, is as popular with the press as the dirt metaphors.

Sexuality

The *Sun* asserted that the women "are not people—they're all burly lesbians."[52] The women's "deviance" is at its most extreme when the press concentrates on their actual and alleged sexuality. The fact that the camp consisted only of women was itself a source of deep irritation and interest. This, coupled with the lack of respectable clothing and strange culinary habits, pointed to the women's "masculinity" and the presence of lesbians at the camp. In truth they were certainly not all lesbians, and even if they were it would not merit the type of attention the press gave this theme.

The *Sun* said, "[The] younger they are, the more butch they are.... Women openly kiss, cuddle and hold hands in camp. They stand in pairs, facing each other with both hands linked, and staring deep into each other's eyes, their bodies swaying." It goes on to describe the "girls" sharing sleeping bags and concludes, "Its [the camp's] reason for surviving and continuing is that it provides an open meeting place for women to reinforce each other's hatred of men." The *Daily Mirror* read, "These women have been described as a bunch of lesbians. Sadly, there's some truth in this, and for some, this is the very reason they are here, and the reason they stay."[53] The idea that the women came to the camp purely to indulge in lesbian sexual behavior is strange, as Blackwood points out:

> As for the lesbians, there were so many comfortable lesbian clubs all over the British Isles. There were so many warm, pleasant places where the lesbians could be just as lesbian as they liked without any harassment. If they were only searching for some ideal place to pursue lesbian activities, they would have to be deranged to choose these awful camps where the battle against cold and hunger made any erotic feeling unimportant.[54]

The *Daily Mail* delves deeper into the alleged "immorality" of their behavior: "And there's Eve breastfeeding by the fire, a vague, amiable, ever smiling lesbian mother from Islington who's camping here with her two children, aged eight and six months, by different fathers, one of them West Indian."[55] This passage juxtaposes a set of signifiers of deviance. Eve is breastfeeding in public (out of place), she is a lesbian, and her children have no father who is present. What's more, her children have separate fathers, indicating promiscuity. The fact that one of the fathers is West Indian sends Eve into an abyss of chaotic and disordered "otherness."

All of the tabloid newspapers, at one time or another, featured the story of a writer who "went undercover" at the camp in order to report the "true facts" to the world. One such case is that of Sarah Bond in the *Daily Express*:

> Half the women I lived among at Greenham were lesbians, striding the camp with their butch haircuts, boots and boilersuits. They flaunt their sexuality, boast about it, joke about it. And some take delight in proclaiming their loathing of men.... I was shocked on my first day when two peace women suddenly went into a passionate embrace in full view of everyone.... And gradually I became annoyed at the way doting

couples sat around the camp fire kissing and caressing.... A lot of women "go gay" after arriving at the camp. With no men around they have to turn to each other for comfort. Other lesbians masquerade as peace women and go to Greenham just for sex.[56]

Clearly, Bond considers lesbian sexual activity to be out of place at Greenham. In the context of a British tabloid full of sexual insinuation, her remarks seem extremely pious and prudish; she is annoyed at the sight of mere kissing when it is between two women. When women express their love for each other they are "flaunting" it. The word "flaunting" implies visibility. Bond is saying that the women are not hiding that which should remain hidden—their sexuality; their affection is out of place. Another implication is that the women's lesbianism is the result of a lack of normality or, more precisely, a lack of men. It is only because men are not present that they turn to each other. Once again the desirability of "home" lurks behind the words. If only they were at home with their husbands, they would not *have to* resort to each other for "comfort."

Angry Newbury residents are even more to the point. The *Daily Telegraph* quotes one resident as saying, "While homosexual practices are no longer illegal, I am among the majority of local people who find such open, constant scenes of lesbian behavior somewhat alarming; our children require explanations." Another resident is quoted in the *Daily Mail* as saying: "It's become a home for lost causes up there. It's no longer just cruise missile demonstrators. There's lesbians, one-parent families, and lost causes." Even more transparently, a third resident says, "We have to put up with those morons and queers for two years.... If I had my way I would put a bomb in the middle of the lot of them."[57]

Hysteria

> *A hysterization of women's bodies: a threefold process whereby the feminine body was analyzed—qualified and disqualified—as being thoroughly saturated with sexuality; whereby it was integrated into the sphere of medical practices, by reason of a pathology intrinsic to it; whereby, finally, it was placed in organic communication with the social body (whose regulated fecundity it was supposed to ensure), the family space (of which it had to be a substantial and functional element), and the life of children (which it produced and had to guarantee, by virtue of biological-moral responsibility lasting through the entire period of the children's education): the Mother, with her negative image*

> of *"nervous woman,"* constituted the most visible form of
> this hysterization.
>   —Michel Foucault, The History of Sexuality

In chapter 2 I discussed the description of graffiti and its perpetrators as "mad." I described how madness is associated with unstable transgressions of boundaries and is considered a threat to order and civilization. The Greenham Women are also labeled mad, but in a way that takes on specific meanings when it is decoded in light of their gender. The women are described as hysterical.

The purpose of the peace camp has clearly been to intervene in the rarified atmosphere of Politics and demand to be heard. This is interpreted by the media as "hysteria." The women are portrayed as hysterical and overemotional—lacking the cool reason necessary for (serious) political participation. The emphasis on women's "emotional nature," I argue, is linked to the historical division between public and private domains. The public domain of politics and business is the male, rational realm; the private domain of "home" is the realm of emotion and passivity. By labeling the women hysterical the press is denying their political (and public) value and relegating the women to the realm of (mere) emotions, of nursing, cooking, and cleaning.

The *Daily Mirror* states that "the peace camp women distinguish themselves with their startlingly swift changes of mood." The *Daily Mail* comments on Helen Johns's change from "an apolitical housewife into a *fervent* feminist." The *Daily Express* refers to the women as "harridans," a word that comes up frequently in all the tabloids. The *Sunday Telegraph* published a letter that read, "After all, would you live in the kind of society that these women propose, a society where emotions rule and women are encouraged to become shrill parasites?" Another letter, this time to the *Daily Mail,* asks, "How can they think their vulgar displays of shouting and yelling...can further their cause?"[58]

This theme of hysterical emotions is prominent in a report in the *Daily Mail* that reports the arrival of the cruise missiles: "Tears streaming down their faces the Greenham Common 'peace women' clawed at barbed wire with their bare hands.... It was a desperate and futile response.... The women never really came to terms with how to respond to the inevitable."[59] Outward displays of extreme emotion mark off the women as "strange." Every "symptom" is noted down and faithfully reported in the media: a "weird wailing that ripped the night air. Their eyes are closed and their bodies rock as they shout out their lament."[60] "At Greenham Common yesterday 144 peace women—many weeping and screaming—were arrested. Their hysterical demo came as two more huge U.S.

planes landed at the Berkshire base."[61] The women are seen bending over their "cauldron"; they sing witches' songs; they are banshees, harridans, and harpies. They are "strident," "fervent," and "hysterical." They are never described as "determined" or "brave" or "steadfast." The descriptions of the women are clearly gendered. In particular they are related to the unusual situation of a large group of women making a public and political point. It is related to the feeling that these women are out of place. Politics is the arena of cool reason and cold (male) logic. Just as a husband tells his wife that she is being overemotional and should calm down to have a "reasonable" discussion, the press tells the Greenham women that they are hysterical. To be hysterical is to continually and loudly proclaim, "This is not so" when others are looking at you curiously and saying, "But it is." The hysteric stands in resistance to some commonsense assumption. The Greenham women are hysterical because they

are living out a physical and mental resistance to a predominant order. They ... are challenging the comfortable prevalence of the familial ideology, by establishing themselves in women-only camps outside a weapons base and by publicly embracing alternatives to authorized heterosexuality and the biological imperative of conventional motherhood.[62]

The Greenham women are hysterical because they touch raw nerves. On the one hand they question the family structure and on the other they wonder about the sanity of weapons of mass destruction. But their hysteria is more than this. They are also hysterical because they are away from home and attempting to participate in a public debate of a political nature. They have transgressed the public/private, male/female boundary, and the press tells them they're crazy. Their "cure" is to return home, as the *Sun* so often remarks. The press presents us and the women with a choice between being a strident, fervent, hysterical pacifist-feminist—a choice that will lead to the breakup of homes—or going home to be an apolitical housewife-mother.

The Rat and the Mole

On visiting Newbury for the first time Caroline Blackwood visited a grocery store, where she was told that they had "got them up here." The store worker was referring to the women and the camps: "The camps were made to sound like invisible sewers and the shopkeepers could have been talking about rats."[63] In fact, the image of the rat and its cousin the mole appeared frequently in press descriptions of the camps. Alison Young provides a perceptive interpretation of the frequent appearance of the rat and mole metaphors in discourse about the Greenham women. She discusses the appearance of stories in the press that spoke of a rat or a mole in the Greenham camp. The implication is that someone in the camp is doing work for "foreign" (namely, Soviet) interests. Rats and moles are individuals who steal the secrets of a society and convey them to another society. These metaphors draw from a well of suppositions about British and Soviet society and (for the metaphor to operate effectively) the notion that rats and moles live underground and come out at night:

> To allege the presence of "a dangerous, anti-western, anti-British 'mole'" (*Daily Express* 8.20.83) at Greenham, links them (as the mole is an image closely aligned with the rat in its ideological location) through the metaphorical selection of the democratically despised condition of secrecy and darkness, with values contradictory to those represented as fundamental to British society.[64]

The rat or mole brings forth images of darkness and secrecy—the underground rather than the surface. The rat and the mole belong in the secretive, closed, dark society of the Soviet Union, not in the "open" society of England. England is the implied opposite of the rat; it is open, democratic, unsecretive, and clean—nothing takes place underground. The rat metaphor extends still further in its implication of dirt and disease. Not only is the rat or mole an individual who gives away secrets while operating secretly and underground; the rat or mole is a classic figure of disease, the carrier of plague. Rats exist where dirt exists. The rat also conveys a radical "out-of-placeness." Rats do not belong in the perfect kitchen. The references to rats or moles in the metaphorical sense of spy exist back-to-back with literal references to the alleged existence of rats in the camp. The *Daily Mail* claimed that "rats have infested the area." The *Daily Mirror* described the experiences of some students: "Gingerly, they helped in the filthy rat-infested kitchen which was littered with discarded food scraps and dirty pots and pans."[65] Here the whole range of metaphors describe the women's alleged out-of-place nature. The rats and the pots and pans are not just literal references; they are also metaphors for displacement. The rat insinuates the women's betrayal of their home in two senses—the home of the perfect kitchen and the home of democracy and freedom. The rat, as Peter Stallybrass and Allon White have described, has been an object of hatred throughout history. In the nineteenth century the emerging discourse connecting physical with moral environments (sanitary science) paid particular attention to the rat as "purveyor of physical and moral dirt."[66] The rat was reconstructed as more than an economic threat (as a spoiler of foods) but also as an object of disgust and a threat to civilized life. It was also a transgressor of boundaries, a creature that lived in the filth of the sewers and came above ground at night. Again, when applied to the Greenham camp, the image of the rat suggests impurity and the presence of a filthy and underground creature in the green and pleasant land.

The descriptions of the women and their camps in the mainstream press clearly attempt to paint a picture of deviance. The descriptions of displacement appear to indicate the "out-of-place" character of the women by suggesting that they belong at home. The second part to the story is the notion that the women were out of place not only because they were away from their "proper place" but also because they were in a particularly improper place—a military base in rural England. By camping and protesting outside a military site the women were profoundly questioning the proper place of women in the military—as "camp followers."

The Carnival at Greenham

The women at Greenham frequently chose to express their refusal to accept "the order of things" in carnivalesque ways. In general they used dancing and singing to keep themselves amused, in addition to wearing painted faces and unusual haircuts. In one of the more famous actions they broke into the base and danced on top of a missile silo. On another occasion they dressed up as bunnies and climbed over the fence to hold a picnic in the base. The press frequently reported the bizarre antics of "these strangely painted women." Occasionally they referred to the "carnival atmosphere."[67] The most notable incidents of carnivalesque behavior occurred in the Newbury district court when the Greenham women were on trial:

> A restrained carnival atmosphere had alternated with echoes of the school room, as the colourfully dressed women, with bouquets and corsages of spring flowers … applauded expert witnesses and co-defendants.… Throughout the day a small group of demonstrators performed outside the court, with a mixture of chanting singing, dancing, juggling, tumbling and embracing.[68]

When the women went to court they did not stop challenging expectations about appropriate behavior. There are few places where behavior is more prescribed than a courtroom. The women's response was therefore startling. The *Daily Telegraph* reports on the court appearance of forty-three Greenham women charged with trespass. The reporter described the "carnival atmosphere in court bordering almost on farce."

He described the singing of peace songs and the waving of flowers. In February the same paper reported on a similar event, in which the women "crowded the narrow corridors singing, dancing and playing pipe music."[69] On other occasions the women responded to the formal procedures by continually shouting "rhubarb." Again in March the women "danced and sang in the corridor of the court," and then, "at one point in the chambers hearing a woman stood in front of the judge wearing a white skull mask, bowler hat, black evening jacket, green trousers and a red carnation. She held up a placard saying 'This time tomorrow we could all be faceless stuffed shirts.' "[70] The *Daily Express* also reported on the court events, describing them as the "Greenham comedy show" starring women "with faces painted white and wearing mock funeral shrouds."[71]

The Newbury courthouse was not the only formal place the women took their carnival. On 17 January 1983 they took it to the center of the legal system—the House of Commons. In a "two-pronged attack" the women heckled and interrupted official proceedings from the "strangers" (visitors) gallery while a group of seventy-three women linked arms and sat down in the lobby and sang. Outside the Commons "women jugglers performed as others paraded a paper-mache head of a woman."[72] The courthouse and the center of government are clearly two very formal and clearly delineated spaces. The singing, dancing, juggling, and disguise of the women have a heightened effect in these places because of the visible and radical contrast of expected formal behavior and surprising, joyous, informal behavior. The spaces demand cool and rational behavior and debate; the women present emotion and carnival in its stead. There is a long history of carnivalesque behavior in the face of authority, which has been the subject of recent empirical and theoretical debate.

Throughout its history carnival has been a time and place of apparent disorder—a deliberate break from normal life and established forms of behavior that is illustrated in Pieter Breughel's painting *The Battle of Carnival and Lent* (1559). The painting shows two separate worlds. One half, the world of Lent, is symbolized by austere black dress and orderly lines of solemn people and emaciated women. The other half, the world of carnival, is full of food, drink, sex, and violence. One side is the world of order and restraint, while the other is that of disorder and excess. Carnival precedes Lent by one to three days, and in contrast to Lent is marked by folly, disregard for order, and "unseemly" behavior:

> During carnival the common people suspended the normal rules of
> behavior and ceremoniously reversed the social order or turned it upside
> down in riotous procession.... Carnival was high season for hilarity,

sexuality, and youth run riot — a time when young people tested social boundaries by limited outbursts of deviance, before being reassimilated in the world of order, submission and Lentine seriousness. It came to an end on Shrove Tuesday or Mardi Gras, when a straw mannequin, King Carnival or Caramantran, was given a ritual trial and execution.[73]

Many authors have described and developed the idea of the "world upside down" that is prevalent in carnival and other forms of popular and folk culture.[74] Carnival represents a ritualized *inversion* of social, moral, and *spatial* orders that is allowed to take place once a year. As Peter Jackson notes, "Carnival takes place, literally, in a world apart, in the city center and in the open air."[75] In this "world apart" many "normal" domains are reversed. Unlike official parades there are no actors and spectators:

> In fact, carnival does not know footlights, in the sense that it does not acknowledge any distinction between actors and spectators. Footlights would destroy a carnival, as the absence of footlights would destroy a theatrical performance. Carnival is not a spectacle seen by the people; they live in it, and everyone participates because its very idea embraces all the people.[76]

Men and women commonly cross-dress; peasants are king for a day; the divisions between private and public space are ignored and the genitals and orifices of the body are celebrated at the expense of the head. The carnival procession is a mirror image of the formal parades and feasts that serve to symbolize the essence and ideal order of society: "The official feast asserted all that was stable, unchanging, perennial: the existing hierarchy, the existing religious, political and moral values, norms and prohibitions. It was the triumph of the truth already established, the predominant truth that was put forward as eternal and indisputable."[77]

It is easy to see the elements of carnival in the behavior of the Greenham women in court and Parliament. These spaces, more clearly than most, represent "all that [is] stable" and "the existing hierarchy." The "truth" presented at the courthouse by the women's prosecutors was clearly the "truth already established." The women reacted to this by dancing in the aisles, juggling, and wearing costumes. As in carnival the women confused the boundaries between "actors" (defendants, lawyers, and so on) and the "audience" by refusing to stay quiet and detached from the formal proceedings of the courthouse stage. The women were acting on a different set of priorities, which, to use Mikhail Bakhtin's highly romanticized language, were of the people. They were not seeing the microscale niceties of legal behavior, they were seeing the world and its potential destruction. As one of the lawyers defending the women said, "Why should courtrooms worry anyone when the threat of utter destruction hangs over us?"[78] The normal rules of behavior were suspended.

Carnival as "symbolic inversion" is a cultural act that "inverts, abrogates and in some fashion presents an alternative to commonly held cultural codes, values and norms."[79] Carnival is a time of revelry and disrespect; a place of dancing, partying, drinking, parades, plays, and mock executions, funerals, and crownings, a time that is set aside from normal activity and everyday life. In addition it deliberately inverts many assumed cultural meanings, social relations, and expected behaviors. In carnival you are not allowed to watch, you must be part of it, dancing, drinking, and doing things otherwise frowned upon by the establishment. "No dogma, no authoritarianism, no narrow-minded seriousness can co-exist with Rabelaisian images; these images are opposed to all that is finished and polished, to all pomposity, to every ready-made solution in the sphere of thought and world outlook."[80] Greenham presents images opposed to the "finished and polished" and ready-made solutions. The Greenham women presented an alternative aesthetic that actively sought to juxtapose objects and actions from radically different contexts. The fence at Greenham is a case in point. Just as the women laughed at the formal territorializations of the courts and parliament, they subverted "proper" places in their continuing transformation of the fence that surrounded the air base (see Figure 5.2). The placing of private things on this cold and public boundary in some sense removed the veil of naturalness from the fence and the goings-on inside it. By taking "rubbish" and transforming it into an aesthetic statement, a secular magic was performed.

> It is not the object itself, familiar to everyone, but the transgression of its "proper" place which carries the psychic charge.... Of course to take on its power, the change of context must assume a compartmentalized, divided world. But at the same time it expresses the desire to break through these divisions and to show that there is nothing sacred or inevitable about them.[81]

The decoration of the fence by the women was carnivalesque in nature, as it transgressed in time and space the formal divisions of territories and acceptable behavior experienced as "common sense" in everyday life. The site of a military base, like those of the court and the parliament, provided an ideal site for these transgressions, as it is a particularly formal type of territory within which behavior is strictly controlled. The transgressions of the women, therefore, are all the more apparent and disturbing.

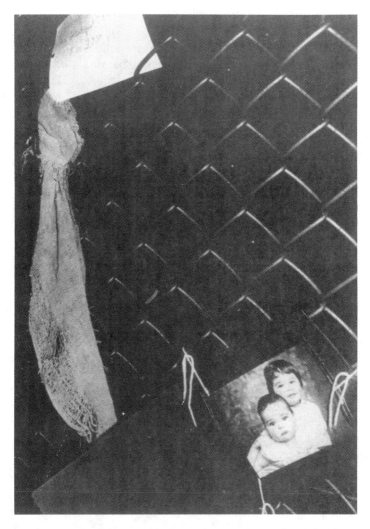

Figure 5.2. Decorating the fence at Greenham. The note reads, "This cloth is from an Inca archaeological site in Peru. It is 2200 years old." (Photo by Tim Malyon, from Guy Brett, *Through Our Own Eyes* [London: New Society Press, 1986]. By permission.)

Bakhtin, the figure responsible for the debates around carnival,[82] believed that carnival denaturalized the dominant order; it showed people that what seemed natural, could, in fact, be otherwise: "In the world of carnival the concerns of the people's immortality is combined with the realization that established authority and truth are relative."[83] Once carnival is experienced in all its comic, grotesque vividness, Bakhtin argues, it becomes impossible to accept as natural the rigidities of established norms. Bakhtin's point is that carnival's antiorder appears to belong to the people. The comedy and laughter inherent in transgressed norms appears to be liberating and subversive because it gives license to violate rules. Indeed, as Stallybrass and White argue, Bakhtin's view of carnivals is extended to the idea of the "carnivalesque" as a "potent, populist, critical inversion of all official worlds and hierarchies in a way that has implications far beyond the specific realm of Rabelais studies."[84] Carnival becomes a metaphor for a people's vision of the world and a critique and inversion of established "high" culture. As the actions of people generally excluded from the establishment, the actions of the Greenham women present such a vision.

Among the general excess and exuberance of carnivalesque activity an important role is given to laughter. Laughter is presented as ambivalent — something mocking and derisory that has the power to revive and reenergize. As history unfolds, Bakhtin shows us, it is accompanied by a laughing chorus of common people. Carnival and its laughter is not just part of a wider culture but is irreducibly "other":

> All these forms of protocol and ritual based on laughter and consecrated by tradition existed in all the countries of medieval Europe; they were sharply distinct from the serious official, ecclesiastical, feudal, and political cult forms and ceremonies. They offered a completely different, nonofficial, extraecclesiastical and extrapolitical aspect of the world, of man and of human relations; they built a second world and second life outside officialdom, a world in which all medieval people participated more or less, in which they lived during a given time of the year. If we fail to take into consideration this two-world condition, neither medieval cultural consciousness nor the culture of the renaissance can be understood.[85]

Carnival is of the people and the people are the "other." Bakhtin's interpretation rests on a recognition of difference that denies the existence of a coherent and systematic "worldview." Rather he asserts the importance of understanding medieval culture as a culture of differences. Carnival is not to be understood as another ritual in some general sense. Rather it is something different. While rituals celebrated the already established truth and sanctioned the established order, carnivals created a whole separate world of laughter and festivity that celebrated the unfinished, the relative, and the everyday.

Bakhtin uses the term "grotesque" to refer to the feeling of carnival. Along with the laughter, "grotesque realism" presents the body in all its imperfect glory. In carnival, "normal" bodily values are undermined by the celebration of orifices and fat. While "normal" culture turns the body into a finished product, carnival celebrates the incomplete by emphasizing the openings—the anus, the genitalia, and large outsized nostrils. Lower regions of the body (particularly the buttocks) are given priority over the head. The celebration of these features in carnival, Bakhtin claims, refers to the importance of everyday life—the toil, the sex, and the defecation rather than the rarified world of reason and spirit celebrated by "high" culture. The big joke, for Bakhtin, is that wherever high-minded seriousness goes on people are always going to be shitting and sweating, eating and pissing. As metaphors these bodily functions refer to the importance of process. Culture, Bakhtin is arguing, is not the finished, rounded, complete, and coherent product that "high" culture would have us believe. Rather it is in constant flux, living and dying, eating and shitting—laughing. Within carnival Bakhtin highlights the process—the mobility and transience.

If we return to the actions of the Greenham women and their representations in the mainstream press, we can see that the carnival behavior in the courtroom was not exceptional and momentary. Once the idea of actual carnival is extended to incorporate Bakhtin's "grotesque realism," we can see that the continued existence of the camp is itself "carnivalesque." The camp was a higgledy-piggledy, forever changing center of real life. It was in a state of flux, its participants always changing. Bodily functions became public out of necessity. The press picked up on the shitting and eating—the grotesque. The Greenham women are the "laughing" (and crying) chorus pointing at the neat, finished, classical body of the air base and screaming, "This is not the truth; it does not have to be like this."

It is no surprise therefore that Stallybrass and White, in their book on transgression, mention the peace camp in their introduction:

The women live "on the wire," "on the perimeter," neither fully outside nor fully inside, and they have triggered powerful associative chains which connect the international issue of nuclear missiles with pig's blood and excremental vandalism: the cosmic with the local, the topographic with the sexual.... [T]he Greenham Common women ... reveal how the grotesque body may become a primary, highly charged intersection and mediation of social and political forces, a sort of intensifier and displacer in the making of identity. The exorbitant contrast between the closed, monumental, classical body of the multi-million dollar American military complex and the open, muddy, exposed huddle of higgledy-piggledy polythene tents is a scandal to hegemonic dignity which it can scarcely sustain. It is indeed wonderful that so little can make such a great difference.[86]

Across the barbed wire that surrounds the base two sets of values confront each other. On one side there is the smooth perfection of the military base, the cold, gray, steely context for a formalized hierarchy of uniformed soldiers who dress and behave according to strict rules and conventions. On the other side there is the chaotic women's encampment of haphazard benders splattered with colorful posters, family photographs, and brightly dressed women, not one of them the same as the next. As Young argues, the two sides represent different abstract representations of the "cultural body":

> [T]he corpus represented by the base is the classical one, smooth, hairless, blond, elevated on high, idealized. Outside the base, there exists an altogether different image: of corporeal physicality and functionalism, a body with orifices exposed, where idealized beauty is irrelevant, replaced with grotesque realism, where the cerebral functions accede to bodily reaction.[87]

Bakhtin's view of carnival and popular culture in general occasionally seems utopian and idyllic. He takes the peasants of medieval Europe and makes them seem carefree and happy as well as rebellious and resistant. His argument seems exaggerated and overly romanticized. Clearly it would be wrong to make the same mistake with the Greenham women, whose lives were far from idyllic, being marked by frequent evictions and constant boredom and frustration. Nevertheless the Greenham women's actions clearly serve to question the assumptions of truth and authority enshrined in the air base:

> Indeed carnival is so vivaciously celebrated that the necessary political criticism is almost too obvious to make. Carnival, after all, is a licensed affair in every sense, a permissible rupture of hegemony, a contained popular blow-off as disturbing and relatively ineffectual as a revolutionary work of art. As Shakespeare's Olivia remarks, there is no slander in an allowed fool.[88]

Some have suggested, as Terry Eagleton does, that carnival is a form of "bread and circuses"—a harmless safety valve through which subordinated groups can let off steam, express their sense of injustice, and then return to normal life and the rule of law. The dominant tendency in theory concerning ritual in general is to conceive of it in terms of its role in facilitating social cohesion. In addition it is commonplace for rituals, including carnival, to be understood in terms of a systematic cultural context. Rituals are explained in functional terms. The goal they serve is often considered to be societal and cultural harmony. Seen from this perspective, carnival becomes a kind of catharsis or safety valve—an exceptional moment in time and space when the normal order is inverted so that it may exist peacefully throughout the remainder of the year. One observer of carnival who follows this line of argument is Max Gluckman in his anthropological studies of ritual, in which he suggests that while "rites of reversal obviously include a protest against the established order ... they are intended to preserve and strengthen the established order."[89] Rituals of inversion provide a license for symbolic struggle that functions to confirm (in the end) social order.

Stallybrass and White make a similar suggestion when they argue that licensed rituals are politically muted affairs in which power allows itself to be contested symbolically in order to more effectively rule in "reality."

This is what Umberto Eco means when he says that carnival only gives apparent license to those who have thoroughly and completely absorbed the rules of normal behavior.[90] In fact, with no "normal structure" carnival is impossible. A *good* carnival thus assumes that the rules must be so pervasively and deeply understood (assumed) as to be "overwhelmingly present at the moment of its violation." It is also necessary that the moment of carnival must be short and once a year. The rest of the year consists of repeated ritual observance of normality. Eco uses Bakhtin's utopian idealization of the people's laughter and turns it around to suggest that laughter cannot be liberating, as it deeply implies the absorption of rules. Indeed the rules have to be so thoroughly absorbed that they do not have to be stated.

LeRoy Ladurie makes a similar argument. He warns us not to take the topsy-turvy world of the carnival in Romans as subversion. Inversion and subversion, he argues, are not the same thing:

> When Guerin and Laroche, in the name of the patrician carnival, proclaimed the February price list, their primary aim was using absurdity to illustrate "an *order* in which Nature and society are soundly unchangeable or untouchable as to facts as opposed to myths." They put forth "an upside down vision, the better to dissipate subversion through amusement." Granted, this vision unwittingly substantiated through its hysteria exactly what it was ridiculing.... [T]he price list had only one meaning. Stripped of its carnival ballyhoo and in view of the way things turned out, it can be summed up in a simple motto: *order, authority, royalty.* If men exchanged roles during Carnival it was only to reaffirm the strength and permanence of the social hierarchy.[91]

In other words the comic freedom of carnival is seen as a safety valve for the otherwise coherent harmonious culture and society.

Michael Bristol, while not accepting Bakhtin's idyllic view of popular culture, cannot accept the "coherence" model. Rulers, he says, do not always have the power to withhold or grant permission; sometimes they just have to accept the people's action. In addition, he argues that the view of society as basically harmonious is "wishful thinking" and that it is just as likely that members of a community are "animated by strong feelings of distrust, animosity and chronic hostility toward one another."[92]

In academic discourse concerning carnival we have a conflict between writers who see carnival as essentially conservative and understandable in terms of a coherent picture of society and culture and those, like Bakhtin, who insist on the "otherness" of carnival—on its irreducibility to any "world picture." In fighting over the conservative or revolutionary nature of an abstract carnival, it seems that academics have "essentialized" carnival and dehistoricized it. Many carnivals probably do serve as control devices or safety valves. Other carnivals have certainly led to major riots and transformations of society.[93] The most famous example of a carnival turned riot is given to us by Ladurie. He describes a carnival in Romans in 1580 that turned into an armed conflict and massacre. Perhaps the only abstract conclusion we can make is that "for long periods carnival may be a stable and cyclical ritual with no noticeably transformative effects but,... given the presence of sharpened political antagonism, it may often act as catalyst and site of actual and symbolic struggle."[94]

One way to "de-essentialize" carnival, and to examine its sociocultural nature, is to look at specific histories and instances of carnival in the places they occur. When we look at the carnivalesque behavior of the Greenham women it clearly seems to be some kind of countercultural movement that does not serve the interests of those in power. At no point was the peace camp "sanctioned" or "licensed." The women were continually evicted and arrested; their presence was a constant thorn in the side of the government. Neither was the peace camp temporary. One of the characteristics of the peace camp that the government and press found most annoying was its refusal to go away. In addition to transgressions of place, the women committed transgressions of time. Traditional political protests took the form of "events," which were temporally circumscribed, usually within the span of a single day. This was not just another march through London; it was ongoing. By camping outside a military base *and* refusing to leave, the women not only transgressed a set of established spatiotemporal boundaries, they also began to create their own lasting sense of place. Greenham Common can no longer be thought of by the average British citizen without some thought of the peace protestors. The peace camp was so effective (and so reviled) not simply because the women were perceived as being away from their proper context (homes and families), but because of *where they were*. The U.S. air base is an extreme example of the "classical body," perfectly "finished" and delineated with a barbed wire fence. The base is smooth and ordered, with a firmly established set of hierarchical relations between the people in it. The reason for the base's existence is a set of "rational" arguments concerning "deterrence" and the protection of "freedom." Aesthetically the base fits into a set of classical norms. This explains the otherwise strange statement in the House of Commons by Lynda Chalker, the undersecretary of state for transport: "I have verified for myself what an eyesore it [the peace camp] is. It offends against the normal standards of airforce establishments. It spoils some pleasant common land and is a potential, if not an actual environmental health hazard."[95] It is somewhat startling that this statement is made about a small group of women in polythene tents camped outside a huge military air base with a nine-mile perimeter fence that sprawls across the common and contains any number of potential health hazards, not the least of which are nuclear warheads. The air base is seen here as an aesthetic model that has been defiled by the women. The aesthetics of the air base fit into the established conception of things, the dominant order, and the women do not. The air base is a monument to power and reason (and the power of reason), while the women are "hysterical," disordered, and out of place.

Chalker's view is supported by some of the residents of Newbury. Mrs. Scull lived in a big old house in Newbury. It was one of the few houses from which it was possible to see the air base and one of the peace camps. She was an active member of RAGE (Ratepayers against Greenham Encampments) and was consistently furious about the presence of the women. She achieved a certain amount of notoriety by leaning out of a window dressed only in a nightie and applauding and cheering as a missile transporter left the base. She was cheering because the women had been unable to prevent the transporter's movement. Her antics were reported, somewhat approvingly, in the national and local press. Caroline Blackwood, intrigued by Mrs. Scull's behavior, decided to call her up and ask about her objections to the peace camp. Mrs. Scull complained bitterly about the aesthetics of the peace camp and about the fact that her money as a ratepayer was being used to police the women. Curiously she did not seem to object to the sight of the base, which dominated the view from her upper windows: "Mrs Scull seemed to be able to blot out the sight of the vast military installation that was right in front of her windows. She appeared to see only a lovely and peaceful English common which had been ruined by the benders of the peace camp."[96] She agreed to show Blackwood the view from her windows.

> She took me to her bedroom. The camp looked rather unimportant from a higher perspective. Mrs. Scull had a really fantastic view of the

desolation of the missile base. From her window, you could see much more barbed wire than you could from the ground. It seemed to roll into infinity.

She asked me to imagine how pretty her view had been before the women had set up their camp. She saw that I was taken aback by the uninterrupted vista of military vehicles and barbed wire.[97]

Mrs. Scull complained that many species of birds had left Newbury since the peace women had arrived. She was convinced that the women's behavior and smell had scared them away. It had not occurred to her that the food the women left in the open might attract birds or, indeed, that they may have been scared away by the sound of air craft landing every day.

One day a couple of older women strolled past Mrs. Scull's house, and "they seemed to be part of an England of a long-lost age."[98] Blackwood, still intrigued by reactions to the peace camp, asked them their views. "It's a crime what these women are doing to this common. And it's such a beautiful spot. Don't you think it's a beautiful spot? But have you ever seen such an eyesore as those camps?" The women continued to bemoan the aesthetics of the Greenham camp while pointing toward it and the (presumably invisible) barbed wire perimeter fence. "It's really a crime what those women are doing to our common," they repeated.

Not all the residents of Newbury displayed such selective blindness. One old gentleman saw the base behind the peace camp: "Those camps can be cleared up in a second. I don't understand the people who make a fuss about the look of the camp. You have a huge rotting carcass on your doorstep and then you start complaining about the flies."[99] The dominant reaction, though, was a distaste for the "eyesore" of the camps and a blind spot for the miles of barbed wire and concrete that covered most of the old common. This was reflected by property values. Houses facing the peace camp areas sold for five thousand pounds less than other, similar houses. The presence of the air base in the views of houses exactly the same had no appreciable effect.

While the blindness to the base may seem surprising at first, there are good reasons why Mrs. Scull and others did not appear to see it. The air base, after all, had been part of the landscape for as long as most Newbury residents could remember—it had become part of the taken-for-granted landscape, part of the geographical doxa. The women, on the other hand, were new and surprising. The residents of Newbury were not used to feminist pacifist peace campers. So while the air base had come to simply exist as part of the landscape, the women were perceived as intrusions. Additionally, the effect of the women may have been to remind the Newbury residents of the base and its lethal contents. Such a reminder may have been disconcerting, scary, and unwelcome. The trans-gressions of the women, in bringing the base into question, may have become the target of the residents' frustrations in the way that the bringer of bad news is feared as much as the news. A third reason for the resi-dents' aesthetic discrimination lies in the way in which the air base fits (more than the women) into the order of the English countryside.

The English Countryside

One of the more striking themes that arises from the press coverage of the peace camp is the juxtaposition of the camp with the town of New-bury and the typically English surrounding countryside of lush, green, rolling hills. The towns and villages of that area appear to conform to the stereotypes of English rural life, thus emphasizing the deviance of the Greenham women. The following quotation plays on this juxtaposition:

> Shirley always used to enjoy her drive home. She would turn off the Basingstoke road, past the freshly cut privet hedge and the neatly tended flowerbeds, then turn right at the gates and along the leafy track to her large Victorian house.... Today it is a trip she dreads. The hedge has been covered in builder's rubble, the flowerbeds long choked by polythene sheeting and rubbish, and her leafy drive is often blocked by cars and vans.... Mrs. Huxtable is one of the many women for whom Greenham Common is not a political cause, or a place for demonstrations or law breaking. For her Greenham Common is home.[100]

Here we have a picture of "normality" disturbed: an English country town with privet hedges (the English equivalent of a white picket fence), flowerbeds (an icon of Englishness), and the large Victorian house. This comforting picture of home and all it connotes is opposed to the peace camp, which in contrast seems unnatural and out of place.

So not only the air base, with its obvious order, is an example of Bakh-tin's classical body. The English countryside of the home counties is also a strictly ordered and cherished landscape. The countryside has tradi-tionally been thought of in opposition to the city. In this scheme the city stands for "culture" and the countryside for "nature." Cowper's famous expression, "God made the country, and man made the town," summa-rized this notion. But, as Raymond Williams has shown in *The Country and the City* (1973), the English countryside is just as much a product of "man" as the town. The English countryside is, in fact, a highly im-portant symbol of order and tidiness: "Seemliness and propriety are re-spected; untidiness, however prevalent, is felt to be ill-mannered and of-fensive; demarcations are clear-cut. Neatness is a matter of boundaries as well as of areas. Roadside verges, hedgerows, fences, and railroad rights-of-way are trim, distinct, unambiguous."[101] David Lowenthal and Hugh Prince go on to suggest that in England, "the absence — or at least the concealment — of disfigurement and squalor often matters more than the presence of beauty."[102] The English countryside, oddly like the air base, is a model of geographical order and tidiness, with everything in its proper place.

Perhaps this idealization of the countryside as a symbol of order partially explains the fact that local residents saw the women as disorder and disfigurement while the air base seemed almost unnoticed. Strangely enough, rural England and Greenham Common air base shared the characteristic of tidiness. Although the air base could not be said to be beautiful in any normal way, it was certainly neat and tidy with everything in its place. The women's camp, on the other hand, must have seemed "untidy" in comparison, with no strict territory and all the transgressions of geographical expectations I have discussed above. The air base fit in with the penchant for order expressed in the countryside, while the women's camp did not.

As well as being ordered, the countryside is an object of great national affection. The countryside (rather than great cities) is England. The "green and pleasant land" — a hopelessly romanticized and bucolic image of the countryside, one not owned by corporate business with the highest levels of mechanization in the world — is a powerful icon in Britain. It was this image that the British prime minister Stanley Baldwin reflected on in the 1920s: "The sounds of England, the tinkle of the hammer and the anvil in the country smithy, the corncrake on a dewy morning, the sound of the scythe against the whetstone, and the sight of the plough-team coming over the brow of the hill ... the one sight of England."[103] This vision, even then, belied the fact that smithies were no longer common, the corncrake was a rare bird, and the tractor had superseded the plough team. This vision of the English countryside (minus modernity) is at the heart of English mythology.

Iain Chambers reflects on the importance of the English countryside to England's "moral economy." He suggests that the English have forsaken the city and romanticized the "timeless sanctuary" of the countryside:

> Symbolically transformed into an empty landscape in the canvases of
> Constable and Gainsborough, the countryside provided a suitably placid
> metaphor, once the potential disturbance of agricultural labourers and
> the rural poor had been literally removed from the picture, for an
> abstractly conceived national culture. It offered a world neatly separated

from the dirty, utilitarian logic of industry and commerce: a world in which it became possible to imagine the lost community and real nature of "Britishness."[104]

For this reason the English landscape is ideologically charged in the conflict over Greenham. The Newbury residents believe that the women's camp is out of place because it is untidy. The peace campers point at the air base and suggest it is out of place in the heart of England. Not only are the missiles foreign technical intrusions; their very presence threatens the existence of the surrounding countryside.

Stephen Daniels has made a similar observation concerning the use of the English countryside in antinuclear art.[105] He describes a montage of Constable's famous *Haywain* loaded with cruise missiles. The landscape behind is bleached with orange light. Daniels suggests that Constable's image was chosen because of its iconic effect. Constable is known as *the* painter of the English countryside, particularly south and east England where the missiles were based, and the *Haywain* is the most popular of his paintings, reproduced on tea towels, postcards, and placemats in homes throughout England. The "landscape with missiles" suggests the intrusion of American technology of mass destruction in England's "green and pleasant land." In addition, the bleached landscape points to the possible result of these missiles being based in deepest England.

Women and the Military

Women have traditionally had very prescribed and marginal roles in relation to the military establishment. As Cynthia Enloe has eloquently argued, "The military camp needs followers." Women have often served many roles for the military, roles that are marginal to its central combat functions. Women have been prostitutes, nurses, military wives, cooks, and workers in defense industries. Women have been "the home front" while the men go to battle at the "real" front. The military is a thoroughly masculine world. No armed service has more than 10 percent of its positions filled by women. Very few indeed include women in combat duty:

> "Camp followers" are kept ideologically marginal to the essential function of militaries—combat. The archetypal image of the camp follower is a woman outcast from society, poor but tenacious, eking out a livelihood by preying on unfortunate soldiers. She is a woman intruding in a "man's" world. Skirts dragging in the battlefield mud, she tags along behind the troops, selling her wares or her body, probably at unfair prices.[106]

The women, despite being marginalized, serve essential functions. They provide a reason for men to join the military in the first place. Men will not stay in an army without sexual access to women. They keep troops healthy and their spirits high; they mend clothes and dress wounds. As wives, daughters, and sweethearts waving them off to another war, they give troops a sense of purpose. The troops can think that the safety of these women depends on them. Finally women provide a cheap and accessible pool of labor to call upon as the men leave for the battlefield—workers who will willingly give the jobs back when the men return. Women associated with the military are often thought of as whores, whatever their actual role. The women's branch of the U.S. Air Force (the Women's Air Force, WAF) is jokingly translated by the men in the air force as "Women All Fuck."[107]

The military itself plays a central role in reinforcing the ideology of masculinity, as the notion of "combat" contributes to concepts of manhood and male superiority. Although men in the military are actually totally subservient to the state, this dependance is hidden behind a myth that says that "to be a soldier means possibly to experience 'combat', and only in combat lies the ultimate test of a man's masculinity."[108] To prove masculinity is to prove that one is not a woman. Drill sergeants training soldiers frequently shout into the faces of recruits, "Woman!" By the time training is finished the soldiers are "real men." This reinforcement of masculinity is underscored in the military by the geographical separation of "front" and "rear." Although women are allowed into the military they are kept away from the "front" and consigned to "supporting" roles. The military structure is metonymic for society at large, allowing women access insofar as they can provide support for the men who go out and do the "real" work.

The idea that women do not belong at the "front" is, of course, anachronistic at best. Women often experience violent confrontation in war, as prostitutes flown to the front line to "service" French troops in Vietnam; as civilian women whose homes are bombed or who are raped by advancing soldiers; as nurses in MASH units.[109] In addition, many of the "frontline" jobs women are denied involve no combat in any traditional sense. Dropping bombs on people from twenty thousand feet or launching a missile from a ship two hundred miles from a target are considered frontline male jobs, while stitching up the wounded five miles behind the front is an acceptable "rear" job for women. Despite all this, the military insists on the separation of rear and front. Enloe suggests (with a wealth of historical and contemporary evidence) that women as *women* must be denied access to "the front," to "combat," so that men can claim a uniqueness and superiority that will justify their dominant position in the social order. And yet because women are in practice often exposed to frontline combat the military has to constantly redefine "the front" and "combat" as wherever "women" are not. Women may serve the military but they can never be permitted to *be* the military. They must remain "camp followers."[110]

The situation at Greenham Common must have been a highly unusual one for the men at the air base. This group of young men had been trained to emphasize their "manhood." They were accustomed to having women around as supporters and "camp followers." They had probably seen advertisements for the military showing young women peering through the fence longing to get a peek at these icons of the masculine dressed in immaculate uniforms. Instead they were in Greenham Common guarding nuclear warheads from a group of hostile and angry women who appeared to have no respect for their exaggerated masculinity:

> Apparently many of the soldiers were under the impression that all the peace women were only camping round the base because they wanted to sleep with them. This was such a vain and deluded assumption, it was comic. Never had any group of men seemed less sexually desirable than the defenders of the cruise missile when seen from the peace camp....
> The foulness of their language as they shouted at the peace camp women befouled them rather than the women. They seemed besplattered with their own oaths and soiled by their own sordid fantasies.[111]

The guards at Greenham clearly believed that the women on the wire *must* have some sexual desire for them. The guards attempted to fit the women into an established category—the category of "camp follower." The presence of the women protesting outside the bastion of masculinity must have been extremely disconcerting. The women were out of place because the military base is a male place.

Other Stories

A key theme in this book is the invocation of meanings for place—the process of creation, reproduction, and transformation of places. I have argued throughout that favored meanings for places are defended and made explicit (taken out of the realm of the assumed) at moments of crisis when transgressions threaten to change a place's meaning, and thus the place itself, from "our" place to "their" place. The press discourse that has been explored here is just such a defense of "common sense." It is a *representation* of the peace camp, not a statement of facts. It is a representation that seeks to devalue and discredit the women at the camp. It works by making the women seem displaced, obscene, and unnatural by suggesting that women do not belong at Greenham Common (that they are out of place) and that they belong instead at "home." It is a surprisingly effective discourse, but it is not the only one. In order to *relativize* the mainstream press reactions it is useful to consider some alternative stories to take the ideological prop of "truth" away from the mainstream story. The alternative stories are those of the liberal press (who supported the women) and the radical feminists (who accused the Greenham women of "selling out.") The aim here is not to validate one story or another but to relativize the stories and outline the way in which the "facts" of the women's existence lead to wildly different representations. It is not that the women are naturally out of place; they are not naturally deviant, dirty, diseased, and hysterical. They are created as such in an attempt to restore normality to the English countryside and to international nuclear politics. The same women in the same place can be and have been seen from a variety of perspectives.

Lynne Jones, in "Perceptions of 'Peace Women' at Greenham Common," discusses the images of the Greenham women in the media from the perspective of a participant (she lived at Greenham for one and a half years). She constructs a table of words used to describe the women in the press and other words that might describe the same people with more positive connotations.

Negative	Positive
Abandoned children	Sacrificed comfort of home
Living in squalor	Living in horrid conditions
Bloody minded/stubborn	Brave/committed
Won't admit defeat	Standing up for beliefs
Don't care about appearance	Suitably dressed
Don't care about property	Not materialistic
Naive	Idealistic
Lost cause	Symbol of resistance
Crazy	Imaginative
No leadership	Egalitarian
Disorganized	Communal
Chaotic	No hierarchy
Tiny minority	Small valiant group

While Jones's thought experiment is useful, it is perhaps more revealing to look at some other stories that did portray the women in ways that differed from the mainstream press.

The Radical Feminist Perspective

To the mainstream press the Greenham women were a group of filthy, hysterical lesbians. To the radical feminists of the women's liberation movement, however, they were women who were "selling out" the larger feminist cause—they were women who behaved in perfectly respectable ways, consistent with patriarchal norms: "Greenham Common looks like the acceptable face of women-only actions to me—legitimized by its falling into women's traditional role of concern for future generations, pacifying etc."[112] The radical feminist critique of Greenham, *Breaching the Peace,* contains a series of essays that seek to question the perceived co-option of the feminist cause by the peace movement and by Greenham in particular. The essays consistently argue that the women's peace camp is "acceptable" to the status quo because of its emphasis on women's nurturing role and its refusal to confront the greater issues of patriarchal domination. The Greenham women had often talked of the future for their children and grandchildren and cited this as a concern that had drawn them to the camp. The radical feminists criticized this as contributing to the continuation of patriarchal, heterosexual, middle-class values:

> On the TV and in the newspapers I see women saying that they are here for the good of their families, that they are simply "ordinary" women who are deeply moved by the urgency of the situation, that they are "naturally" concerned to preserve life and defend their children, that if there were no nuclear threat, they would go on being very nice, ordinary women and all would be OK.[113]

Beneath this image, Lynn Alderson argues, is a dangerous notion of women's "natural" concerns for family:

> The idea that women are naturally non-violent, could not be responsible for wars and the development of nuclear technology, that is, wouldn't even if we had access to weapons and science; that it is a particular female characteristic to respect life—this is a dangerous one for us to hold. It goes along with some biological notion that we inherit our behavior with our genitals or that we are protectors of life because we bear children and that this is right and proper.[114]

The radical feminists also noted the use of strategies like "embracing" the base and "decorating" the fence with pictures of children and diapers. All this, they claim, "is precisely the kind of protest that is expected of and allowed to women. It is the traditional voice of the poor woman left at home who can only use emotional appeals ... to influence those that do have power."[115] The efforts of the Greenham women were seen as attempts to use stereotypes of the nurturing woman to bring out as many women as possible. While this may work, they argue, it does not provide a solid critique of patriarchy; rather it contributes to its continuation: "There are many advantages in cultivating the emotive significance of nappies and toys on barbed wire fences. The ensuing positive publicity fosters respectability as pregnant women are dragged away by reluctant policemen."[116] The Greenham women, according to the radical feminists, are choosing an easy target (nuclear weapons) and in doing so are glossing over the more everyday forms of "war" against women: "So, it's OK to link arms and hold hands around a military base, in the cause of peace, but to do it in the streets for the love of it and it's another matter, as any dyke who's been beaten up can tell you."[117] What Frankie Green is saying here is that the women at the base have created a place where usually unacceptable behavior is acceptable and even expected. In a sense the Greenham women are "in place." She suggests that the more important battles are fought in everyday spaces where similar behavior (holding hands) leads to severe consequences. The attention to the nuclear threat diverts attention from the everyday continuing occurrence of male domination and violence against women at home and on the streets. Even if nuclear weapons were to go, there would be no "peace" for the women who continue to be abused and dominated by men:

> As far as I'm concerned the ultimate act of male violence happens everyday. And when I'm walking around thinking of this and I hear phrases like "women for life on earth" and "women for peace" I feel completely bemused. What on earth do they mean? What peace? Being "against cruise," "against nuclear arms" I can understand, but what is the idea of "peace"?[118]

> Holding hands and weaving webs is not enough. While you are getting your sisterly buzz with yet another trip to Greenham I am walking up the street wondering if I'll make it to my front door or behind it. I want freedom from all male violence, not a variety of "peace." I want women's liberation.[119]

In summary, the story told by the radical feminists about Greenham argues that the women presented the acceptable face of protest because (1) the women used claims of a special feminine concern for peace and nurturing, which fit into a dominant heterosexual patriarchal ideology, and (2) the women, by protesting cruise missiles and arguing that their removal would further the cause of "peace," diverted attention from the everyday "war" on women. In addition the radical feminist authors wanted to dispel the myth that the camp's all-women status in itself constituted a radical statement:

> Everywhere in recorded history there are women-only activities, tolerated and even encouraged.... Certainly they can work best together at their women's work—in menstrual huts, in purdah, making jam, spinning and weaving, having babies and caring for them, being the custodians and understanders of LIFE ... and saving the world from nuclear disaster, making it safe for children and for men. When we are together, women only, because we love each other only and because we are working for women, for ourselves, that is ... more likely to change the world.[120]

The Liberal Perspective

The liberal account of the Greenham camp was largely sympathetic and consistently appeared in the *Guardian* daily newspaper as well as the Sunday *Observer*. Occasional accounts in the *Daily Mirror* and even some of the more conservative "quality" newspapers (*Daily Telegraph, Times*) also saw the women in a favorable light. A typical liberal account of the Greenham women is given by the *Sunday Times* under the headline "The Day Mummy Went on a Demo."[121] The tale is an everyday story concerning the Wilkinsons. They are described as a "normal" family with a large home, dogs, and clarinet-playing children. The image is one of middle-class respectability. All that upsets the picture of affluent normality is that Mrs. Wilkinson (who is pursuing a degree in cultural studies) is in prison as a result of her participation in the Greenham protest. The reason given for her participation is a genuine "concern for family" and the future of her children. While in prison she keeps herself amused with knitting projects sent to her by her husband. The picture is one of acceptability and respectability. The story is saying that this woman is a "normal" woman with a home and family (as are, by implication, many others), who is genuinely disturbed by the threat of nuclear destruction and decides to take part in the Greenham protest. In short, the message is that "these women deserve our support because they are normal."

This theme is replicated in other accounts. The *Observer*, in a color supplement spread entitled "Women on the Wire," says that "by far the majority are ordinary women who have never taken a strong line."[122] It continues, stating they have jobs and studies and often husbands. In another edition the paper reads:

Any woman from anywhere in the world can come, go, return; and be welcomed. No questions are asked. There is no hierarchy, no structure. There is no distinction of race, creed, colour, money, age, class or nationality. These unpretentious women in their beat-up warm clothes, have become a world-wide symbol and model for countless *ordinary* people who also say NO.[123]

The generally less sympathetic *Daily Telegraph* goes as far as to say, "Most of the women look and sound healthy and apart from their mud-stained clothing, fairly clean.... [S]ome women abandoned or postponed studies, or left good jobs to go to Greenham. Others have left apparently approving husbands at home to look after children, returning home from time to time to pick up the threads of family life."[124] Although this description is, at best, ambivalent, it nevertheless makes some attempt to place the women in the context of "normality." The *Daily Mirror* makes perhaps the most poetic defense of the women in an editorial piece entitled "Pickets of Peace," which reads:

> *They were not sluts or harridans as the Daily Express, for one, viciously described them.* ... the press was hostile to them ... the soldiers in the Greenham base called them "smellies." ... A local restaurant refused to serve them.... It was to avert that fate [nuclear catastrophe] that some of the women left their homes and families, and were called lesbians for it by those who never felt such passions for peace.[125]

An extended liberal perspective of the peace camp is given in Caroline Blackwood's book *On the Perimeter*. Blackwood had read the mainstream press reports and was disturbed by the description of the women.

> I was curious to meet the Greenham women, for the press had decorated them with such loathsome and frightening adjectives, they had been made to sound almost mythical in their horror.... They'd been accused of being sex-starved.... They were also described as being in the pay of the Soviet Union, and it was said that many of them were Russian spies.... I found the charge that the Greenham women lived like dogs and that they were smearing Newbury with their excrement almost the most chilling one.... The claim of Auberon Waugh that the Greenham women smelt of "fish paste and bad oysters" also haunted me for it had such distressing sexual associations.... As these women had been attributed with almost every unsavory characteristic, I had become very curious to see why they aroused such violent hatred and to discover how evil-smelling and odious the Greenham women could be.[126]

When she arrived at the camp she was confronted with the sight of the air base: "Nothing could look less beautiful than the cruise missile base itself, with its vast expanse of concrete, its hideous military buildings and vehicles and the warheads resting in their silos. Within the perimeter fence, the Americans had created Lowell's 'unforgivable landscape.' "[127] And then she found a peace camp with a lonely old lady sitting in the middle knitting. Despite the image of harmlessness, Blackwood was overcome with fear fed by the memories of the press portrayals of the women:

> The ugly newspaper descriptions of the Greenham women had stirred up ridiculous images in my unconscious. I saw that she was quite old, that she had grey hair. If she was a Greenham witch I hated the idea that she might get up and scream at me. If she was as destructive as I'd been told, she might give me a viscous stab with her knitting needles. But above all, I dreaded that she might suddenly behave like a dog and defecate.[128]

As Blackwood gets to know the women she begins to portray them as "normal" but concerned women doing as their conscience dictates. The image is given of a group of women who *didn't want* to be camped in the mud and disorder, who were not deliberately annoying people but trying their best to be comfortable in an uncomfortable situation: "Pat was a gentle and intelligent woman. She was sensibly dressed for the awful conditions her conscience had forced her to live in. She was wearing trousers and heavy boots and a bulky jacket."[129] It is interesting to consider other terms in which this might have been stated. "Sensibly dressed" could be "unfeminine" and "awful conditions" could be described as "squalor." How different the impression that would have been given of Pat.

Blackwood also tells us that the local council had made the women's lives harder by refusing to provide them with water, banning any tents or caravans, and stopping the use of chemical toilets. In fact, many of the "disordered" elements of the peace camp's appearance were a direct result of the local government's attempts to make the women's life uncomfortable. Even the things the women could do to improve appearances seemed useless in the face of council actions: "She pointed apologetically to the disordered appearance of the camp. 'We used to keep things much tidier. But now that we've heard that there's an eviction order and we are only really waiting for the bailiffs, there just doesn't seem much point in trying to keep the camp neat."[130] One camp even had a sign that read, "Please leave things as you would like to find them." The vision of normality contrasts starkly with the Danteesque pictures of manifest deviance painted by the *Sun*, the *Mail*, the *Express,* and others.

Underlining this contrast is the way the women's relationship to children is used by Blackwood: "It was the protest of all the women who have ever looked after children. It gave a black warning that came direct from personal experience. 'If you let children play with dangerous instruments, it won't be very long before there's a hideous accident.' "[131] In the mainstream press the women are accused of either abandoning their children or exposing them to immorality at the camp. In Blackwood's account the women's relationship to children is used to defend them and their actions; it is *because* they are mothers that they feel the need to be at Greenham.

The point of this discussion of radical and liberal accounts of Greenham is to relativize the mainstream story. The same situation—the presence of pacifist-feminist women in a ramshackle camp outside Greenham Common air force base—leads to wholly different *representations*. The mainstream press portrays the women as "deviant" by pointing to their perceived displacement, using metaphors and descriptive terms of dirt, disease, and hysteria. The radical press argues, on the contrary, that the women *are* mainstream, because they consciously use female stereotypes of mother and nurturer to promote their cause. The radical press's view of the women is also negative, but for the opposite reasons (mainstream says women are "bad" because they are "deviant"; radical press says women are "bad" because they are "normal"). Finally the liberal press seeks to portray the women as normal women with heightened moral awareness who deserve support *because* they are normal.

In this illustration we see a conflict over different notions concerning what is out of place, the missiles or the women. The story that the women were out of place became the dominant story. It was the story told by the mainstream press. The radical account, which argued that the women were, in fact, in place and behaving in accord with societal norms, remained marginalized. The liberal account, although slightly more widespread, became a subordinate story, particularly as the peace camp remained in place. The Greenham women's own story—the story that said that the missiles did not belong in Greenham—was more or less ignored as the arguments over the appropriateness or inappropriateness of the peace camp became the point of contention.

Conclusion

The story told in this illustration is a complicated one that is centered on a struggle over place and ideology—over "what belongs where." It has been a story with multiple characters all saying very different things about nuclear weapons, about women, and about England. In the end the story told by the press that the women are "out of place" became dominant. This is hardly surprising, given the sheer number of homes reached by the various popular newspapers with their tales of sordid deviance. What is surprising is that a relatively small number of women could make as much difference as they did. Transgression of the rules of place is an extremely effective form of protest that points toward the historical nature of assumed boundaries. It is a testimony to the women of Greenham that the place Greenham Common will long be associated with the politics of peace in addition to the politics of mass destruction.

Part 3

Conclusions

Chapter 6

Place and Ideological Strategies

The geographical ordering of society is founded on a multitude of acts of boundary making—of territorialization—whose ambiguity is to simultaneously open up the possibilities for transgression. In order to fully understand the range of a society's geographical values, it is enlightening to map out geographical deviance and transgressions. By concentrating on the marginal and the "low," the "other," we achieve a novel perspective upon its *central* workings. The geographical classification of society and culture is constantly structured in relation to the unacceptable, the other, the dirty. Graffiti, the Greenham protest, and the Stonehenge convoy help define the delineations of culture, the geography of common sense. Simultaneously, these marginal(ized) events question the naturalness and absoluteness of assumed geographies. Like Bakhtin's carnivalesque-comic view of the world, these marginal events foster "a realization that established authority and truth are relative."[1]

My analysis of transgression has not been a contemplation of the extraordinary for its own sake. Rather it has been to circuitously contemplate the center, the classical body, *which defines itself in relation to* these grotesque moments. Each illustration has been layered with transgressions—geographical, social, and cultural. In each case the reaction of the media has involved an unavoidable and always already existing linkage of the spatial, the social, and the cultural. Every social entity and every meaning has its place. Looking at reactions to transgressions helps us see this.

Marginal, grotesque, extraordinary elements and events in society are interesting in themselves, but they are more interesting when we examine the role they play in defining the "normal," the classical, the dominant. The center could not exist without the margin. There could be no moral geography without an immoral geography. Peter Stallybrass and Allon White make a strong case for the importance of transgression. They argue that "what is socially peripheral is often symbolically central." Matter out of place, they argue, is far from a residual and deviant category of experience. The forms of cultural "negation" are essential to a proper understanding of symbolic processes in general.[2] Similarly, attention to the geographically marginal tells us a great deal about the geographically central.

There are two principle lessons, then, to be learned from my analysis of reactions to heretical geographies. One concerns the way place is implicated in the creation and maintenance of ideological beliefs; the other is about the uses and limits of transgression as a way of challenging and transforming these beliefs. The former is a lesson in continuity and the latter a lesson in change. It is time now to reflect on these two lessons and outline what it is we have learned. Let us take the question of the relationship between place (meaningful segments of space) and ideology (ideas about what is good and just) first. In the final chapter we will return to the question of transgression.

The illustrations concerned the reactions to events judged by those with powerful opinions to be "deviant" because (at least in part) they were "out of place." I have argued throughout that the meanings of places are historically constituted and vary through time. In each case the taken-for-granted meanings of place were not natural but were socially and historically constructed. In addition I suggested that the socially constructed meaning of places directly affected judgments of the events in them. The meaning of New York affected the judgment of graffiti, for example. Simultaneously the events (such as graffiti) affected the meaning of the place. What results is a cycle of meanings, actions, and places influencing, constituting, and structuring each other.

Recent geographical literature has concerned itself with this social construction of place. It has become commonplace to make assertions concerning the social and historical nature of places and to delineate some of the ways in which this has occurred in particular instances. Recent cultural geography and much "postmodern" geography discuss these issues. A typical statement is made by David Harvey: "The first step down the road is to insist that place in whatever guise is, like space and time, a social construct. The only interesting question that can be asked is; by what social process(es) is place constructed?"[3] This is surely an overstatement. While I agree that the social construction of place is an interesting question, other types of analysis are necessary. Harvey, Edward Soja, and others frequently assert that place is a powerful tool for manipulating social action. It still remains to ask, Why is place such a powerful container of social power? More specifically, What is it about place that makes it an effective signifier of ideological values? In asking these questions I hope to link the literature on "society and space"[4] with the tradition in geography of closely examining the *nature of place*.[5]

An illustration will help. If we need to build a shelf we know that there are certain mechanical properties of a tool that will help us achieve this aim. In general it is a good idea to use a hard and heavy substance to hammer in nails. Leverage of some kind will also help us apply force to the nail. For these reasons it is unlikely that we would use a bedsheet or a piece of cheese; usually we would choose a hammer. Given the mechanical properties we have identified, we can see how the hammer fulfills them; it has a heavy compact head and a long narrow handle for leverage. We know that the hammer will not do anything without a person to use it. We could therefore analyze the hammer in terms of the intentions of the user. We could also, however, discuss the qualities of hammers in general (or the materials that go to make a hammer) and outline how these qualities make it useful for its task. I intend to do the second kind of analysis in what follows.

The point of this exercise is to recognize that while it is true that places are always socially constructed and that they are created in some image rather than in others, it is also true that every society and culture has places of some (socially constructed) kind. Any imagined or theorized future society will have places. To propose a radical transformation is not to propose the abolition of place but to propose transformations in the types of places. Place in a general sense is transhistorical and universal. It is a fundamental element of human existence, a product of the intentional transformation of the natural environment by humans.

If we did not think that there was something important and unique about space and place, some set of powers and potentials in social interaction, why would we be concerned about delineating its use? Harvey, and others in radical geography, must accept that space and place *are* distinctive (regardless of who uses them) and not simply a matter of "mere" ideology. The reasons space and place are used by powerful groups, I argue, are reasons internal to the very nature of space and place.

This chapter is structured around a list of *ideological strategies* extracted and generalized from recent work on ideology.[6] Writers in social theory, literary theory, and cultural studies have asked how ideology works and have begun to make some sense out of a historically "fuzzy" area. The question they have asked is, What characteristic mechanisms are mobilized in the creation of ideas about what is good and just? Ideologies are typically used to classify, differentiate, naturalize, and link ideas to action. Each of these can be related to characteristics of place.

Place and Classification

We take for granted the spatial arrangement of things—fences, buildings, roads, shops. Space is both a socially constructed arrangement of things and the medium of all these historical arrangements. Indeed space, along with time, has long been understood as a basic dimension of all things natural and mental. Our perception is primarily oriented visually and spatially.[7] Space and time are also the most basic forms of classification. When and where things occur are basic categorizations familiar to all but the youngest child. They form the knowledge most fundamental for everyday survival. Needless to say, the details of the classifications are variable across cultures. Nonetheless it is indisputable that an understanding of space is universally important to people's everyday existence. Try living for a day disregarding the expectations that come with divisions of space. Space is a primal dimension of existence in a way that something like census categorizations are not.

Space and place are such fundamental categories of experience that the power to specify the meanings of places and expectations of behavior in them is great indeed. Pierre Bourdieu has argued that classifications are the site par excellence of struggle. The primary forms of classification, he suggests, "owe their special efficacy to the fact that they function below the level of consciousness and language, beyond the reach of introspective scrutiny or control by the will."[8] Such primary forms of classification, as Kant and Durkheim have shown, include classification by space. Indeed, Bourdieu often talks in terms of "knowing one's place" and a "sense of limits." These primal classifications add up to doxa. Classifications that remain unarticulated are, in Bourdieu's view, the strongest of ideological weapons. An important struggle, then, is to recognize these classifications and change them from internalized limits (doxa) to explicit boundaries (orthodoxy):

> Only in and through the struggle do the internalized limits become
> boundaries, barriers that have to be moved. And, indeed, the system of
> classificatory schemes is constituted as an objectified, institutionalized
> system of classification only when it has ceased to function as a sense of
> limits so that the guardians of the established order must enunciate,
> systematize and codify the principles of production of that order, both
> real and represented, so as to defend them against heresy.[9]

Classifications that remain unstated are powerful because they are not recognized discursively but practically. The division of space is just such a primary form of classification, as Bourdieu himself has shown in his ethnography of the Kabyle of Algeria in *Outline of a Theory of Practice,* in which he describes the ways the Kabyle structure their lives in accordance with unsaid spatial norms.

Place and Differentiation

One form of classification that has been the object of much "poststructuralist" thought is an emphasis on "difference" and the "other." Although all classification is a form of differentiation, the differentiation here is between "us" and "them." People (both dominant and subordinate) create themselves as subjects in relation to opposites and differences. White people contrast themselves to nonwhite people, men to women, capitalists to communists, and so on. Although all groups do this, the more powerful ones in any given context will create the distinctions that become most widely accepted. Thus citizens of the West are more likely to be influenced by notions of nonwhite people as "primitive" and white people as "civilized" than, for instance, by Afrocentric ideas of black superiority. Equally they are more likely to abide by the middle-class definition of order and cleanliness than by the Gypsy's definition, which is formed in relation to their perception of house dwellers as nonhygienic.

This process of differentiation is a characteristic mechanism by which ideological values are transmitted. Goren Therborn argues that every ideology has an "alter-ideology."[10] Ideologies are set up in opposition to something else. Thus the ideology of masculinity is "not-feminine" and the alter-ideology of order is "disorder." The structure of this book has centered on the definition of the geographically appropriate through reaction to the geographically inappropriate. John B. Thompson refers to the process of fragmentation.[11] This process occurs through "differentiation," which is an emphasis on the differences between groups that is used to prevent unity, and "expurgation of the other" — the creation of enemies who are evil and threatening to everyone else, who are expected to gang up on the helpless "other." Differentiation divides the subjected while the expurgation of the other unites disparate groups by identifying a common enemy. Each serves ideological purposes and relies on the creation of normative difference. At one time or another Jews, communists, gays, feminists, and a variety of youth subcultures have served as the "common enemy."

Differentiation, then, is an important ingredient in the construction of ideologies. One fundamental way to differentiate is by place. In our everyday life we unavoidably experience difference as we move through the landscape. If we stay in one place and insulate ourselves from visitors, we experience a reasonably continuous and unchanging context. As soon as we move we experience change. One room is different from the next, one house from another, a neighborhood is marked off from others. Regions, countries, and continents are all different—inhabited by strangers. Differentiation may also occur through time, but the past and the future are not coexistent with the present and are not immediately and visibly juxtaposed. It is hard to create enemies out of different times. Still, we are reminded of past "mistakes" like "trusting the Germans" (assuming we are British), or we are told that a place far away also exists, metaphorically, in a different time: "they are backward there."

The visibility of place makes it especially important in creating differences:

> Vision is our intellectual sense par excellence. It discriminates and defines. "We prefer seeing to everything else," says Aristotle, "because, above all the other senses, sight makes us know and brings to light the many differences between things." Sight provides us with a spatially structured universe. All the objects are visible at the same time, and they are stable long enough to apprehend their relationship to each other.[12]

Sight is our most important sense, and it is used to distinguish spatially and direct us through the complicated and dangerous world of everyday life. The definition of difference, though, goes beyond simply seeing it. Places also have associated characteristics that influence our characterizations of the people in them or from them.

Places are fundamental creators of difference. It is possible to be inside a place or outside a place. Outsiders are not to be trusted; insiders know the rules and obey them. The definition of *insider* or *outsider* is more than a locational marker. Just as place has objective and subjective facets, the designations of difference through place mean two connected things. An outsider is not just someone literally from another location but someone who is existentially removed from the milieu of "our" place—someone who doesn't know the rules.

Recall that in the graffiti story, graffiti and its creators were associated with other places in order to present them as aberrant and deviant. Graffiti was associated with the third world in order to emphasize its apparent disorder. In the case of the Greenham women, the media played on their supposed connections to the Soviet Union. In doing so they questioned the women's loyalty to their place and the honesty of their aims. The use of place and space to differentiate between "us" and "them" is a key ideological tool.[13] The classification and differentiation of things by place have important effects on the way we perceive and make sense of the world. More important, though, these perceptions affect our practice—our actions.

Place and Practice

> *A successful ideology must work both practically and theoretically, and discover some way of linking these levels. It must extend from an elaborated system of thought to the minutiae of everyday life, from a scholarly treatise to a shout in the street.*
>
> —*Terry Eagleton*, Ideology: An Introduction

Ideology is often thought of as synonymous with a rigid, doctrinaire set of ideas—a dogma—separate from the experience of the world. This is the way the word *ideology* is often used in conversation by laypeople; they mean abstract and narrow-minded. In critical theory, however, ideology has been just the opposite. Ideologies are "action-oriented" beliefs—ideas that promote some actions while discouraging others. A patriarchal ideology not only involves ideas about male superiority but, far more important, also supports and legitimates actions that contribute to actual domination.

This linkage of the abstract and the everyday has been a key problematic in recent social theory. Raymond Williams's idea of "structure of feeling" is one attempt to deal with this connection. Williams was concerned with the way "the social" is always defined in the past tense, as if it were complete and finished. Thus the "present" is always other than social: "If the social is always past in the sense that it is always formed, we have indeed to find other terms for the undeniable experience of the present: not only the temporal present, the realization of this and this instant, but the specificity of the present being, the inalienably physical."[14] If something is not fixed and forever but in flux and moving as it is experienced, it is taken out of the "social" and described as "personal" and "subjective." Williams, in developing the notion of "structure of feeling," sought to make the social less fixed and the subjective more structured: "We are talking about characteristic elements of impulse, restraint, and tone: specifically affective elements of consciousness and relationships: not feeling against thought, but thought as felt and feeling as thought: practical consciousness of a present kind, in a living and interrelating continuity."[15] The word *structure* indicates a set of internal relations, while the word *feeling* implies an active sense of process perhaps unrecognizable as social. Similarly, the apparently rigid social structures of the past were always partially in flux—being changed by people's actions.

Thus, in Williams's formulation of structure of feeling, a whole range of ideas from the seemingly fleeting and everyday "practical consciousness" to the rigid doctrines of "official consciousness" is encapsulated. A similar reformulation of ideology is Bourdieu's idea of *habitus*. Through this formulation Bourdieu attempts to describe the way ideology takes hold of, and is maintained through, everyday activity. A *habitus* is a set of dispositions that generate particular practices. As people act, apparently spontaneously, in accordance with internalized systems of belief, certain norms are reproduced. The concept of *habitus*—a structured and structuring structure—is one that attempts to get away from the idea of formal *rules* and toward *strategies*. People in their actions simply act as they think they are supposed to. In so doing they reinforce the basis of these actions. Like "structure of feeling," *habitus* concentrates on the importance of practical knowledge—the savoir faire—as opposed to the formal delineation of discursive knowledge.

In the work of both Williams and Bourdieu we see the importance of practice to the theory of ideology. Ideology is seen as a set of practices derived from beliefs and beliefs derived from practice. Ideologies, to be successful, connect the metaphysical to the everyday. Thus the Catholic religion connects the idea of transubstantiation to the eating of bread.

These discussions of ideology as a middle ground between the fixed and structured and the fluid and personal clearly match discussions about the nature of place. While some discussions of place have emphasized location, others have emphasized the material structure of place. Still others have chosen to concentrate on the subjective qualities of place—the sense of place. Recently geographers have begun to unravel the objective and subjective elements of place.

Place can be described in terms of three elements: location, locale, and sense of place.[16] A location is a point in space with specific relations to other points in space. A set of coordinates provides a location. The term *locale* refers to a broader context for social relations, while *sense of place* refers to subjective feelings associated with a place. In most geography, one or another of these notions predominates. Spatial analysis and economic geography have focused on location, while cultural geographers have examined sense of place. All three ideas of place constitute a more total idea of what place is, ranging from more objective facets to more subjective ones.

Place always exists in a state between objective fact and subjective feeling.[17] Because we live in place, as part of place, and yet simultaneously view place as something external, place can be thought of as a center of meaning and an external context for action—as ideal and material. Place combines realms that theory has sought to hold apart.[18] Place, as a phenomenological-experiential entity combines elements of nature (elemental forces), social relations (class, gender, and so on), and meaning (the mind, ideas, symbols). Experience of place, from a phenomenological perspective, is always an experience of all three realms, each of which affects our actions in place.

Similar discussions have centered on the concept of landscape. Stephen Daniels talks of the "duplicity of landscape," by which he means the irreducibility of landscape to either its material or its ideological dimensions.[19] Following the Marxist sociologist Fred Inglis, Daniels argues that landscape is a concept that "stands at the intersection of concepts a sociologist would strain to hold apart: 'institution,' 'product,' 'process' and 'ideology.'"[20] Landscape, like place, "can neither be completely reified as an authentic object in the world nor thoroughly dissolved as an ideological mirage."[21] Landscapes and places are products we have to live in and use. Art and literature are products made for contemplation, and we can leave them at any time. A place forces us to make interpretations and to act accordingly. As Daniels argues, landscape cannot be seen as just a solid piece of reality, but neither can it be reduced to the whimsy of the establishment. It exists in between.[22]

Places and landscapes are ideas set in stone that, like it or not, we have to act in. Our actions are interpretations of the text of a place that are recognizable to other people and are thus reinforced. Antonio Gramsci has suggested that "each man [sic] ... carries on some form of intellectual activity, that is, he is a 'philosopher,' an artist, a man of taste, he participated in a particular conception of the world, has a conscious line of moral conduct, and therefore contributes to sustain a conception of the world or to modify it, that is, to bring into being new modes of thought."[23] We are all philosophers because ideas are related to practice by our behavior in place. Our interpretations of the world are revealed in the way we act.

Ideology, then, is not just a set of ideas but ideas related to practices—ideas connected to what we do. Place and landscape also connect the mental to the material as our actions in them constitute interpretations. There is clearly a link between the two problematics, if we think of a place as a text where the words have become spatial divisions and subdivisions. To read this text we act in it; places force us to link ideas to actions almost constantly. We walk on the sidewalk, kneel in the church, and drink only in the bar. The interpretation of a place is, in everyday life, a practical interpretation. Our beliefs about place are usually indistinguishable from actions in place. Ideology seeks to link the concrete and the abstract. What better way than through place?

Place as Natural

One of the more frequently noted ideological strategies is the removal of beliefs from the realm of history and their placement into the realm of nature. The word *natural* (like *cultural*) is a complicated one that requires some explanation.[24] Nature is commonly thought of as the opposite of culture. In this sense it means "nonmental." It includes the totality of all things physical, excluding only things mental. But when we talk of "enjoying nature," we are not usually discussing our appreciation of plastic kettles or interstate highways (both in the set of all things nonmental). A "nature lover" loves the nature of plants and animals and things not apparently created by humans. There is also "human nature," which refers to the characteristics of humans that are thought of as instinctual and irrepressible. Nature also means the essence of something. When we say it is the nature of metal that it is heavy, we mean that heaviness is a defining characteristic of metal. Related to this is the sense in which natural means "normal." So what does it mean to say that ideologies appear as "natural"? Part of the problem is that the different definitions of nature are often conflated. To say that homosexuality is unnatural is to say that this does not conform to "nature" (instincts, for example) and that it is not normal. The definitions of nature as "normal" and as essential characteristics are often confused. Likewise the ideal of nature as the nonhuman is held up as an irrefutable lawlike set of standards.

Often the ideological use of nature is to present something as though there were never, and could never be, any alternative. In other words something "just is." Again this conflates the idea of nature as the nonhuman (and beyond our control) and nature as "essential characteristic." Through this process the historical and social nature of ideas are ignored, concealed, or forgotten.[25] They exist in the same way that trees exist. Ideologies are ideally matched to people's "common sense." Ideology "goes without saying." Of course some things *are* natural (that is, not created by sociocultural forces), such as sleeping, eating, dying, and being born. There may be ideological beliefs about ways to eat or when to sleep, but the basic needs are surely there. The majority of ideas and behaviors, however, do not fall into this basic and limited list. Living together in families and eating meat every day are examples of behaviors that are thought of as natural but that are not. In everyday life we hear people say, "It's only natural" about a bizarre array of thoughts and behaviors. In academic discussion, too, there have been endless at-tempts to "prove" that something is natural. The alleged superior intel-ligence of whites is an obvious example. The naturalizing technique is used by oppositional groups, too. While homophobes claim the "unnat-ural" nature (?) of gay sex, elements of the gay community defend them-selves as "born that way."

The most successful ideologies make no explicit claims to nature. The most powerful expectations remain unnoticed and assumed. The supposed naturalness of ideas remains implicit in behavior. Discursive claims to naturalness need only be made once the doxa has been questioned and orthodoxy needs to be imposed. The natural way is not the "best" way; it is the only way.

Place displays an air of obviousness. Geography has often been thought of as "so much common sense." I remember a friend at high school ques-tioning my choice of geography for advanced study. He asserted that ge-ography was "the science of the obvious." His preferred subjects were pure mathematics and physics, and I found it hard to argue with him. The subject matter of geography — places, landscapes, regions — seems static and bound. Space appears to freeze time and remain unshifting and dull. Compared with the dynamism of time, space and place appear inert — like a wet towel thrown over a world in flux. Place can certainly appear to be monolithic and insensitive to change. Concrete and brick have a certain inertia even in the postmodern world. Once a monument is built it tends to stay there. Place and space also obfuscate their social roots. Places appear to have their own rules, not the rules constructed for them. It is in recognition of this that Mayor Koch was able to claim that Grand Central Station was obviously for traveling and not sleep-ing. This wasn't *his* idea; it was obvious. Foucault touched on this atti-tude to space as dead and fixed:

> It is surprising how long the problem of space took to emerge as a historico-political problem. Space used to be either dismissed as belonging to "nature" — that is, the given, the basic conditions, "physical geography," in other words a sort of "prehistoric" stratum; or else it was conceived as the residual site or field of expansion of peoples, of a culture, a language or a state.[26]

Foucault argues that space was reduced by philosophy to a secondary consideration after time. Space, he argues, was reduced to the dead, the fixed, and the inert because it seems unchanging and "natural."

It did not require philosophers to decide that space and place were fixed and inert. Geographers themselves, for much of the subject's history, have assumed a certain naturalness about their subject matter. Chorology spoke of regions as pseudonatural givens that were considered pre-existent entities to be discovered and described ad infinitum. Recent geography has taken up the task of describing the ways spaces and places are socially constructed. Robert Sack's theory of territoriality explicitly calls into question the idea that territoriality is a product of nature—a genetic drive like that displayed by animals. He replaces this notion with the idea that territoriality is a strategy of control used to obfuscate other, more direct forms of power. Since territoriality is a strategy, the questions about territory that need to be asked concern the circumstances under which territory is or is not a favored strategy of control.[27] David Harvey's work has raised similar questions about space and time. Throughout his work he has emphasized that the command over space is fundamental to social (usually capitalist) power. Like any other fetish, he argues, space is powerless without social forces behind it.

But places are not *just* social. Sack argues that place incorporates elements from the realms of nature, social relations, and meaning and is irreducible to any one of these realms.[28] While analytically separable, the social, the natural, and the cultural are indistinguishable in everyday life. A place is clearly more than just a set of cultural meanings, as it represents social forces and is solid, material, and composed of elemental forces. The phenomenological experience of place involves a holistic experience of meanings, social forces, and natural forces. So what does it mean when we refer to "the nature of New York's subway system" or "the nature of big cities"? Several different meanings of the word *nature* get confused in such statements. They mean both "the essential characteristics of X" and "the normal characteristics of X." Both of these meanings relate to the idea of nature as "the physical (nonsocial) world." Thus the materiality of place (its nature in the sense of its being physical) obscures its social origin and appears as a freestanding power in itself with its own rules and expectations.

A shopping mall, for instance, is a building made from certain materials that hold together because of certain forces (nature in the sense of "all things nonmental"). It is also the result of sets of social relations involved in capitalism, and it holds certain meanings portrayed in the advertising world and elsewhere. The materiality of a shopping mall (nature in the sense of "all things physical"), however, is conflated with the idea of nature as "what just is." An ideology that seeks to conceal its own historical roots uses the physical naturalness of place to make claims about the essential nature of place and forgets the social realm. An ideology emphasizes the realm of nature and conceals the realm of social relations. Social theory, as a critical mode of inquiry, has simply reversed the emphasis and underscored the social elements of place.

In my illustrations the question of naturalness appeared several times. In each case the transgressions, in some way, upset expectations and revealed the historical and social nature of particular places and particular spatial norms. In the reactions I have analyzed, there were frequent attempts to call the transgressions "unnatural." Women gathering outside an air base is unnatural while the air base itself is almost natural—part of the system that protects and preserves England against unwelcome advances from communists everywhere. Similarly the graffiti on the subway in New York called into question assumptions about the "nature" of the subway and of New York City.

Conclusion

It is useful at this stage to summarize the ways place contributes to the efficacy of ideological strategies and thus to the creation and maintenance of ideological beliefs.

1. Place is a fundamental form of classification. Classification is a basic ideological mechanism. The classification of things by place structures our judgment of those things (objects, actions).
2. We differentiate through place between "us" and "them," "in" and "out," "high" and "low," "central" and "marginal." The process of differentiation through which "others" are created is a basic ideological mechanism.
3. Ideological beliefs, to be effective, must connect thought to action, theory to practice, the abstract to the concrete. Place, insofar as it is the material context of our lives, forces us to make interpretations and act accordingly. Place thus contributes to the creation and reproduction of action-oriented (ideological) beliefs.
4. Ideologies involve the removal of beliefs and actions from their social roots and their placement in the realm of "nature." The materiality of place gives it the aura of "nature." The "nature" of place can thus be offered as justification for particular views of what is good, just, and appropriate.

Place, then, plays an important role in the creation and continuation of ideological beliefs. The story, however, does not end here. It has been a feature of cultural studies and recent cultural geography that more attention has been given to challenges to ideological beliefs and, sometimes, transformations of them. Ideologies are not only created and maintained in some monolithic fashion; they are also challenged, resisted, and transgressed, leading to revisions, adaptations, and denunciations. It is in this spirit that this project has been tinged throughout with optimism about the power of human action. In each of my illustrations people acted against established norms of social-geographic behavior. Despite the formidable array of representations lined up against people such as Greenham women, "hippies," and graffitists, they have each had lasting effects. New York is now represented in Disneyland by bright and colorful graffiti, Greenham Common is associated with peace as much as with war, and Stonehenge is recognized as a site of festivities as well as a museum of the past. All of the transgressions left lasting impressions. Chambers has recently noted that

> the confusion of "place," of voices, histories and experiences speaking
> "out of place," forms part of the altogether more extended sense of
> contemporary semantic and political crisis. A previous order and
> organization of place, and their respective discourse, has had increasingly
> to confront an excess of languages emerging out of the histories and
> languages of feminism, sexual rights, ethnicity, race and the environment,
> that altogether undercut its authority.[29]

Indeed the arrangement of spaces and places can be thought of as a "metanarrative" — a text of established meanings. Parts of this narrative include monuments like Stonehenge, military sites like Greenham Common, and "world" cities like New York. All of these are easily recognizable parts of the "way things are," and they are intertwined in a continuing story about the modern world, about the West, about England, about freedom. Against this metanarrative are arrayed an increasingly diverse set of alternative stories and alternative places. Movements such as gay rights, feminism, ecological defense, and peace activism make up an increasingly complex set of voices discussing a plethora of previously unspoken issues and promoting new geographies. In addition, less politicized groups such as youth subcultures have frequently disobeyed the expectations that come along with place.

This book has not been a story of monolithic and unidirectional power over a huge, apparently stupid, majority by a small, smart elite. Although I have outlined the ways in which place is used to convey ideological values, there has been significant resistance to these processes. Just as place has features that make it useful in the manipulation of people, in the control of behavior, and in the creation of values, it also has features that make it efficacious as a site and object of struggle.

Chapter 7

Place, Transgression, and the Practice of Resistance

The fact that space and place are useful surrogates for more direct forms of power leads to an interesting, albeit unintended, consequence. Robert Sack has pointed out that, for a variety of reasons, space is often used to control people and things.[1] A father who wants to stop his restless child from breaking valuable plates can either explain in detail the problems that arise when small hands handle big plates, or he can, to the same effect, declare the kitchen a "no-go-zone." Capitalist bosses can control workers by controlling the space of production. Police can keep a watchful eye on activities at Stonehenge that might lead to damage, or they can simply ban any person who counts as a "hippy" from anywhere within an eight-mile radius of the monument. These strategies of power are relatively effective and simple. The unintended consequence, however, is to give space a heightened symbolic significance. If the child wants to deliberately make parents angry it is no longer necessary to break plates; she simply has to enter the forbidden zone of the kitchen. The workers, to frustrate the capitalists, no longer have to directly control the tools of production. It suffices to stage a sit-in on the factory grounds or to prevent scab labor from entering. Similarly the "hippies" no longer need to actually get to Stonehenge in order to upset the police; they simply have to enter the eight-mile radius. The unintended consequence of making space a means of control is to simultaneously make it a site of meaningful resistance.

Peter Stallybrass and Allon White have remarked on how surprising it is that the Greenham Common women could have such a powerful influence by camping outside an air base.[2] The contrast of the closed, monumental base and a small disordered group of women was a "scandal to hegemonic dignity." The women appeared to enter the base with ease. They often cut through the perimeter fence and danced on top of missile silos. Several women spent three hours inside the air traffic control tower without being noticed. These tactical forms of symbolic resistance were effective because of the value placed on territorial integrity. No site is more territorially organized than a military base, where every action during the day has its assigned place. Few symbols more clearly define a territory than rolls of barbed wire fence. For women to hold picnics inside the base and to dance on missile silos was a tremendous affront to and unintended consequence of the strict territoriality of the base. The territorial basis of control in the military world opened up novel forms of resistance for the women.

Similarly, the graffiti artist in New York could, intentionally or not, upset so many because of the territorial organization of New York into what Yi-Fu Tuan calls a "segmented world."[3] The graffitists were not actually harming anyone; they were marking surfaces with paint. Because of the fine division into "proper places," this in itself was a cause for alarm and was considered to be violence. Since spaces in New York had become surrogates for other forms of control and power, the marking of the spaces constituted a symbolically violent offense against the forces of property and order. Graffiti was a crime against place and against the forces that represented themselves through place. This is the story that Michel de Certeau recounts of the strategy and the tactic, the static and the mobile, the proper and the transgressive.[4] The tools of the weak are those which already exist as strategies of the strong. The father can declare and enforce territories in his house, while the child can only use these spaces tactically. Although graffitists are involved in territory-making in New York, they do not have the power to enforce it in the same way that the New York police do. The powerful in any given context can tabulate, build, and create spaces and places, while the relatively powerless can only "use, manipulate and divert these spaces."[5]

In short, the qualities of space and place that make them good strategic tools of power simultaneously make them ripe for resistance in highly visible and often outrageous ways. The creation of property leads to the existence of trespass. The notion of "in place" is logically related to the possibility of being "out of place."

Denaturalizing Place

While powerful groups may exploit the natural aspects of place, the resistant may point to its social aspects as a rejoinder. I have already suggested that a powerful ideological strategy is to "naturalize," to hide and obfuscate the social and the historical. "Deviant" groups can point (intentionally or otherwise) to the social aspects of place in order to denaturalize the claims of the powerful. This, in fact, is one of the few things that links someone like David Harvey to a "hippy" convoy. Harvey has sought to portray the sociohistorical roots of places and spaces in capitalism in order to "demystify" them. "Hippies" pointed out that the National Trust idea of Stonehenge is a recent and controversial view and that Stonehenge is intended for use. Equally they revealed the historic nature of property and rootedness by presenting alternatives.

I have already shown that place links ideas to actions in an ideological fashion and makes us all practical philosophers. Most of the time we obey taken-for-granted rules of place and the proper. By the repetition of our actions we reinforce the established norms of behavior in space. But since our behavior in space is linked to ideas, this behavior also has the seeds of rebellion in it.

A key event that occurred during the process of writing this book was the Chinese rebellion of students and workers at Tiananmen Square. Although the philosophy of the rebels was not systematically outlined, their actions told us a lot. The power of their protest was drawn from the official inappropriateness of their actions in that particular place. The square, normally, is a symbol of Communist China. It is a place where the military holds parades and people celebrate the revolution. Normally the behavior of people is perfectly matched to the ideas of order and "common sense" that have prevailed in that country. The continuous and repeated acts of people behaving themselves have contributed to the continuation of the ideas that are enshrined there. The actions of the students in this symbol of Maoist order (as opposed to some less symbolic street) became a powerful and moving protest against the particular "normality" of modern China.

What this example shows — and my illustrations show somewhat less dramatically — is the power of inappropriate actions. Action in space is, as I have already suggested, a reading of a text. Because the reading is particularly visible, heretical readings immediately draw attention to themselves. People acting "out of place" suggest different interpretations. If enough people follow suit, a whole new conception of "normality" may arise. In effect, the "reading" of people acting in space is also a kind of "writing" as new meanings are formed. The consumption of place becomes the production of place. Graffitists, by disobeying the expectations of place, provided a heretical reading of the subway. Eventually, after thousands upon thousands of names appeared across New York, Disney World decided to portray the whole of New York with a graffiti-covered train. The graffiti artists had (mis)read the city and produced a new one in its place. In the final pages of this book I examine the potentials and limits of this misreading. To what degree can transgression provide a blueprint — a dress rehearsal — for radical change?

The Uses and Limits of Transgression

Transgression, as I have defined it, depends on the preexistence of some form of spatial ordering. Forms of transgression owe their efficacy to types of space, place, and territory. Transgressions do not form their own orders. Boundaries are critiqued, not replaced. This observation is symptomatic of a bigger question—the question of construction versus deconstruction, creation versus critique. Resistance, deconstruction, criticism—all of these are reactions, hostages to wider events and topographies of power. Temporally they always come second or third. Transgression has limits. Constant transgression is permanent chaos.

Yet within transgression lie the seeds of new spatial orderings. Certainly within the transgressions of the Greenham women was the suggestion of a nonmilitaristic, nonpatriarchal, nonhierarchical way of life. Yet few would suggest that the peace campers' often horrendous living circumstances represent a model for all of us. The Greenham camp's existence was contingent on the air base and the missiles. Similarly, the existence of graffiti in New York's public spaces hinted at the possibility of a less authoritarian public space more reflective of polyvocal points of view. And yet it would, in my view, be foolish to put forward the lifestyle of the graffitist as the basis for the proverbial "revolution." And the travelers, too, had suggestions for new and different notions of sacred space, mobile lifestyles, and common rights to land. But I, for one, do not care to give up my comfortable house and resolutely immobile belongings for the traveling way of life.

Although all of these transgressions had utopian elements in their more articulate moments, none of them provide an "answer." They were all "making geography" but not in situations of their own choosing. They were often desperate *responses* to the power-laden imposition of norms and boundaries that they did not create. The lack of space for public expression, the militarization of society, and the existence of 10 percent unemployment and low-paying jobs are all elements of life that the transgressors did not choose and can only react to. In the absence of these conditions the transgressions, too, would disappear.

Given these limitations, what are the possibilities of transgression as a deliberate political strategy? To answer this question I will take you on a journey that starts in the specialized world of art and ends in the Paris Commune.

Transgression in Art

One area in which transgression has been used in subversive ways is in art. The traditions of the situationist international and dadaism are two examples.[6] More recently transgression has been used by British photographer Ingrid Pollard and Polish artist Krzysztof Wodiczko. Ingrid Pollard, a black British woman, has used her own body as a form of transgression into the landscape of the Lake District. Her works *Cost of the English Landscape* and *Pastoral Interlude* involve pictures of herself in the British landscape. When she enters the Lake District, the meaning of the landscape is brought into question. Her experience of the area is very different from mine as a teenager on holiday or from that of the members of ramblers' associations or fell runners. The "Englishness" that the landscape has been constructed to convey essentially ignores Pollard's existence. Black people in Britain (certainly more so than in the United States) are overwhelmingly associated with the inner city; their landscape is that of Brixton and Toxteth. The pictures of Pollard in the "natural" surroundings are thus startling.

Pollard's *Pastoral Interlude* is a series of prints of Pollard in the Lake District and other areas of rural beauty accompanied by text. The prints show Pollard in various typical hiking poses with the green scenery as a backdrop. The only surprising element is Pollard herself. The effect of seeing Pollard in the Lake District is heightened by the text, which links the history of the slave trade (and Britian's part in it) with her presence in the "green and pleasant land," presumed to be owned and used by a homogeneous white population. Pollard makes it clear that while others may feel relaxed in such an environment she feels a sense of unease and dread.

The prints of Pollard in the Lake District, Suffolk, Derbyshire, and Saint Andrews provoked a personal reaction in me of some surprise. I spent many hours hiking in the Lake District in my teenage years. My memories of it are good ones. Seeing Pollard's black face among the trees and sheep forced me to think back and search for other black faces. There were none. The image is startling. The prints and text prompted me to see the invisible and to think of the landscape as a topography that excluded.

Pollard conveys this exclusion in her photographic collages. In *Cost of the English Landscape* we see Pollard in the Lake District. In one shot she is rowing across a lake, in another she is walking down a footpath. In still another she stands on the deck of a boat among white tourists with the Union Jack flying in the background. These photographs appear to be simple holiday snapshots, much the same as those in family albums across the country.

On each side of the large collage are three larger prints arranged vertically showing Pollard climbing a style. Separating the prints are large signs that read Keep Out and No Trepass.

Interspersed with the snapshots are picture postcards and sections of topographic maps. Finally there are textual snapshots—pieces of text superimposed on the landscape. Some of these are quotes from the lakes' past by Wordsworth and references to Beatrix Potter and John Ruskin. Others are labels of anonymous origin saying "a chance to see the real Lake Country" and "a whole day of spectacular scenery." The final element of the collage is the representation of nuclear power. Superimposed on the topographic maps are red nuclear energy symbols. Overlaid on pictures of mountains with threatening clouds are the words "So what is radiation?" Among the picture postcards is one from the Nuclear Power Industry attempting to portray nuclear power in a "green" setting. The main elements are Pollard, the landscape, nuclear power, and the literary past.

The combined effect of the collage is to examine the meaning of this potent ideological landscape. Pollard takes this symbol of nationhood and nature that supposedly binds the British people together and reveals the usually invisible forces that keep people apart. On the one hand there are the hedged fields, sheep, and cottages and on the other are sites of nuclear power and a multinational population.

At first glance the red nuclear power warnings and references to Sellafield seem somewhat superfluous to Pollard's immediately apparent desire to examine the relations between the ideological landscape and race. The link, of course, is invisibility and danger. Radiation is invisible and fatal. Racism, too, is made invisible in a landscape that does not reveal its roots but sits like so much nature waiting for the camera's eye. Pollard makes the invisible visible from two angles and each complements the other. Pollard, through her juxtapositions and use of text, fractures the harmony of the famous land—she slips doubt into the fault lines of landscape representation and makes visible the taken-for-granted. She calls the effect of the landscape into question and asks us to assess the "cost."

Pollard's placing of her own black skin in the context of Britishness—her transgression of the Lake District—gives the landscape a heightened symbolic significance. She is clearly out of place—her transgression points to the possibilities of other interpretations. By entering the landscape, both figuratively and literally, she uses, manipulates, and diverts the meanings of this familiar landscape.

Until recently Pollard's art has been exhibited in art galleries. While the subject of her art has involved the transgression of familiar places, the presentation of her art has remained quite orthodox.[7] Most recently, though, an example of her work made to resemble a picture postcard has been displayed on twenty-five billboards around the British Isles. The project, titled *Wordsworth's Heritage,* includes four shots of the Lake District surrounding an oval within which the viewer sees Wordsworth's head. In each of the four photographs there are black people looking at maps and "enjoying nature." This project, displayed in urban areas, attempts to question the spaces in which art is consumed.

In the same vein Krzysztof Wodiczko is interested in going outside the art gallery and questioning the assumptions implicit in the urban environment.[8] As an artist Wodiczko is highly aware of the geographical nature of transgression. Much of his work involves the projection of images onto the walls of public buildings, memorials, and monuments. Examples of his art include the projections of missiles onto victory arches and columns, body parts of suited businessmen onto office blocks, and a swastika onto the South African embassy in London. In order to raise questions about the exclusion of homeless people in New York from public space, Wodiczko projected padlocks onto trendy SoHo art galleries. Art galleries do not usually advertise their own role in the displacement of low-cost housing. Under the cover of night he challenges the authority of these spaces. "The attack," he says, "must be unexpected, frontal, and must come with the night when the building, undisturbed by its daily functions, is asleep." The effect of the unexpected is to cause people to look again at the spaces he has temporarily defaced. Wodiczko knows that the spaces of the city give shape to ideology: "Superficially we resent the authority of its massive monumental structure . . . yet in our heart of hearts . . . we will allow ourselves to become intoxicated by its structural ability to embody, and to artistically grasp our intimate, unspoken drive for the disciplined collaboration with its power."[9] So he attacks these buildings with symbols, jarring our consciousness, making the familiar (and thus unnoticed) strange and worthy of attention. Finally, he knows the limits of transgression. He knows that his images shock us into a new, more conscious relationship with urban space. He also knows that these symbol attacks can only be temporary, for extended action would only result in the return of familiarity and neglect.

Both Pollard and Wodiczko take significant elements of the landscape and challenge them through transgression. Their strategies, however, illustrate the anterior nature of transgression. While Pollard assumes the history that made the English countryside mean what it does, Wodiczki's projections rely on the already existing meanings of monuments and urban spaces. Their work could not exist without the preexisting spaces they transgress.

Art into Protest

ACT-UP (Aids Coalition to Unleash Power) self-consciously connects the transgressions of art to more practical political protest. The best-known symbol of ACT-UP is the phrase SILENCE = DEATH (white on a black background) under a pink triangle pointing up. The triangle is an inversion of the pink triangle (pointing down) that gay men were forced to wear in Nazi concentration camps. The combined effect is to question the silence surrounding the issue of AIDS and the oppression of gay people. To wear a T-shirt bearing this symbol is to become visible in a landscape that most often ignores or conceals gay identity. The phrase "coming out" also points toward the issue of visibility in a homophobic environment. The SILENCE = DEATH symbol is highly provocative. It is a pink, black, and white statement that is hard to ignore. It is almost permanently "out of place" in its refusal to remain silent. No doubt it is a way of "fitting in" in gay or progressive enclaves, but it does not remain confined to these select places. It multiplies like a pop cultural icon and appears on people's bodies across the globe.

The SILENCE = DEATH symbol is but one aspect to ACT-UP's larger program of "appropriation art."[10] By appropriating already familiar symbols and styles, ACT-UP artists make a postmodern challenge to the idea of "originality" and "authorship." Instead they point toward the socially created nature of "the self" and suggest a Foucauldian creation of individuals through preexisting images and discourses. To gay people and people with AIDS this makes a good deal of sense, as their public identity often appears to be imposed by discourses that are out of their control. Much of ACT-UP's symbolism involves an appropriation of words and images used to label them as transgressive. The use of the pink triangle is mirrored in the use of the word "queer" as a signifier of pride and defiance.

Much appropriation art is more subtle. A public service announcement posted on city buses in San Francisco and New York showed well-dressed young couples kissing under the caption Kissing Doesn't Kill: Greed and Indifference Do. The poster was made to imitate the style of a Benetton ad, with the important difference that the kissing couples included lesbians and gay men. Again the preexisting symbolism added to the power of ACT-UP's statement.

Douglas Crimp describes how ACT-UP was in danger of being co-opted (as graffiti had been) by the institution of art:

> For AIDS activist artists, rethinking the identity and role of the artist also entails new considerations of audience. Postmodernist art advanced a political critique of art institutions—and art itself as an institution—for

the ways they constructed social relations through specific modes of address, representations of history, and obfuscations of power.[11]

Even the most politically critical postmodern art had been successfully institutionalized into chic reviews, catalogs, and exhibitions. ACT-UP participants, however, were activists first and artists second. Their designs have been used primarily as posters and T-shirts — as activist slogans and confrontations. ACT-UP art has sought to permanently transgress established boundaries. The point has been to remain loud and visible. To be reduced to a gallery exhibit would defeat this purpose.

Combined with ACT-UP's artistic visibility is an uncanny sense of political staging. Just as the group appropriates images, they subvert and appropriate places. The SILENCE = DEATH symbol is a constant subversion of place. Combined with this have been more specific place-based actions. ACT-UP's first major demonstration was at Wall Street on 24 March 1987. The point of the demonstration was to raise awareness about the price and availability of drugs to combat AIDS. The pharmaceutical company Burroughs-Wellcome had been granted a monopoly on the drug AZT, the only legal drug for AIDS treatment. The company had announced it would charge ten thousand dollars annually for treatment. To raise awareness of the normally hidden relationship between the drug industry and the Federal Drug Administration, ACT-UP activists hung an effigy of FDA commissioner Frank Young in front of Trinity Church. In addition they held up traffic for several hours by blocking the street and handing out broadsheets detailing the links between the drug industry, the government, and the price of drugs for AIDS patients. The demonstration made national news. Two and half years later (14 September 1989), a group of activists entered the New York Stock Exchange with fake name tags. Once inside they unfurled a huge banner that read Sell Wellcome, chained themselves to bannisters, and blew fog horns, which stopped trading on Wall Street for five minutes. Other ACT-UP activists successfully smuggled out film of the protest, and again the AIDS issue made headline news.

Another example of ACT-UP's political savvy was the use of Saint Patrick's Cathedral (see Figure 7.1). A presidential commission on the HIV epidemic visited New York to conduct hearings in February 1988. One member of the commission was Cardinal John O'Connor, a well-known homophobe and opponent of safe-sex education. ACT-UP held a protest at his church to raise awareness about O'Connor's positions and to protest the makeup of the Reagan-appointed commission. In December 1989 ACT-UP returned to the cathedral to protest O'Connor's recent opposition to a National Conference of Catholic Bishops' ruling

Figure 7.1. ACT-UP demonstration, Saint Patrick's Cathedral, New York City, 10 December 1989. (Photo by Ben Thornberry, from Douglas Crimp and Adam Rolston, *Aids Demo Graphics* [Seattle: Bay Press, 1990]. By permission.)

that condom use to curtail the AIDS epidemic might be tolerable. In an operation known as Stop the Church, several thousand people turned up while the cardinal was giving mass. Some played dead on the streets outside; others held banners saying Danger, Narrow-Minded Church Ahead and other inventive slogans. More controversially, demonstrators inside the church forced O'Connor to abandon his sermon by shouting, throwing condoms in the air, chaining themselves to pews, and playing dead in the aisles. The media portrayed the protest as a sacrilege. The protestors, the media argued, by entering the cathedral had gone too far. In the minds of ACT-UP, though, the protest was a success, as it kept the AIDS crisis in the spotlight. The preexisting meanings of Wall Street and Saint Patrick's Cathedral lent power to ACT-UP's message in much the same way as the pink triangle challenged the silence around AIDS and gay bashing. ACT-UP's art of appropriation extended the subversion of images and symbols to the symbolic aspects of place.

A Utopian Moment

As Kristin Ross has argued, the moment of the Paris Commune represented the brief existence of a "revolutionary urban space." The communards, in their seventy-three-day rebellion against the regimentations of the Second Empire in 1871, set out to deconstruct the sociospatial order of a strictly hierarchical Paris. The most obvious symbolic act in this attempt was the demolition of the Vendôme Column. The column was a monument to the victories of Napoleon's army. If it had been present in the 1980s it would have been a perfect target for one of Wodiczko's symbol attacks. The communards, lacking slide projectors, simply leveled the column (see Figure 7.2). The commune decree read:

> Considering that the imperial column at the Place Vendôme is a monument to barbarism, a symbol of brute force and glory, an affirmation of militarism, a negation of international law, a permanent insult to the vanquished by the victors, a perpetual assault on one of the three great principles of the French Republic, Fraternity, it is thereby decreed:
> Article One: The column at the Place Vendôme will be abolished.[12]

The anticommunard poet Catulle Mendès referred to the act of demolition as a "youthful prank," as though the communards were engaging in graffiti on New York's subway. Instead the demolition of the monument was just one — very visible — act to demolish the hierarchy of social space.

Another spatial symbol of the Commune was provided by the barricades. While the ill-fated monument at Vendôme was situated in a special and unique "proper place," the barricades were makeshift and spontaneous. They were made from whatever was available. Perfection in construction was of no concern. Ross describes the construction of the barricades as the "wrenching of everyday objects from their habitual context to be used in a radically different kind of way."[13] This reminds me of the

Figure 7.2. The Vendôme Column, five minutes before its fall. (Courtesy Bibliothèque Nationale, Paris.)

transgressions of the Greenham women, redecorating the barbed wire fence with everyday objects. The monumental perfection of the Vendôme Column is replaced, in the utopian moment of the commune, with the haphazard barricades, a more appropriate symbol for the communards.

The military tactics of the communards relied on constant mobility in order to confront and confuse the more stationary and orthodox republican army. One tactic was to "pierce" the houses alongside the streets so that communards could move between buildings. This involved making holes in the walls between buildings so that the communards could move freely in many directions while undercover. "Street fighting," Ross writes, "depends on mobility or permanent displacement. It depends on changing houses into passageways—reversing or suspending the division between public and private space ... the interior becomes a street."[14]

Superficially, these transgressions and reversals of established geographies do not seem to add up to much. They can be interpreted as more serious and ultimately deadly forms of graffiti. The net effect of these transformations or reversals of spatial expectancies, though, represents a sustained attempt to reinvent space and produce a permanent heretical geography. Recall that Paris was, and still is, the product of a grand piece of social and spatial engineering that excluded the urban proletariat from the public spaces of central Paris. The communards repossessed and transfigured this deliberate spatial order. In the process they created a new, nonhierarchical urban spatial order.

Conclusion—and Social Transformation?

What the journey from art to commune shows is the power of transgression. In each case individuals and groups sought to question and resist the "way things are" by (mis)using and appropriating already existing places and by crossing boundaries that often remain invisible. The effect of such actions ranges from causing art gallery visitors to think about their holidays in the Lake District to momentarily rearranging the oppressive spaces of Paris. In each case the existing landscape is brought into question and alternative ones are hinted at.

Each of these deliberate cultural-political protests exists in a parasitic relationship to an already powerful set of spaces and places. Pollard's art is effective because it appropriates the iconic power of the Lake District, ACT-UP gains national attention by subverting well-known meaningful buildings, and the communards' demolition of Vendôme is significant because of the already existing meanings of monumental Paris. These political acts divert and manipulate the power of established geographies.

While this is a source of strength, it is also transgression's main limit. Transgression's efficacy lies in the power of the established boundaries and spaces that it so heretically subverts. It is also limited by this established geography; it is always in reaction to topographies of power.

It is this problem that lies behind a significant tension in cultural politics—between the aim to shock and critique and the need to appear sensible and to be taken seriously. The crossing of established sociogeographical boundaries upsets the status quo and appears shocking. It is perceived as grotesque, as threatening, and as deviant. The power of transgression lies in its ability to reveal topographies of power that surround us. The limits to transgression lie in the fact that it is not enough to constantly deconstruct and destabilize.

During the writing of this book many transgressions occurred that have become iconic in recent political history—the social transformations of Eastern Europe in 1989, the students in Tiananmen Square, the destruction of the Berlin Wall, the shelling and rebuilding in marble of the "white house" in Moscow. Such events reveal the continuing power of transgression. They also point beyond transgression to the possibilities of social transformation. The transgressions of the Paris communards transformed Paris for seventy-three days. What happens when transgression becomes permanent? Successful social transformation is the culmination of transgression and is grounded in the spatiality of everyday life. Just as the power of the territory and of the strategy is profoundly sociospatial, so the resistance of the tactic and of the transgression combines the social and spatial in a fundamental way. Any social transformation, to be successful, has to be understood as a spatial transformation. The irreducible spatiality of transgression forces us to accept this. The French Revolution, like the Commune, involved creative acts of transgression that were central to its success. Carnival, for instance, was a tactical ploy of the revolutionaries.[15] The carnivalesque transgressions of the revolutionaries culminated in social tranformation, and a new game board was formed upon which further transgressions would inevitably occur. The Paris uprisings of 1968 attempted to transgress and thus change the board once again with the assertion that beneath the paving stones lay the beach.

Social transformation usually implies an end state—a utopian dream. Trangression, on the other hand, can only play on the ephemeral. Wodiczko understands this well, limiting his terrorist projections to short nocturnal moments. Wodiczko is concerned that his projections not become part of the scenery—things that themselves demand transgression. Monuments are the stuff of imagined eternities, while transgressions demand temporality. Writing about his projections, Wodiczko wrote: "Warning: Slide projectors must be switched off before the image loses its impact and becomes vulnerable to the appropriation by the building as decoration."[16] As parts of the Berlin Wall enter museums and theme parks around the world, this warning should be applied to the dreams of transformation within the simplest of transgressions. The new social spaces that result from the transgression of old social spaces will themselves become old social spaces pregnant with the possibility of transgression.

Notes

CHAPTER 1. INTRODUCTION

1. G. Therborn, *The Ideology of Power and the Power of Ideology* (London: Routledge, 1980), 19.

2. My use of the word *place* continues a tradition in geography originating in the rather idealist formulations of humanistic geography. I wish to maintain the emphasis on subjectivity that these studies insisted upon and have therefore used the word *place* rather than "social space." That said, my insistence on the social nature of place meaning resonates with the work of Henri Lefebvre, who uses the term *social space* to great effect in *The Production of Space* (Oxford: Blackwell, 1991). Pierre Bourdieu also writes of "social space," but appears to use it in an almost entirely metaphorical way (see Bourdieu, "The Social Space and the Genesis of Groups," *Theory and Society* 14 [November 1985]: 723–44).

3. By "ideology" I mean "meaning in the service of power." I return to this concept in chapter 2.

4. Ed Koch, quoted in R. Deutsche, "Uneven Development: Public Art in New York City," *October* 47 (1988): 5.

5. See Deutsche, ibid., for an in-depth analysis of this event.

6. P. Williams, *The Alchemy of Race and Rights* (Cambridge, Mass.: Harvard University Press, 1991), 58–59.

7. *New York Times*, 24 December 1986, quoted in ibid., 67.

8. For a detailed analysis of the legal proceedings at New Bedford, see K. Bumiller, "Fallen Angels: The Representation of Violence against Women in Legal Culture," in M. A. Fineman and N. S. Thomadson, eds., *At the Boundaries of Law: Feminism and Legal Theory* (New York: Routledge, 1991), 95–111.

9. This story is told by A. Sacharov, "All the World's (Literally) a Stage for Theater of the Oppressed," *In These Times*, 6–12 May 1992, 20. See also M. Schutzman and J. Cohen-Cruz, eds., *Playing Boal: Theatre, Therapy, Activism* (London: Routledge, 1994).

10. P. Bourdieu, *Outline of a Theory of Practice* (Cambridge: Cambridge University Press, 1977).

11. Ibid., 163.

CHAPTER 2. GEOGRAPHY, IDEOLOGY, AND TRANSGRESSION

1. See D. Massey, *Spatial Divisions of Labour* (London: Macmillan, 1984), 52.

2. N. Smith, *Uneven Development: Nature, Capital, and the Production of Space* (Oxford: Blackwell, 1984); E. Soja, *Postmodern Geographies* (London: Verso, 1989); R. Sack, *Human Territoriality: Its Theory and History* (Cambridge: Cambridge University Press, 1986); D. Harvey, *The Condition of Postmodernity* (Oxford: Blackwell, 1989).

3. See D. Cosgrove and P. Jackson, "New Directions in Cultural Geography," *Area* 19, no. 2 (1987): 95–101; P. Jackson, *Maps of Meaning* (Boston: Allen and Unwin, 1989); D. Cosgrove, "Towards a Radical Cultural Geography," *Antipode* 15, no. 1 (1983): 1–11; S. Daniels, "Marxism, Culture and the Duplicity of Landscape," in N. Thrift and R. Peet, eds., *New Models in Geography*, vol. 2 (Boston: Allen and Unwin, 1990).

4. See L. Grossberg, C. Nelson, and P. Treichler, eds., *Cultural Studies* (London: Routledge, 1992); S. Hall et al., eds., *Culture, Media, Language* (London: Hutchinson, 1980).

5. See R. Williams, "Base and Superstructure in Marxist Cultural Theory," *New Left Review* 82 (1973).

6. See J. Duncan, "The Superorganic in American Cultural Geography," *Annals of the Association of American Geographers* 70 (1980): 181–91.

7. But see the essays in K. Anderson and F. Gale, eds., *Inventing Places: Studies in Cultural Geography* (Cheshire: Longman, 1992).

8. For humanistic reactions, see Yi-Fu Tuan, *Space and Place: The Perspective of Experience* (Minneapolis: University of Minnesota Press, 1977); E. Relph, *Place and Placelessness* (London: Pion Press, 1976); and J. N. Entrikin, *The Betweenness of Place* (London: Macmillan, 1991). For radical reactions, see J. Agnew, *Place and Politics* (Boston: Allen and Unwin, 1987); J. Agnew and J. Duncan, eds., *The Power of Place* (Boston: Unwin Hyman, 1990); and R. Shields, *Places on the Margin* (London: Routledge, 1991).

9. J. Duncan, *The City as Text: The Politics of Landscape Interpretation in the Kandyan Kingdom* (Cambridge: Cambridge University Press, 1990); T. Barnes and J. Duncan, eds., *Writing Worlds: Discourse, Text and Metaphor in the Representation of Landscape* (London: Routledge, 1992); H. Moore, *Space, Text and Gender* (Cambridge: Cambridge University Press, 1986).

10. Therborn, *Ideology of Power*, 15.

11. J. B. Thompson, *Ideology and Modern Culture* (Cambridge: Polity Press, 1990).

12. Therborn, *Ideology of Power*, 25.

13. I do not mean to suggest that the taken-for-granted idea of "position" is unproblematic. See N. Smith and C. Katz, "Grounding Metaphor: Towards a Spatialized Poetics," in M. Keith and S. Pile, eds., *Place and the Politics of Identity* (London: Routledge, 1993), 67–83.

14. For important discussions of practice, see Moore, *Space, Text and Gender*; P. Bourdieu, *Outline of a Theory of Practice* (Cambridge: Cambridge University Press, 1977); M. de Certeau, *The Practice of Everyday Life* (Berkeley: University of California Press, 1984).

15. For an innovative "dramaturgical" approach to the role of place in defining the appropriate, see E. Goffman, *The Presentation of Self in Everyday Life* (New York: Overlook Press, 1973) and *Asylums* (New York: Anchor, 1961).

16. D. Hebdige, *Subculture: The Meaning of Style* (London: Routledge, 1979), 12–13; emphasis in original.

17. A. Gramsci, *Prison Notebooks* (London: Lawrence and Wishart, 1973); R. Williams, *Culture* (London: Fontana, 1981).

18. Bourdieu's ideas in many ways resemble Antonio Gramsci's conception of hegemony. Gramsci's ideas have been well covered in geography and cultural studies. See, for instance, Jackson, *Maps of Meaning*, and J. Burgess and J. Gold, eds., *Geography, the Media and Popular Culture* (London: Croom Helm, 1985).

19. P. Bourdieu, *Distinction: A Social Critique of the Judgment of Taste* (Cambridge, Mass.: Harvard University Press, 1984), 468.

20. Bourdieu, *Outline*, 164; emphasis in original.

21. Bourdieu, *Distinction*, 471.

22. Bourdieu, *Outline*, 166.

23. Bourdieu, *Distinction*, 480.

24. H. Garfinkel, *Studies in Ethnomethodology* (Englewood Cliffs, N.J.: Prentice Hall, 1967).

25. G. Canguilhem, *The Normal and the Pathological* (New York: Zone Books, 1989).

26. J. C. Scott, *Weapons of the Weak: Everyday Forms of Peasant Resistance* (New Haven, Conn.: Yale University Press, 1985), 290.

27. H. S. Becker, *Outsiders: Studies in the Sociology of Deviance* (New York: Free Press, 1963), 9; emphasis in original.

28. See C. Castleman, *Getting Up* (Cambridge, Mass.: MIT Press, 1982); R. Lachmann, "Graffiti as Career and Ideology," *American Journal of Sociology* 94, no. 2 (1988): 229–50.

29. D. Sibley, *Outsiders in Urban Society* (New York: St. Martin's Press, 1981). See also J. Okely, *Gypsy-Travellers* (Cambridge: Cambridge University Press, 1983).

30. Hebdige, *Subculture*.

31. See J. Burgess, "News from Nowhere: The Press, the Riots and the Myth of the Inner City," in Burgess and Gold, eds., *Geography, the Media and Popular Culture*; J. Hartley, *Understanding News* (London: Methuen, 1982); S. Hall, "Culture, the Media and the 'Ideological' Effect," in J. Curran, M. Gurevitch, and J. Wollacott, eds., *Mass Communication and Society* (London: Edward Arnold, 1977), 315–49.

32. H. Lefebvre, *The Production of Space* (Oxford: Blackwell, 1991), 56.

CHAPTER 3. HERETICAL GEOGRAPHY 1

1. See K. Auletta, *The Streets Were Paved with Gold* (New York: Random House, 1974); W. K. Tabb, *The Long Default: New York City and the Urban Fiscal Crisis* (New York: Monthly Review Press, 1982).

2. Quoted in Tabb, *Long Default*, 42.

3. Ibid., 31.

4. *New York Times*, 21 July 1971, 37.

5. See *New York Times*, 26 January 1973, 39.

6. An excellent pictorial report on New York subway graffiti is given by M. Cooper and H. Chalfant, *Subway Art* (New York: Holt, Rinehart and Winston, 1984).

7. See C. Castleman, *Getting Up* (Cambridge, Mass.: MIT Press, 1982) for an excellent extended description of the subway graffiti world.

8. *New York Times*, 28 March 1973, 51; and 14 January 1973, 14.

9. *New York Times*, 7 August 1975, 29.

10. See *New York Times*, 8 December 1972, 49.

11. Ibid.

12. Quoted in Castleman, *Getting Up*, 119.

13. *New York Times*, 16 September 1973, 27.

14. For wide discussions of SoHo, gentrification, and the art world, see S. Zukin, *Loft Living: Culture and Capital in Urban Change* (Baltimore, Md.: Johns

Hopkins University Press, 1982), and B. Wallis, ed., *If You Lived Here* (Seattle: Bay Press, 1991).

15. H. Foster, *Recodings: Art, Spectacle, Cultural Politics* (Seattle: Bay Press, 1985), 108.

16. *New York Times*, 30 June 1975, 28.

17. *New York Times*, 21 May 1972, 66.

18. Castleman, *Getting Up*, 177.

19. M. Douglas, *Purity and Danger* (London: Routledge, 1966), 36.

20. J. Kristeva, *The Powers of Horror* (New York: Columbia University Press, 1983), 69.

21. Ibid.

22. *New York Times*, 15 September 1972, 41.

23. *New York Times*, 30 June 1973, 13.

24. S. Stewart, "Ceci tuera cela: Graffiti as Crime and Art," in J. Fekete, ed., *Life after Postmodernism* (New York: St. Martin's Press, 1987), 169.

25. *New York Times*, 26 November 1972, sec. 7, 1.

26. *New York Times*, 16 September 1973, 27.

27. *New York Daily News*, 6 May 1973, 33.

28. *New York Daily News*, 18 August 1974, 3.

29. Quoted in P. Hagopian, "Reading the Undecipherable: Graffiti and Hegemony," *Polygraph* 1 (1988): 106.

30. Yi-Fu Tuan, *Landscapes of Fear* (New York: Pantheon, 1979).

31. F. Driver, "Moral Geographies: Social Science and the Urban Environment in Mid-Nineteenth Century England," *Transactions of the Institute of British Geographers*, n.s., 13 (1988): 277.

32. Ibid., 278.

33. Ibid., 279; see also D. Ward, *Poverty, Ethnicity and the American City, 1840–1925* (Cambridge: Cambridge University Press, 1989), and K. Anderson, "Cultural Hegemony and the Race Definition Process in Chinatown," *Environment and Planning D: Society and Space* 6, no. 2 (1988): 127–50.

34. S. Sontag, *AIDS and Its Metaphors* (New York: Farrar, Straus and Giroux, 1988).

35. M. Foucault, *Madness and Civilization: A History of Insanity in the Age of Reason* (London: Tavistock, 1967).

36. *New York Times*, 29 August 1972, 66.

37. *New York Times,* 5 June 1972, 32; and 28 September 1972, 46.

38. R. Rosenblatt, quoted in Hagopian, "Reading," 105.

39. N. Mailer, quoted in Hagopian, "Reading," 106.

40. N. Glazer, "On Subway Graffiti in New York," *Public Interest* 54 (1979): 4.

41. See Castleman, *Getting Up,* and Chalfant and Cooper, *Subway Art.*

42. C. Oldenburg, quoted in Castleman, *Getting Up,* 142.

43. This story is told by Hagopian, "Reading."

44. R. Rosenblatt, quoted in ibid., 109.

45. See Anderson, "Cultural Hegemony."

46. S. Laws, *Issues of Blood: The Politics of Menstruation* (London: Macmillan, 1990), 36.

47. Charles Brace, quoted in Ward, *Poverty, Ethnicity,* 16.

48. Ibid.

49. Ward shows that while the perception of immigrant and working-class life in the slums of New York may have been one of filth and disorder, their actual lifestyles were often very ordered and sanitary (*Poverty, Ethnicity,* 79–82). Similarly the graffiti artists are perceived as chaotic and spontaneous while they maintain a very strict order and hierarchy within their own world. One type of order does not recognize another type of order and calls it disorder.

50. F. Fanon, *The Wretched of the Earth* (Harmondsworth: Penguin, 1963). See also Fanon, *Black Skin, White Masks* (New York: Grove Press, 1967).

51. In conflicts between the United States and third world upstarts, the enemy is frequently portrayed in terms of irrationality. Qaddafi was called the "Mad Dog." In the recent Gulf conflict, the "bad" country (Iraq) was often represented in terms of strangeness and madness, while a "good" country (Egypt) was referred to simply as "Western," implying reason and good sense.

52. *New York Times,* 25 August 1972, 30.

53. Atlanta and Alexander, "Wild Style: Graffiti Painting," in A. McRobbie, ed., *Zoot Suits and Second-Hand Dresses* (Boston: Unwin Hyman, 1988), 166.

54. Stewart, "Ceci tuera cela," 168.

55. Rosenblatt, quoted in Hagopian, "Reading," 105.

56. Stewart, "Ceci tuera cela," 168; my emphasis.

57. For discussions of graffiti as art, see S. Gablik, *Has Modernism Failed?* (New York: Thames and Hudson, 1984); and H. Foster, *Recodings: Art, Spectacle, Cultural Politics* (Seattle: Bay Press, 1985).

58. Stewart, "Ceci tuera cela," 173.

59. Hagopian, "Reading."

60. Atlanta and Alexander, "Wild Style," 163–64.

61. Quoted in Stewart, "Ceci tuera cela," 172.

62. Norman Mailer, quoted in ibid., 173.

63. Atlanta and Alexander, "Wild Style," 166.

64. P. Stallybrass and A. White, *The Politics and Poetics of Transgression* (Ithaca, N.Y.: Cornell University Press, 1987), 2.

65. Ibid., 3–4.

66. E. Said, *Orientalism* (New York: Vintage, 1979).

67. Stallybrass and White, *Politics and Poetics,* 126.

68. Ibid., 5–6.

69. Ibid., 5.

70. A. Bonnett, "Art, Ideology and Everyday Space: Subversive Tendencies from Dada to Postmodernism," *Environment and Planning D: Society and Space* 10 (1992): 69–86.

71. P. Osborne, quoted in Bonnett, "Art, Ideology," 70.

72. See Wallis, *If You Lived Here.*

73. R. Williams, *Culture* (London: Grenada, 1981), 13.

74. R. Williams, *Marxism and Literature* (Oxford: Oxford University Press, 1978), 113.

75. Stewart, "Ceci tuera cela," 170.

76. Lee, quoted in Atlanta and Alexander, "Wild Style," 166.

CHAPTER 4. HERETICAL GEOGRAPHY 2

1. As with other chapters I focus on representations here. For ethnographic material based on the words of the travelers themselves, see R. Lowe and W. Shaw, *Travellers: Voices of the New Age Nomads* (London: Fourth Estate, 1993).

2. *Daily Mail,* 28 July 1992, 6–7.

3. *Daily Mail,* 30 July 1992, 6.

4. My major sources for the ideas expressed here are S. Hall et al., *Policing the Crisis: Mugging, the State, and Law and Order* (New York: Holmes and Meier, 1978); S. Cohen, *Folk Devils and Moral Panics: The Creation*

of Mods and Rockers (London: MacGibbon and Kee, 1972); and S. Hall, *The Hard Road to Renewal: Thatcherism and the Crisis of the Left* (London: Verso, 1988).

5. There is a danger of assigning a whole set of ideas to one symbolic figure. Thatcher was certainly not the only person responsible for the values of the eighties. "Thatcherism" is a broad term widely used to describe those values.

6. Hall, *Hard Road,* 23.

7. Ibid., 25.

8. Ibid., 36.

9. Ibid., 37.

10. *Guardian,* 23 May 1986.

11. The convoy members did not refer to themselves as hippies. The use of this term by the media in itself suggests to the reader young, lazy, drug-taking, relatively privileged adolescents. In the youth subculture of 1980s Britain few people would call themselves "hippies." In this chapter I refer to the participants as travelers, festival-goers, or "hippies" (in quotation marks).

12. *Daily Telegraph,* 4 June 1985, 5.

13. P. Vincent-Jones, "Private Property and Public Order: The Hippy Convoy and Criminal Trespass," *Journal of Law and Society* 13, no. 3 (1986): 343–70.

14. *Times* (London), 21 June 1991, 14.

15. C. Chippindale, *Stonehenge Complete* (Leipzig: Thames and Hudson, 1983), 20.

16. quoted in ibid., 25.

17. From William Wordsworth, "Guilt and Sorrow," quoted in ibid., 98.

18. Chippindale, *Stonehenge,* 253.

19. Helen O'Neil, quoted in ibid., 255.

20. Ibid.

21. C. Rojek, "The Convoy of Pollution," *Leisure Studies* 7 (1988): 26.

22. P. Bourdieu, *Distinction: A Social Critique of the Judgment of Taste* (Cambridge, Mass.: Harvard University Press, 1984), 6.

23. Ibid., 7.

24. M. Bakhtin, *Rabelais and His World* (Bloomington: Indiana University Press).

25. See Rojek, "Convoy."

26. Ibid., 28.

27. J. Wilson, *Politics and Leisure* (London: Unwin Hyman, 1988), 28.

28. Ibid., 21.

29. Rojek, "Convoy," 28.

30. See *Guardian*, 9 June 1986, 1, 30.

31. *Sun*, 7 June 1986, 4, 5.

32. *Daily Telegraph*, 4 June 1986, 1, 36.

33. *Daily Mail*, 31 May 1986, 2.

34. *Daily Telegraph*, 27 May 1986, 1.

35. *Guardian*, 25 June 1986, 5.

36. *Guardian*, 23 May 1986, 3.

37. *Daily Telegraph*, 23 May 1986, 5.

38. *Daily Mail*, 1 June 1986, 2.

39. *Guardian*, 29 May 1986, 1.

40. Telegram from landowners to Thatcher, quoted in *Daily Telegraph*, 4 June 1986, 1, 36.

41. *Daily Telegraph*, 3 June 1986, 1.

42. *Daily Telegraph*, 28 May 1986, 20.

43. *Daily Mail*, 1 June 1986, 1.

44. *Daily Mirror*, 27 May 1986, 16.

45. *Manchester Guardian*, 31 May 1986, 4.

46. See G. L. Mosse, *Nazi Culture: Intellectual, Cultural and Social Life in the Third Reich* (New York: Grosset and Dunlap, 1966).

47. C. A. Berry, *Gentlemen of the Road* (London: Constable, 1978).

48. D. P. Singhal, *Gypsies: Indians in Exile* (Berkeley, Calif.: Folklore Institute, 1982).

49. D. Sibley, *Outsiders in Urban Society* (New York: St. Martin's Press, 1981), 19.

50. P. Archard, "Vagrancy: A Literature Review," in *Vagrancy: Some New Perspectives*, ed. T. Cook (New York: Academic Press, 1979).

51. J. Okely, *The Traveller-Gypsies* (Cambridge: Cambridge University Press, 1983), 9.

52. Ibid., 89.

53. Sibley, *Outsiders*, 38–39.

54. *Sun*, 7 June 1986, 6.

55. *Daily Telegraph*, 10 June 1986, 1.

56. *Daily Mirror*, 2 June 1986, 4.

57. *Daily Mirror*, 10 June 1986, 4–5.

58. *Daily Mirror*, 30 June 1986, 23.

59. *Sun*, 7 June 1986, 4–5.

60. *Daily Mirror*, 30 June 1986, 23.

61. *Sun*, 4 June 1986, 6.

62. *Daily Telegraph*, 28 May 1986, 20.

63. *Daily Telegraph*, 5 June 1986, 18.

64. *Sun*, 30 June 1986, 4. Here we see the distinction between people who can trespass and people who can't. The distinction rests on ideas of "normal leisure," as defined by Rojek, "Convoy." Rambling and bird-watching, we can assume, are "healthy" leisure activities and are thus excused from the laws of property.

65. Vincent-Jones, "Private Property," 354.

66. Ibid., 345.

67. Ibid., 348.

68. Vincent-Jones shows that none of these claims are true and some are just the opposite. For instance, 71 percent of squatters improved properties rather than destroyed them, and the great majority of squatters were motivated by necessity.

69. *South London Press*, 24 January 1975, quoted in Vincent-Jones, "Private Property," 351.

70. *Daily Telegraph*, 16 July 1975, quoted in Vincent-Jones, ibid.

71. Vincent-Jones, ibid., 352.

72. *Daily Mirror*, 27 May 1986, 16.

73. *Daily Mail*, 7 June 1986, 3.

74. *Sun*, 3 June 1986, 6.

75. *Daily Mail*, 28 May 1986, 6.

76. *Sun*, 9 June 1986, 2.

77. Agriculture Minister John Gummer, quoted in *Daily Mirror*, 27 May 1986, 16.

78. Vincent-Jones, "Private Property," 353.

79. Sir Havers claimed that he did not know of any homes being left empty for long periods, at a time when there were 700,000 empty homes in England.

80. Bowden, quoted in Vincent-Jones, "Private Property," 356.

81. Mellors, quoted in ibid., 362.

82. Bourdieu, *Distinction*, 7.

83. *Daily Mail*, 28 May 1986, 6.

CHAPTER 5. HERETICAL GEOGRAPHY 3

1. C. Blackwood, *On the Perimeter* (Harmondsworth: Penguin, 1984), 10.

2. G. Brett, *Through Our Own Eyes* (London: New Society Press, 1986), 134.

3. Blackwood, *On the Perimeter*, 3.

4. See J. Liddington, *The Long Road to Greenham* (London: Virago, 1988).

5. Quoted in A. Young, *Femininity in Dissent* (London: Routledge, 1990), 16.

6. *Daily Standard*, 2 December 1981, quoted in L. Jones, "Perceptions of 'Peace Women' at Greenham Common, 1981–85: A Participant's View," in *Images of Women in Peace and War*, ed. S. MacDonald, P. Holden, and S. Ardener (Madison: University of Wisconsin Press, 1987), 179–201, at 181.

7. Brett, *Through Our Own Eyes*, 139.

8. I do not mean to imply that these varied and different groups were in complete agreement. They were united, however, by their opposition to nuclear weapons.

9. See Young, *Femininity*, for a full description of the government-press relationship.

10. See L. Krasniewicz, *Nuclear Summer: The Clash of Communities at the Seneca Women's Peace Encampment* (Ithaca, N.Y.: Cornell University Press, 1992).

11. Jones, "Perceptions of 'Peace Women' "; for Young, see n. 5.

12. *Daily Mail*, 13 December 1982, 17.

13. *Sunday Telegraph*, 19 December 1982.

14. Michael McNair-Wilson, MP, House of Commons, 25 July 1986.

15. *Daily Express*, 11 January 1983.

16. Blackwood, *On the Perimeter*, 50.

17. *Daily Express*, 2 June 1983, 6.

18. *Daily Mail,* 14 November 1983, 7.

19. *Daily Mail,* 16 February 1983, 18.

20. *Guardian,* 2 June 1983, 6.

21. *Daily Mail,* 14 November 1983, 7.

22. *Daily Telegraph,* 3 May 1984, 18.

23. A. Corbin, *The Foul and the Fragrant* (Cambridge, Mass.: Harvard University Press, 1986).

24. J. Kristeva, *Powers of Horror: An Essay on Abjection* (New York: Columbia University Press, 1983), 71.

25. See S. Laws, *Issues of Blood: The Politics of Menstruation* (London: Macmillan, 1990), and L. Lander, *Images of Bleeding: Menstruation as Ideology* (New York: Orlando Press, 1988).

26. M. Douglas, quoted in Laws, *Issues,* 17.

27. Ibid., 30.

28. Ibid., 42.

29. A man discussing menstruation in ibid., 44.

30. Laws, *Issues,* 45.

31. E. Martin, "Science and Women's Bodies: Forms of Anthropological Knowledge," in M. Jacobus et al., eds., *Body/Politics: Women and the Discourses of Science* (London: Routledge, 1990), 69–82. Interestingly, the words used to describe sperm production were more likely to be "remarkable," "amazing," and "sheer magnitude."

32. Ibid., 80.

33. Blackwood, *On the Perimeter,* 64.

34. See D. Ward, *Poverty, Ethnicity and the American City, 1840–1925* (Cambridge: Cambridge University Press, 1989); K. Anderson, "Cultural Hegemony and the Race Definition Process in Chinatown," *Environment and Planning D: Society and Space* 6, no. 2 (1988): 127–50.

35. Brett, *Through Our Own Eyes,* 146.

36. Ibid., 146.

37. J. Berger, *Ways of Seeing* (Harmondsworth: Penguin, 1972).

38. *Times,* 10 December 1982; *Sunday Telegraph,* 19 December 1982; *International Herald Tribune,* 11 January 1983.

39. *Times,* 10 December 1982.

40. *Sun,* 7 November 1983, 9.

41. *Daily Mirror,* 11 July 1983.

42. *Daily Mail,* 12 March 1983.

43. *Daily Mirror,* 11 July 1983. For a thorough engagement with the anxiety produced by clothing out of place, see M. Garber, *Vested Interests: Cross Dressing and Cultural Anxiety* (London: Routledge, 1992).

44. *Daily Mail,* 8 January 1983, 11.

45. *Daily Mirror,* 24 February 1983, 9.

46. Blackwood, *On the Perimeter,* 26, 115.

47. *Daily Express,* 11 January 1983; *Daily Mail,* 2 June 1983, 8; *Daily Telegraph,* 7 January 1983, 3.

48. *Daily Mail,* 11 May 1983.

49. *Sun,* 26 February 1983; *Daily Express,* 9 March 1983; *Guardian,* 2 June 1983, 6.

50. *Daily Telegraph,* 13 December 1982, 1.

51. *Daily Telegraph,* 19 December 1982.

52. *Sun,* 19 November 1983, 23.

53. *Sun,* 7 November 1983, 9; *Daily Mirror,* 11 July 1983, 6–7.

54. Blackwood, *On the Perimeter,* 65–66.

55. *Daily Mail,* 13 January 1983, 16–17.

56. Quoted in Young, *Femininity,* 74–75.

57. *Daily Telegraph,* 3 May 1984, 18; *Daily Mail,* 1 February 1983, 6; *Daily Mail,* 9 December 1983, 10.

58. *Daily Mirror,* 11 July 1983, 6–7; *Daily Mail,* 8 January 1983, 1; *Daily Express,* 9 March 1983; *Sunday Telegraph,* 19 December 1982; *Daily Mail,* 15 February 1983, 22.

59. *Daily Mail,* 2 November 1983, 2.

60. *Sun,* 7 November 1983, 9.

61. *Sun,* 16 November 1983.

62. Young, *Femininity,* 84.

63. Blackwood, *On the Perimeter,* 3.

64. Young, *Femininity,* 97.

65. *Daily Mail,* 11 May 1983; *Daily Mirror,* 11 July 1983, 6–7.

66. P. Stallybrass, and A. White, *The Politics and Poetics of Transgression* (Ithaca, N.Y.: Cornell University Press, 1986), 143.

67. *Daily Mail,* 2 April 1983; *Daily Telegraph,* 12 December 1983, 28.

68. *Times,* 17 February 1983.

69. *Daily Telegraph,* 4 January 1983, 3; 23 February 1983, 3.

70. *Daily Telegraph,* 11 March 1983, 1.

71. *Daily Express,* 16 April 1983.

72. *Daily Telegraph,* 18 January 1983, 1.

73. R. Darnton, *The Great Cat Massacre and Other Episodes in French Cultural History* (New York: Basic Books, 1984), 83.

74. See P. Burke, *Popular Culture in Early Modern Europe* (London: Temple Smith, 1978); M. Gluckman, *Custom and Conflict in Africa* (Oxford: Blackwell, 1956); M. Ozouf, *Festivals and the French Revolution* (Cambridge, Mass.: Harvard Univeristy Press, 1989); G. Pearson, *Hooligan: A History of Respectable Fears* (London: Macmillan, 1983).

75. P. Jackson, *Maps of Meaning* (London: Routledge, 1989), 80.

76. M. Bakhtin, *Rabelais and His World* (Bloomington: Indiana University Press, 1984), 7.

77. Ibid., 9.

78. Brett, *Through Our Own Eyes,* 132.

79. Barbara Babcock, quoted in Stallybrass and White, *Politics and Poetics,* 17.

80. Bakhtin, *Rabelais,* 3.

81. Brett, *Through Our Own Eyes,* 152.

82. But see also Burke, *Popular Culture*; J. S. McIntyre, *Rituals of Disorder: A Dramatistic Interpretation of Radical Dissent,* Journalism Monographs 112 (Columbia, S.C.: Association for Education in Journalism and Mass Communication, 1989); Jackson, *Maps*; M. D. Bristol, *Carnival and Theatre: Plebian Culture and the Structure of Authority in Renaissance England* (New York: Routledge, 1985).

83. Bakhtin, *Rabelais,* 10.

84. Stallybrass and White, *Politics and Poetics,* 7.

85. Bakhtin, *Rabelais,* 5–6.

86. Stallybrass and White, *Politics and Poetics,* 24–25.

87. Young, *Femininity,* 36–37.

88. T. Eagleton, *Walter Benjamin: Towards a Revolutionary Criticism* (London: Verso, 1981), 148.

89. Gluckman, *Custom,* 109.

90. U. Eco, *Travels in Hyperreality* (New York: Harcourt Brace Jovanovitch, 1986).

91. L. Ladurie, *Carnival at Romans* (New York: Braziller, 1979), 192.

92. Bristol, *Carnival.*

93. Ozouf, *Festivals,* makes a compelling argument that festivals of all kinds actually played a central role in the transformation of France during the French revolution.

94. Stallybrass and White, *Politics and Poetics,* 14.

95. Parliamentary Debates, 1983.

96. Blackwood, *On the Perimeter,* 84.

97. Ibid., 98.

98. Ibid., 90.

99. Quoted in Blackwood, *On the Perimeter,* 92.

100. *Daily Mail,* 1 February 1983, 6.

101. D. Lowenthal, and H. Prince, "English Landscape Tastes," *Geographical Review* 55, no. 2 (1965): 198.

102. Ibid., 200.

103. Ibid., 187.

104. I. Chambers, *Border Dialogue* (London: Routledge, 1990), 32–33.

105. S. Daniels, "Marxism, Culture and the Duplicity of Landscape," in R. Peet and N. Thrift, eds., *New Models in Geography,* vol. 2. (Boston: Allen and Unwin, 1990), 177–220.

106. C. Enloe, *Does Khaki Become You?* (Boston: South End Press, 1983), 2.

107. Ibid., 2.

108. Ibid., 13.

109. Ibid., 15.

110. Ibid.

111. Blackwood, *On the Perimeter,* 14.

112. F. Green, "Not Weaving but Frowning," in B. Whisker et al., eds., *Breaching the Peace* (London: Only Women Press, 1983), 7–8.

113. L. Alderson, "Greenham Common and All That ... A Radical Feminist View," in Whisker et al., eds., *Breaching the Peace,* 11.

114. Ibid., 12.

115. Ibid., 11.

116. Bellos et al., "Is Greenham Feminist?" in Whisker et al., eds., *Breaching the Peace*, 19.

117. Green, "Not Weaving," 8.

118. Ibid., 9.

119. Margrit, "Getting out of Greenham," in Whisker et al., eds., *Breaching the Peace*, 40.

120. L. Mohin, "Essay," in Whisker et al., eds., *Breaching the Peace*, 22.

121. *Sunday Times*, 21 November 1982, 4.

122. *Observer*, 12 December 1982, 10–13.

123. *Observer*, 2 December 1984.

124. *Daily Telegraph*, 7 January 1983, 3.

125. *Daily Mirror*, 5 April 1984, 2.

126. Blackwood, *On the Perimeter*, 1–2.

127. Ibid., 3.

128. Ibid., 5.

129. Ibid., 6.

130. Ibid., 11.

131. Ibid., 35.

CHAPTER 6. PLACE AND IDEOLOGICAL STRATEGIES

1. M. Bakhtin, *Rabelais and His World* (Bloomington: Indiana University Press, 1984), 10.

2. P. Stallybrass and A. White, *The Politics and Poetics of Transgression* (Ithaca, N.Y.: Cornell University Press, 1986).

3. D. Harvey, "From Space to Place and Back Again" (Paper presented at the Tate Gallery, London, 1990), 5.

4. See E. Soja, *Postmodern Geographies: The Reassertion of Space in Critical Social Theory* (London: Verso, 1989), and D. Harvey, "From Space to Place and Back Again" (Paper presented at the Tate Gallery, London, 1990).

5. See J. N. Entrikin, *The Betweenness of Place* (London: Macmillan, 1990); R. D. Sack, *Place, Consumption and Modernity* (Baltimore, Md.: Johns Hopkins University Press, 1992); Yi-Fu Tuan, *Space and Place: The Perspective of Experience* (Minneapolis: University of Minnesota Press, 1977); J. Agnew, *Place and Politics* (Boston: Unwin Hyman, 1987).

6. See G. Therborn, *The Power of Ideology and the Ideology of Power* (London: Verso, 1980); R. Geuss, *The Idea of a Critical Theory* (Cambridge: Cambridge University Press, 1980); J. B. Thompson, *Ideology and Modern Culture* (Cambridge: Polity Press, 1990); T. Eagleton, *Ideology: An Introduction* (London: Verso, 1991); and R. Williams, *Marxism and Literature* (Oxford: Oxford University Press, 1978).

7. See J. Berger, *Ways of Seeing* (Harmondsworth: Penguin, 1972); Yi-Fu Tuan, *Space and Place* (Minneapolis: University of Minnesota Press, 1977).

8. P. Bourdieu, *Distinction: A Social Critique of the Judgment of Taste* (Cambridge, Mass.: Harvard University Press, 1984), 467.

9. Ibid., 480.

10. G. Therborn, *The Power of Ideology and the Ideology of Power* (London: Verso, 1980).

11. J. B. Thompson, *Ideology and Modern Culture* (Cambridge: Polity Press, 1990).

12. Yi-Fu Tuan, *Segmented Worlds and Self* (Minneapolis: University of Minnesota Press, 1982), 118.

13. See, for example, E. Said, *Orientalism* (New York: Vintage, 1979); and R. Shields, *Places on the Margin* (London: Routledge, 1991).

14. Williams, *Marxism and Literature* (Oxford: Oxford University Press, 1978), 128.

15. Ibid., 132.

16. J. Agnew, *Place and Politics* (Boston: Unwin Hyman, 1988).

17. J. N. Entrikin, *The Betweenness of Place: Towards a Geography of Modernity* (London: Macmillan, 1991).

18. R. D. Sack, "The Consumer's World: Place as Context," *Annals of the Association of American Geographers* 78, no. 4 (1988): 622–64.

19. S. Daniels, "Marxism, Culture and the Duplicity of Landscape," in N. Thrift and R. Peet, eds., *New Models in Geography*, vol. 2 (Boston: Allen and Unwin, 1990), 177–220.

20. F. Inglis, quoted in ibid., 206.

21. Daniels, "Marxism, Culture," 206.

22. See also J. Duncan, *The City as Text* (Cambridge: Cambridge University Press, 1990).

23. A. Gramsci, quoted in "Antonio Gramsci," in *Culture, Ideology and Social Process*, ed. T. Bennett, G. Martin, C. Mercer, and J. Woollacott (London: Open University Press, 1981), 212.

24. For a complete investigation into the many and confused meanings of the word *nature,* see R. Williams, *Keywords* (London: Fontana Press, 1983), 219–24. I draw on only some of the meanings explained there.

25. See chapter 2 in N. Smith, *Uneven Development* (Oxford: Blackwell, 1984), for an excellent discussion of the ideology of nature.

26. M. Foucault, *Power/Knowledge* (New York: Pantheon, 1980), 149.

27. R. Sack, *Human Territoriality: Its Theory and History* (Cambridge: Cambridge University Press, 1986).

28. R. Sack, *Place, Consumption and Modernity* (Baltimore, Md.: Johns Hopkins University Press, 1992). By "nature" Sack means the realm of things physical, but he also refers to it as a force (as in "natural laws" such as gravity).

29. I. Chambers, "A Miniature History of the Walkman," *New Formations* 11 (1990): 3.

7. PLACE, TRANSGRESSION, AND THE PRACTICE OF RESISTANCE

1. R. Sack, *Human Territoriality: Its Theory and History* (Cambridge: Cambridge University Press, 1986).

2. P. Stallybrass and A. White, *The Politics and Poetics of Transgression* (Ithaca, N.Y.: Cornell University Press, 1986), 25.

3. Yi-Fu Tuan, *Segmented Worlds and Self* (Minneapolis: University of Minnesota Press, 1982).

4. M. De Certeau, *The Practice of Everyday Life* (Berkeley: University of California Press, 1984).

5. Ibid., 30.

6. A. Bonnett, "Art, Ideology and Everyday Space: Subversive Tendencies from Dada to Postmodernism," *Environment and Planning D: Society and Space* 10 (1990): 69–86.

7. I saw Pollard's work in a traveling exhibit titled *Interrogating Identity* while it was at the Madison, Wisconsin, Civic Center in May 1992.

8. See N. Smith, "Homeless/Global: Scaling Places," in J. Bird, B. Curtis, T. Putnam, G. Robertson, and L. Tickner, eds., *Mapping the Futures* (London: Routledge, 1993), 87–119; R. Deutsche, "Uneven Development: Public Art in New York City," *October* 47 (1988): 3–52.

9. Walker Art Center, *Public Address: Krzysztof Wodiczko,* exhibition notes (Minneapolis, Minn.: Walker Art Center, 1992), 1, 2.

10. See D. Crimp, *Aids Demo-Graphics* (Seattle: Bay Press, 1990).
11. Ibid., 20.
12. K. Ross, *The Emergence of Social Space: Rimbaud and the Paris Commune* (Minneapolis: University of Minnesota Press, 1988), 5.
13. Ibid., 36.
14. Ibid., 38.
15. See M. Ozouf, *Festivals and the French Revolution* (Cambridge, Mass.: Harvard University Press, 1988).
16. Quoted in P. Boswell, "Krzysztof Wodiczko: Art and the Public Domain," in K. Wodiczko, *Public Address* (Minneapolis: Walker Art Center, 1992), 20.

Index

ACT-UP, 170–73
AIDS, 41–42

Bakhtin, Mikhail, 78, 123, 125–27, 149
Basquiat, Jean-Michel, 36
Battle of the Beanfield, 67
Becker, Howard, 24–26
Berger, John, 111
Blackwood, Caroline, 110, 116, 119, 131, 142–43
Boal, Augusto, 7
Bonnett, Alastair, 56
Bourdieu, Pierre, 8, 9, 18–21, 57, 76–79, 94, 152–53, 156
Bristol, Michael, 129
Brett, Guy, 102
Byron, Lord, 44

Callaghan, James, 63
Campaign for Nuclear Disarmament (CND), 101
Canguilhem, Georges, 22
carnival, 78; Greenham Women and, 121–31; laughter and, 126; meaning of, 122; ritual and, 126; as safety valve, 128; as world upside down, 123–24
Certeau, Michel de, 164
Chambers, Iain, 134, 162
city, image of, 46
classical body, 100, 128, 149
consensus, 63–64

Corbin, Alain, 108
countryside: as object of national affection, 134; as ordered landscape, 133; rustic images of, 83
Crimp, Douglas, 170–71
cultural capital, 77
cultural studies, 12, 13
culture: definition of, 57

Dadaism, 56, 166
Daniels, Stephen, 155, 157
defecation, 107
deterrence, nuclear, 101
Deutsche, Rosalyn, 4
deviance, 24–27
dirt: in construction of deviance, 81; definition of, 38; graffiti as, 38–40; Greenham women as, 105–6; menstruation as, 109; travelers as, 82
disease: graffiti as, 40–42
Disney World, 37, 49
disorder, moral, 49
dominant ideology thesis, 17
Douglas, Mary, 38–39, 109
doxa, 18–21, 152
Driver, Felix, 41
druids, 74, 94
Duchamp, Marcel, 56

Eagleton, Terry, 128
Eco, Umberto, 129

Enloe, Cynthia, 135
English Heritage, 67, 75, 94
ethnomethodology, 22
everyday space, 54

Fanon, Frantz, 45
folk devils, 65
Foucault, Michel, 41–42, 159
front line, 112–13, 115, 135–36

Garfinkel, Harold, 22
gentrification, 56
Glazer, Nathan, 42
Gluckman, Max, 129
graffiti: as art, 35–36, 50–55; artists,
    25; criminality of, 46; definition
    of, 32; descriptions of, 37–50; in
    Disney World, 37; as disorder,
    37–50; ethnicity and, 42–46;
    history of, 32–37; measures
    against, 33–35; as primitive, 51;
    style of, 47; as vandalism, 58
Gramsci, Antonio, 18, 157
Greenham Common Air Base: images
    of, 99, 101; location of, 98;
    masculinity of, 100
Greenham Common Women's Peace
    Camp, 98; air base and, 131;
    children and, 114-15, 144;
    clothing and, 113–14, 143;
    culinary disorder in, 112–13;
    history of, 100–105; hysteria and,
    117–19; liberal perspectives on,
    141–44; media interest in, 102;
    radical perspective on, 139–41;
    sexuality and, 115–17
grotesque realism, 100, 126–27
Gypsies, 26; deviant images of, 85;
    romantic images of, 84; sense of
    cleanliness of, 86; sites for, 85–86

Hagopian, Paul, 50
Hall, Stuart, 63
Haring, Keith, 36

Harvey, David, 11, 12, 150, 160, 164
Heath, Edward, 62
Hebdige, Dick, 16–17, 26–27
hegemony, 18
Heseltine, Michael, 104
high and low domains, 52–55, 78
hippies (see also travelers): deviance of,
    70; strategies for dealing with, 92
Holzer, Jenny, 36
home, 99–100
homelessness, 4–5, 56
Howard Beach, 5–8
Hurd, Douglas, 69, 82
hysteria, 117–19

ideological strategies, 151–62
ideology, 14–21; common sense and,
    18; definition of, 14; dogma and,
    155; inclusive, 15; positional, 15

Jackson, Peter, 13, 123

Koch, Mayor Ed, 4–5, 36
Kristeva, Julia, 39, 108

Labour Party, 101
Ladurie, Leroy, 129–30
Lady Pink, 43
landscape: hegemonic, 57; as text,
    13
law: legitimation of, 93; and order,
    65–66; trespass, 88–94
Laws, Sophie, 44, 108
Lefebvre, Henri, 27
leisure: normal, 78–80, 186n; social
    geography of, 80
Lindsay, Mayor John, 31, 36, 42, 46
Lowenthal, David, 134

madness, 42, 45, 118–19
Mailer, Norman, 42
Martin, Emily, 109–10
menstruation, 107–10
methodology, 9–10, 21–22

military: masculinity and, 136;
    metaphors, 83; women and,
    135–37
miner's strike, 67
mobility: deviance of, 81, 87, 88, 95;
    graffiti and, 52; legitimate forms
    of, 83; as lifestyle, 80, 82, 95
moral panics, 64

national heritage, 76
National Trust, 67, 75
new cultural geography, 12
New York City, 4–5; Central Park, 6;
    fiscal crisis of, 31–32; homeless in,
    6; image of, 46; immigration and,
    44; infrastructure of, 31
normality, geography of, 94–96

obscenity, 39–40
odor, 106–8
Okely, Judith, 85–86
Oldenburg, Claes, 43
Orientalism, 51, 53
outsiders, 25–26, 154

Paris Commune, 173–75
place, 3, 13, 47, 150, 156, 177n;
    classification and, 152–53;
    creation of, 59; differentiation
    and, 153–55; meaning of, 49,
    59–60; nature of, 151, 158–61;
    sense of, 156; social construction
    of, 150
plague, 41–42
Pollard, Ingrid, 167–69
pollution, 39
practice, 16–18, 155–58
Prince, Hugh, 134
property, 48, 88–89, 111
public space: and private space, 47,
    108, 110, 118

rape, 6, 8
rat, as metaphor, 119–21

resistance, 22–24
Rojek, Chris, 81
rootedness: ideology of, 84
Rosenblatt, Roger, 42, 44, 48
Ross, Kristin, 173–75

Sack, Robert, 11–12, 160, 163
Said, Edward, 53
sanitary science, 41
Scott, James, 22–23
sexuality, 115–17
Sibley, David, 26, 84–85
Situationists, 56, 166
Smith, Neil, 11
social space, 3, 177n
sociospatial dialectic, 12
Soja, Edward, 11–12, 150
Sontag, Susan, 41–42
specialized space, 55
squatters, 89–94
Stallybrass, Peter, 52, 54, 126–27,
    149–50, 163
Stewart, Michael, 52, 55
Stewart, Susan, 47, 58
Stonehenge: alternative meanings
    of, 75–76; description of, 70;
    English cultural identity and,
    70–71; festival at, 66–67; in
    myth, 71; in painting and
    literature, 71–74, 94; meanings
    of, 70–80; modern popularity of,
    74–75

TAKI 183, 32–33, 36, 43–44
Thatcher, Margaret, 63–64, 89, 101,
    184n
Thatcherism, 63–65, 184n
Therborn, Goren, 14, 153
Thompson, John B., 14, 153
Tiananmen Square, 165, 176
transgression, 8–9, 21–27, 39, 59–60,
    149; definition of, 21; in art,
    166–73; resistance and, 22; social
    transformation and, 175–76

travelers, 62; as dirty, 81–82, 86; laws
    against, 84
trespass, 69, 88–95
Tuan, Yi-Fu, 164

vagabonds, 82
vagrancy, 84–85
Vincent-Jones, Peter, 89–94

Ward, David, 44–45, 182n
White, Allon, 52, 54, 126–27,
    149–50, 163
Williams, Patricia, 6
Williams, Raymond, 18, 133, 155
Wodiczko, Krzysztof, 167–69

Young, Alison, 104, 119, 128

Tim Cresswell is currently a lecturer in geography at the University of Wales in Lampeter. His master's and Ph.D. degrees are from the University of Wisconsin, Madison, where he was supervised by Yi-Fu Tuan. Cresswell taught briefly at the University of Connecticut at Storrs as a visiting assistant professor in 1993. He has published papers on geography and transgression in a number of geography journals (*Antipode, Society and Space,* and *Transactions*) and is currently working on a book on mobility as a sociocultural phenomenon.